Longman
Shakes

A Midsummer Night's Dream

John O'Connor
l Consultant: Dr Stewart Eames

e Editor: John O'Connor

Assessment Practice:
utcliffe (AQA)
aylor (Edexcel)
et Graham (WJEC)

Longman
Part of Pearson

Longman is an imprint of Pearson Education Limited, a company incorporated in England and Wales, having its registered office at Edinburgh Gate, Harlow, Essex, CM20 2JE. Registered company number: 872828

www.pearsonschoolsandfecolleges.co.uk

Longman is a registered trademark of Pearson Education Limited

© Pearson Education Limited 2010

The rights of Dr Stewart Eames, John O'Connor, Chris Sutcliffe, Pam Taylor and Margaret Graham to be identified as the authors of the work have been asserted by them in accordance with the Copyright, Designs and Patents Act 1988.

First published 2010

12 11 10
10 9 8 7 6 5 4 3 2 1

British Library Cataloguing in Publication Data
A catalogue record for this book is available from the British Library

ISBN 9781408236857

Typeset by Juice Creative Ltd, Hertfordshire
Cover photo © Photostage, Ltd.
Printed and bound in Great Britain by Henry Ling Limited, at the Dorset Press, Dorchester DT1 1HD

We are grateful to the following for permission to reproduce copyright photographs:

Getty Images: *page 157*: Andrea Pistolesi/The Image Bank

Every effort has been made to contact copyright holders of material reproduced in this book. Any omissions will be rectified in subsequent printings if notice is given to the publishers.

CONTENTS

ACT 1: SCENE BY SCENE

1 Theseus and Hippolyta discuss their approaching wedding. Egeus demands that his daughter Hermia should marry Demetrius, although she is in love with Lysander. Learning what will happen if she disobeys her father, Hermia secretly agrees to run away with Lysander. They tell Helena what they are going to do. Helena is in love with Demetrius and decides to tell him what Hermia is planning to do.

2 A group of Athenian workmen (the 'Mechanicals') meet to plan a play that they hope to perform on Theseus's wedding night. Peter Quince hands out the parts and they agree to rehearse the following night in the woods outside the city.

ACT 2: SCENE BY SCENE

1 In the woods, a Fairy meets Puck, a hobgoblin servant of Oberon the Fairy King. They discuss the quarrel between Oberon and his queen, Titania. When the King and Queen meet, Oberon demands that she give him a little changeling boy that she is looking after, but she refuses. Oberon plots with Puck to gain his revenge and instructs him to find a flower with magic properties. While Titania sleeps, Oberon will squeeze some juice from the flower onto her eyes, so that she will fall in love with the first thing she sees on awakening. Oberon takes pity on Helena when he observes her being rejected by Demetrius and tells Puck to use the juice on Demetrius too.

2 Oberon squeezes the magic juice onto Titania's eyes as she sleeps. Hermia and Lysander get lost in the woods and decide to sleep where they are for the night. Puck mistakenly anoints Lysander's eyes instead of Demetrius's and, when Lysander awakes, he sees Helena and falls in love with her. She runs away and he chases after her. Hermia wakes up to find herself alone and goes to look for Lysander.

ACT 3: SCENE BY SCENE

1 The Mechanicals meet in the woods to rehearse their play. They discuss how to solve some of its problems and begin their rehearsal. Puck mischievously puts an ass's head on Bottom and the others run off in terror. Awaking at the sound of Bottom's voice, Titania falls in love with him and takes him off to her bower.

2 To correct Puck's mistake, Oberon anoints Demetrius's eyes, and he falls in love with Helena when he awakes. Both Lysander and Demetrius now claim to be in love with Helena, who thinks they are mocking her. Hermia turns on Helena for having stolen Lysander, and then the two men prepare to fight it out. Puck keeps Lysander and Demetrius apart. All four lovers are exhausted and they fall asleep.

ACT 4: SCENE BY SCENE

1 Oberon releases Titania from the spell and Puck removes the ass's head from Bottom. Then Oberon and Titania make peace. Out hunting, Theseus and Hippolyta discover the four lovers asleep. Theseus overrules Egeus and allows Hermia to marry Lysander. Both pairs of lovers will be married at the same time as Theseus and Hippolyta. Bottom wakes up full of wonder at his amazing dream.

2 The Mechanicals gloomily discuss the loss of Bottom and the money they might have been given if their play had been performed. Bottom unexpectedly arrives with the exciting news that their play has been shortlisted for performance.

ACT 5: SCENE BY SCENE

1 Theseus discusses the lovers' experience with Hippolyta and then selects the Mechanicals' *Pyramus and Thisby* as the wedding-night performance. The Mechanicals perform their play and round off the evening's entertainment with a dance. Oberon and Titania bless the married couples and Puck asks the audience to applaud.

THE ATHENIAN COURT

THESEUS
Duke of Athens
He has defeated Hippolyta,
Queen of the Amazons,
in battle and is soon to
marry her.

HIPPOLYTA
Queen of the Amazons, a
tribe of warrior women
She will marry Theseus at the
end of the play, but is not
afraid to disagree with him.

EGEUS
An Athenian lord
He insists that his daughter
Hermia must marry
Demetrius rather than
Lysander.

PHILOSTRATE
In charge of Theseus's
entertainments
He recommends that
Theseus should reject the
Mechanicals' play.

THE LOVERS

HERMIA
Egeus's daughter
She is in love with Lysander
and agrees to run away with
him when her father orders
her to marry Demetrius.

HELENA
Hermia's friend
She is in love with Demetrius
and reveals to him Hermia's
plan to run away with
Lysander.

LYSANDER
Hermia's lover
Puck mistakenly puts the
juice of a magic flower on
his eyes and he awakes
to fall in love temporarily
with Helena.

DEMETRIUS
Helena's former lover
He wants to marry Hermia
and follows her when she
runs away with Lysander.

THE ATHENIAN WORKMEN ALSO KNOWN AS 'THE MECHANICALS'

PETER QUINCE
A carpenter
He organises the
Mechanicals' *Pyramus
and Thisby* play and
performs the role of
Prologue.

NICK BOTTOM
A weaver
He plays Pyramus.
Titania falls in love
with him after Puck
has given him an
ass's head.

FRANCIS FLUTE
A bellows-mender
He takes the role of
Thisby despite his
reluctance to play
a woman.

TOM SNOUT
A tinker
He plays the part of the
Wall in *Pyramus and
Thisby.*

ROBIN STARVELING
A tailor
He plays the part of
Moonshine in *Pyramus
and Thisby.*

SNUG
A joiner
He plays the part of
Lion in *Pyramus and
Thisby.*

THE FAIRY WORLD

OBERON
King of the Fairies
He wants a changeling boy
belonging to Titania. She
refuses, and to punish her he
orders Puck to use the juice
of a magic flower to make
her fall in love with the next
thing she sees.

TITANIA
Queen of the Fairies
She falls in love with Bottom
when he is wearing an ass's
head, after Puck has put
magic juice on her eyes.

ROBIN GOODFELLOW
also known as **PUCK**
*A hobgoblin in
Oberon's service*
He carries out his
master's orders and
sprinkles the magic
juice onto people's
eyes.

**PEASEBLOSSOM, COBWEB,
MOTH** and **MUSTARDSEED**
*Titania's fairy
attendants*

A FAIRY
*One of Titania's
attendants*

5

THE ATHENIAN COURT

THESEUS *Duke of Athens*

HIPPOLYTA *Queen of the Amazons, soon to marry Duke Theseus*

EGEUS *a lord, Hermia's father*

PHILOSTRATE *master of entertainments for Duke Theseus*

Other lords, ladies and attendants

THE LOVERS

HERMIA *Egeus's daughter, in love with Lysander*

HELENA *in love with Demetrius*

LYSANDER *in love with Hermia*

DEMETRIUS *Egeus's choice as husband for Hermia*

THE MECHANICALS (ATHENIAN WORKMAN)   *Their parts in 'Pyramus and Thisby'*

PETER QUINCE *a carpenter*	*the* PROLOGUE
NICK BOTTOM *a weaver*	PYRAMUS
FRANCIS FLUTE *a bellows-mender*	THISBY
TOM SNOUT *a tinker*	WALL
ROBIN STARVELING *a tailor*	MOONSHINE
SNUG *a joiner*	LION

THE FAIRIES

PUCK *a hobgoblin, also called Robin Goodfellow*

OBERON *King of the Fairies*

TITANIA *Queen of the Fairies*

PEASEBLOSSOM

COBWEB

} *Titania's attendants*

MOTH

MUSTARDSEED

A FAIRY *in Titania's service*

The scene is Athens and the woods outside the city.

In this scene ...

- Theseus and Hippolyta discuss their approaching wedding.
- Egeus demands that his daughter Hermia should marry Demetrius, but she is in love with Lysander. Theseus tells Hermia what will happen if she disobeys her father.
- Lysander and Hermia tell Helena of their plans to elope.

Theseus and Hippolyta are talking about their coming wedding, when they are interrupted by Egeus. He wants his daughter Hermia to marry Demetrius, but she is in love with Lysander.

THINK ABOUT for GCSE

Performance and staging
- Imagine you were directing the play for stage or screen. What would the set and characters look like at the moment when Theseus speaks the opening line? Think about the setting, costume and the arrangement of the characters.

Relationships
- What do we learn here about the background to the marriage between Theseus and Hippolyta? How might it have affected their relationship?

Structure and form
- The opening mood is generally happy. At what point does it change?

1–2 **our ... apace**: it will soon be our wedding day

2–3 **Four ... moon**: It will be a new moon in four days' time

4 **wanes**: gets smaller
lingers: delays

5 **step-dame**: old stepmother
dowager: widow

6 **withering out**: using up
revenue: inheritance / income

7 **steep**: drown

9 **silver bow**: Diana was the Roman goddess of hunting and the moon.

11 **solemnities**: marriage ceremony

13 **pert**: lively

14 **Turn melancholy forth**: send gloominess away

15 **The pale ... pomp**: there is no place for melancholy in our celebrations

16–17 **I wooed ... injuries**: Theseus won Hippolyta's love by defeating her in battle.

18 **key**: mood

19 **pomp**: splendour
triumph: spectacular public celebrations
revelling: lively festivities

22 **vexation**: distress / anger

8

Athens: Duke Theseus's palace.

Enter THESEUS *and* HIPPOLYTA, *with* PHILOSTRATE *and other attendants.*

THESEUS	Now, fair Hippolyta, our nuptial hour	
	Draws on apace. Four happy days bring in	
	Another moon – but O, methinks, how slow	
	This old moon wanes! She lingers my desires	
	Like to a step-dame or a dowager,	5
	Long withering out a young man's revenue.	

HIPPOLYTA	Four days will quickly steep themselves in night;	
	Four nights will quickly dream away the time –	
	And then the moon, like to a silver bow	
	New bent in heaven, shall behold the night	10
	Of our solemnities.	

THESEUS	Go, Philostrate –	
	Stir up the Athenian youth to merriments.	
	Awake the pert and nimble spirit of mirth;	
	Turn melancholy forth to funerals:	
	The pale companion is not for our pomp.	15

Exit PHILOSTRATE.

Hippolyta, I wooed thee with my sword,
And won thy love doing thee injuries –
But I will wed thee in another key,
With pomp, with triumph, and with revelling.

Enter EGEUS *and his daughter* HERMIA, *followed by* LYSANDER
and DEMETRIUS.

EGEUS	Happy be Theseus, our renownèd Duke!	20
THESEUS	Thanks, good Egeus. What's the news with thee?	
EGEUS	Full of vexation come I, with complaint	
	Against my child, my daughter Hermia.	
	Stand forth, Demetrius. – My noble lord,	
	This man hath my consent to marry her.	25
	Stand forth, Lysander! – And, my gracious Duke,	

Egeus accuses Lysander of having used witchcraft to win Hermia's affections and wants Theseus to force her by law to marry Demetrius. Theseus reminds Hermia of the duty she owes her father.

27 **bewitched ... child**: (Lysander) won Hermia's heart with magic charms
28 **rhymes**: love poems
29 **interchanged**: exchanged
31 **feigning ... feigning**: soft ... deceitful
32 **stolen ... fantasy**: wormed his way into her mind
33–4 **gawds ... sweetmeats**: flashy gifts, trinkets, knick-knacks, little presents, flowers, sweets
34–5 **messengers ... youth**: gifts likely to have a powerful influence on an impressionable girl
36 **filched**: stolen
38 **stubborn harshness**: hostile disobedience
39 **Be it so**: if
41 **privilege**: legal right
45 **Immediately ... case**: specifically created for cases like this
46 **Be advised**: Think carefully
48 **composed your beauties**: gave you your physical characteristics
49 **but as a form**: no more than an imprint
51 **disfigure**: deface / destroy

THINK ABOUT for GCSE

Characterisation
- What are your early impressions of Hermia? Look at the way she replies to Duke Theseus, for example.

Performance and staging
- Theseus tells Hermia that to her father she is 'but as a form in wax' – no more than his imprint. In performance, how would you advise (a) Hermia and (b) Hippolyta to react to this?

54 **in this kind**: in a situation like this
    wanting ... voice: lacking your father's approval
56 **would**: wish

58 **entreat**: beg

60 **concern my modesty**: suit well with my reputation as a young woman

This man hath bewitched the bosom of my child.
Thou, thou Lysander, thou hast given her rhymes,
And interchanged love-tokens with my child.
Thou hast by moonlight at her window sung,   30
With feigning voice, verses of feigning love,
And stolen the impression of her fantasy
With bracelets of thy hair, rings, gawds, conceits,
Knacks, trifles, nosegays, sweetmeats, messengers
Of strong prevailment in unhardened youth.   35
With cunning hast thou filched my daughter's heart –
Turned her obedience, which is due to me,
To stubborn harshness! And, my gracious Duke,
Be it so she will not here before your Grace
Consent to marry with Demetrius,   40
I beg the ancient privilege of Athens.
As she is mine, I may dispose of her –
Which shall be either to this gentleman
Or to her death, according to our law
Immediately provided in that case.   45

THESEUS   What say you, Hermia? Be advised, fair maid.
To you your father should be as a god,
One that composed your beauties; yea, and one
To whom you are but as a form in wax
By him imprinted – and within his power   50
To leave the figure, or disfigure it.
Demetrius is a worthy gentleman.

HERMIA   So is Lysander.

THESEUS   In himself he is –
But in this kind, wanting your father's voice,
The other must be held the worthier.   55

HERMIA   I would my father looked but with my eyes.

THESEUS   Rather your eyes must with *his* judgement look.

HERMIA   I do entreat your Grace to pardon me.
I know not by what power I am made bold,
Nor how it may concern my modesty   60
In such a presence here to plead my thoughts –
But I beseech your Grace, that I may know

Theseus confirms that Hermia has three choices: to marry Demetrius, become a nun, or suffer the death penalty. Demetrius and Lysander each argue why they should be allowed to marry her.

THINK ABOUT for GCSE

Performance and staging
- Theseus argues that although the life of a nun is a fine thing, it is better for a girl to make the most of her beauty and marry. How might each of the other characters present on stage react to this?

Themes and issues
- What does the scene so far reveal about the **authority** of a father over a daughter, or men over women?

Structure and form
- Which moments so far have been mainly light-hearted and which mainly serious? What effect does this combination of light-heartedness and seriousness have?

63 **befall me**: happen to me
65 **die the death**: be put to death
   abjure: give up
67 **question your desires**: consider what you really want
68 **Know of**: learn from
   blood: feelings / passions
69 **yield not**: do not give in to
70 **livery**: clothing (and life)
71 **aye**: ever
   in shady cloister mewed: cooped up in a dark convent
72 **barren sister**: childless nun
73 **fruitless**: childless
75 **maiden pilgrimage**: the religious life of a virgin
76 **earthlier happy**: happier / more fortunate on earth
80 **Ere**: before
   yield ... up: give up my right to remain a virgin
81-2 **unwishèd ... sovereignty**: the mastery of a man in marriage whom my soul refuses to accept as its lord
83 **pause**: think it over
84 **sealing-day betwixt**: wedding day between
88 **would**: wishes
89 **Diana**: the goddess of chastity
89-90 **protest for aye**: solemnly vow forever
90 **austerity**: harsh life (of a nun)
92 **crazèd title**: flawed claim

94 **Do you marry *him***: you marry him

96 **render**: give to

98 **estate unto**: formally give to

99 **as well derived**: from as good a family

The worst that may befall me in this case,
If I refuse to wed Demetrius.

THESEUS   Either to die the death, or to abjure   65
For ever the society of men.
Therefore, fair Hermia, question your desires,
Know of your youth, examine well your blood –
Whether, if you yield not your father's choice,
You can endure the livery of a nun,   70
For aye to be in shady cloister mewed,
To live a barren sister all your life,
Chanting faint hymns to the cold fruitless moon.
Thrice blessèd they that master so their blood
To undergo such maiden pilgrimage –   75
But earthlier happy is the rose distilled
Than that which, withering on the virgin thorn,
Grows, lives, and dies in single blessedness.

HERMIA   So will I grow, so live, so die, my lord,
Ere I will yield my virgin patent up   80
Unto his lordship, whose unwishèd yoke
My soul consents not to give sovereignty.

THESEUS   Take time to pause, and by the next new moon –
The sealing-day betwixt my love and me
For everlasting bond of fellowship –   85
Upon that day either prepare to die
For disobedience to your father's will,
Or else to wed Demetrius as he would –
Or on Diana's altar to protest
For aye austerity and single life.   90

DEMETRIUS Relent, sweet Hermia – and Lysander, yield
Thy crazèd title to my certain right.

LYSANDER   You have her father's love, Demetrius:
Let me have Hermia's. Do you marry *him*.

EGEUS   Scornful Lysander! True, he hath my love,   95
And what is mine my love shall render him –
And she is mine, and all my right of her
I do estate unto Demetrius.

LYSANDER   I am, my Lord, as well derived as he,

13

Lysander points out that Demetrius previously wooed Helena, who still loves Demetrius. Theseus leaves to discuss matters with Egeus and Demetrius. Hermia and Lysander are left together.

THINK ABOUT for GCSE

Characterisation

- Look at Theseus's speeches up to line 126. What has he said to suggest that he is on (a) Egeus's side and (b) Hermia's? Who do you think he most sympathises with?

Relationships

- What do you think prompts Theseus to ask Hippolyta, 'what cheer, my love?' (line 122)? Hippolyta says nothing after her opening words to Theseus. How might she be reacting to the way Theseus has dealt with Egeus's complaint? How would you describe Egeus and Hippolyta's relationship?

100 **well possessed**: wealthy

102 **with vantage**: better

105 **prosecute**: follow up
106 **avouch ... head**: say it to his face

109 **dotes in idolatry**: worships him like a god
110 **spotted and inconstant**: stained with unfaithfulness

113 **self-affairs**: my own personal matters
114 **My mind did lose it**: I forgot about it

116 **schooling**: serious advice
117 **arm**: prepare
118 **fancies**: desires

120 **by ... extenuate**: I am powerless to soften

125 **Against our nuptial**: in preparation for our wedding
126 **nearly that**: that closely

130 **Belike**: Perhaps
131 **Beteem**: 1 allow; 2 teem (pour with rain)
    tempest: i.e. weeping
132 **aught**: anything

	As well possessed. My love is more than his;	100

As well possessed. My love is more than his;   100
My fortunes every way as fairly ranked,
If not with vantage, as Demetrius' –
And, which is more than all these boasts can be,
I am beloved of beauteous Hermia.
Why should not I then prosecute my right?   105
Demetrius, I'll avouch it to his head,
Made love to Nedar's daughter, Helena,
And won her soul – and she, sweet lady, dotes,
Devoutly dotes, dotes in idolatry,
Upon this spotted and inconstant man!   110

THESEUS   I must confess that I have heard so much,
And with Demetrius thought to have spoke thereof –
But, being over-full of self-affairs,
My mind did lose it. But Demetrius, come,
And come, Egeus. You shall go with me.   115
I have some private schooling for you both.
For you, fair Hermia, look you arm yourself
To fit your fancies to your father's will;
Or else the law of Athens yields you up –
Which by no means we may extenuate –   120
To death, or to a vow of single life.
Come, my Hippolyta – what cheer, my love?
Demetrius and Egeus, go along –
I must employ you in some business
Against our nuptial, and confer with you   125
Of something nearly that concerns yourselves.

EGEUS   With duty and desire we follow you.

Exit THESEUS *with* HIPPOLYTA, *followed by* EGEUS, DEMETRIUS
and attendants.

LYSANDER *and* HERMIA *remain.*

LYSANDER   How now, my love? Why is your cheek so pale?
How chance the roses there do fade so fast?

HERMIA   Belike for want of rain, which I could well   130
Beteem them from the tempest of my eyes.

LYSANDER   (*Sighing*) Ay me! For aught that I could ever read,
Could ever hear by tale or history,

Hermia and Lysander talk about the problems that lovers often face. Lysander has a plan for them to elope and stay with his aunt. She lives some distance from Athens and they can get married there, because Athenian law does not apply there.

135 **blood**: birth (i.e. social class, rank)

136 **O cross!**: What a barrier!
too high … low: too high-born to be enslaved by someone of low birth

137 **misgraffèd … years**: badly matched in age

139 **stood … friends**: depended on your family choosing for you

141 **if … choice**: if the lovers had chosen each other

145 **collied**: black / dark

146 **spleen**: fit of temper
unfolds: reveals

147 **ere**: before

149 **quick**: 1 quickly; 2 living
confusion: ruin

150 **ever crossed**: always thwarted / frustrated

151 **edict in destiny**: law of fate

153 **customary cross**: the kind of obstacle lovers usually face

154 **due to**: much a part of

155 **fancy's**: love's

156 **persuasion**: argument

157–8 **dowager … revenue**: very wealthy widow

159 **remote seven leagues**: i.e. about twenty-one miles away

160 **respects**: regards

164 **steal forth**: secretly leave

165 **without**: outside

167 **do observance … May**: celebrate May Day

168 **stay**: wait

THINK ABOUT for GCSE

Performance

• In lines 128 to 140, the lovers list some of the obstacles to true love, such as difference in social class (lines 135 to 136) or age (lines 137 to 138). How would you advise the actors to speak this dialogue? What effect would you want to achieve?

• What images does Lysander employ to describe the nature of love (lines 143 to 149)? What aspect of love do the images help to convey?

	The course of true love never did run smooth.	
	But either it was different in blood –	135
HERMIA	O cross! – too high to be enthralled to low.	
LYSANDER	Or else misgraffèd in respect of years –	
HERMIA	O spite! – too old to be engaged to young.	
LYSANDER	Or else it stood upon the choice of friends –	
HERMIA	O hell! – to choose love by another's eyes!	140
LYSANDER	Or, if there were a sympathy in choice,	
	War, death, or sickness did lay siege to it –	
	Making it momentary as a sound,	
	Swift as a shadow, short as any dream,	
	Brief as the lightning in the collied night,	145
	That in a spleen unfolds both heaven and earth,	
	And, ere a man hath power to say 'Behold!',	
	The jaws of darkness do devour it up.	
	So quick bright things come to confusion.	
HERMIA	If then true lovers have been ever crossed,	150
	It stands as an edict in destiny.	
	Then let us teach our trial patience,	
	Because it is a customary cross,	
	As due to love as thoughts, and dreams, and sighs,	
	Wishes and tears – poor fancy's followers.	155
LYSANDER	A good persuasion. Therefore hear me, Hermia:	
	I have a widow aunt, a dowager	
	Of great revenue, and she hath no child.	
	From Athens is her house remote seven leagues,	
	And she respects me as her only son.	160
	There, gentle Hermia, may I marry thee –	
	And to that place the sharp Athenian law	
	Cannot pursue us. If thou lov'st me, then,	
	Steal forth thy father's house tomorrow night.	
	And in the wood, a league without the town,	165
	Where I did meet thee once with Helena	
	To do observance to a morn of May,	
	There will I stay for thee.	
HERMIA	My good Lysander,	

Hermia agrees to meet Lysander the following night in the woods outside the city. Helena arrives, miserable that Demetrius does not return her love or find her attractive, but loves Hermia instead.

THINK ABOUT for GCSE

Performance and staging
- What advice would you give to the actor playing Helena in her first speech to Hermia (lines 181 to 193)? For example, where might she be angry, bitter, jealous or bewildered? Should the audience sympathise with her or laugh at her, or both?

Language
- How might the actors perform lines 194 to 201 so that the effect is different from Hermia and Lysander's complaints about love (lines 128 to 140)?

169 **Cupid**: The son of Venus, goddess of love, was usually portrayed as a winged, blindfolded child with a bow and arrow.

171 **simplicity**: harmless innocence
doves: These birds drew Venus's chariot.

173 **the Carthage Queen**: Dido, Queen of Carthage, fell in love with Aeneas ('the false Troyan') and threw herself on a funeral pyre when he deserted her.

174 **under sail**: sailing away

180 **Whither away?**: Where are you going?

181 **fair**: beautiful
unsay: deny

182 **fair**: beauty

183 **lode-stars**: guiding stars
air: tune

184 **tuneable**: pleasant sounding / harmonious

186 **favour**: looks / physical appearance

190 **bated**: excepted (she would give the whole world *except* Demetrius)

191 **translated**: transformed

192 **art**: skill (possibly magic)

193 **sway the motion**: control the impulses

200 **folly**: foolishness

201 **would**: I wish

I swear to thee by Cupid's strongest bow,
By his best arrow with the golden head,   170
By the simplicity of Venus' doves,
By that which knitteth souls and prospers loves,
And by that fire which burned the Carthage Queen
When the false Troyan under sail was seen,
By all the vows that ever men have broke –   175
In number more than ever women spoke –
In that same place thou hast appointed me,
Tomorrow truly will I meet with thee.

LYSANDER   Keep promise, love. Look – here comes Helena.

Enter HELENA.

HERMIA   God speed, fair Helena! Whither away?   180

HELENA   Call you me fair? That 'fair' again unsay.
               Demetrius loves *your* fair. O happy fair!
               Your eyes are lode-stars, and your tongue's sweet air
               More tuneable than lark to shepherd's ear
               When wheat is green, when hawthorn buds appear.   185
               Sickness is catching. O, were favour so,
               Yours would I catch, fair Hermia, ere I go!
               My ear should catch your voice, my eye your eye,
               My tongue should catch your tongue's sweet melody.
               Were the world mine, Demetrius being bated,   190
               The rest I'd give to be to you translated.
               O teach me how you look – and with what art
               You sway the motion of Demetrius' heart!

HERMIA   I frown upon him, yet he loves me still.

HELENA   O that your frowns would teach my smiles such skill!   195

HERMIA   I give him curses, yet he gives me love.

HELENA   O that my prayers could such affection move!

HERMIA   The more I hate, the more he follows me.

HELENA   The more I love, the more he hateth *me*.

HERMIA   His folly, Helena, is no fault of mine.   200

HELENA   None but your beauty – would that fault were mine!

Hermia and Lysander comfort Helena and reveal their plan to elope. By running away, they will give her a chance to win back Demetrius's love.

203 **fly**: run away from

209 **Phoebe**: (another name for the moon goddess)
210 **visage**: face
      glass: mirror (of water)
211 **liquid pearl**: dew
212 **still**: always
213 **devised to steal**: planned to slip away
215 **faint**: pale
      were wont to: used to
216 **Emptying ... counsel**: sharing our inmost thoughts
219 **stranger companies**: the company of strangers

223 **lovers' food**: the joy of seeing each other

224 **adieu**: goodbye
225 **As you ... you!**: May Demetrius be as infatuated with you as you are with him!
226 **some ... some**: some people more than others

230 **errs**: goes astray

232 **base**: cheap and shoddy
      quantity: value
233 **transpose ... dignity**: change for the better

THINK ABOUT for **GCSE**

Relationships
• What do we learn about Hermia and Helena's past relationship from Hermia's speech (lines 214 to 223)?

HERMIA	Take comfort. He no more shall see my face.
	Lysander and myself will fly this place.
	Before the time I did Lysander see,
	Seemed Athens as a paradise to me.	205
	O then, what graces in my love do dwell,
	That he hath turned a heaven unto a hell!

LYSANDER	Helen, to you our minds we will unfold.
	Tomorrow night, when Phoebe doth behold
	Her silver visage in the watery glass,	210
	Decking with liquid pearl the bladed grass –
	A time that lovers' flights doth still conceal –
	Through Athens' gates have we devised to steal.

HERMIA	And in the wood, where often you and I
	Upon faint primrose-beds were wont to lie,	215
	Emptying our bosoms of their counsel sweet,
	There my Lysander and myself shall meet,
	And thence from Athens turn away our eyes
	To seek new friends and stranger companies.
	Farewell, sweet playfellow. Pray thou for us –	220
	And good luck grant thee thy Demetrius.
	Keep word, Lysander. We must starve our sight
	From lovers' food, till morrow deep midnight.

| LYSANDER | I will, my Hermia. |

Exit HERMIA.

| | – Helena, adieu. |
| | As you on him, Demetrius dote on you! | 225 |

Exit LYSANDER.

HELENA	How happy some o'er other some can be!
	Through Athens I am thought as fair as she.
	But what of that? Demetrius thinks not so.
	He will not know what all but he do know.
	And as he errs, doting on Hermia's eyes,	230
	So I, admiring of his qualities.
	Things base and vile, holding no quantity,
	Love can transpose to form and dignity.
	Love looks not with the eyes, but with the mind,

Helena thinks about how Demetrius used to find her attractive. She decides to tell Demetrius about Hermia's plan to elope to earn his thanks.

235 **winged Cupid**: The son of Venus, goddess of love, was usually portrayed as a winged, blindfolded child with a bow and arrow.

236 **Nor hath ... taste**: And love doesn't have the least bit of common sense

237 **figure**: represent / symbolise
unheedy: unwise

239 **beguiled**: deceived

240 **As waggish ... forswear**: Just as mischievous boys break their word in jest

241 **is perjured**: breaks his word

242 **eyne**: eyes

245 **dissolved**: 1 broke his promises; 2 'melted' with love

248 **intelligence**: information

249 **it is a dear expense**: it will be a high / loving price to pay (for Demetrius's gratitude, as he will then run after Hermia)

250 **enrich**: get something back from

THINK ABOUT _for_ GCSE

Themes and issues
• **Love**: Cupid (called Eros by the Greeks) is usually portrayed as a little boy, often blindfolded, carrying a bow and arrow. Why, according to Helena, is 'winged Cupid painted blind' (line 235)? What else does she say about Cupid and love?

Characterisation
• What do you think Helena hopes to gain by revealing Hermia's plan to elope with Demetrius (lines 246 to 251)? What impression have you formed of Helena?

And therefore is winged Cupid painted blind.   235
Nor hath Love's mind of any judgement taste –
Wings, and no eyes, figure unheedy haste –
And therefore is Love said to be a child,
Because in choice he is so oft beguiled.
As waggish boys in game themselves forswear,   240
So the boy Love is perjured everwhere.
For ere Demetrius looked on Hermia's eyne,
He hailed down oaths that he was only mine –
And when this hail some heat from Hermia felt,
So he dissolved, and showers of oaths did melt.   245
I will go tell him of fair Hermia's flight.
Then to the wood will he tomorrow night
Pursue her – and for this intelligence,
If I have thanks, it is a dear expense.
But herein mean I to enrich my pain,   250
To have his sight, thither and back again.

Exit.

In this scene ...

- A group of Athenian workmen (the 'Mechanicals') meet to plan a play that they hope to perform for Theseus and Hippolyta on their wedding night.
- Peter Quince hands out the parts and they agree to meet in the woods outside the city the following night.

Nick Bottom urges Peter Quince to tell them all about the play that they hope to perform on Duke Theseus's wedding night. The play is about two lovers, Pyramus and Thisby. Bottom boasts how passionately he will play the part of Pyramus.

THINK ABOUT for GCSE

Performance and staging

- Each workman's name suggests his trade or a physical characteristic: weavers' yarn is wound onto a 'bottom'; 'Quince' is perhaps from 'quoins', a carpenter's wedges; 'Snug' presumably makes snugly fitting joints; 'Flute' might refer to wooden organ pipes, operated by bellows; Snout possibly has a big nose or, as a tinker, mends kettle spouts; Starveling is a tailor, supposedly skinny. How would you represent these characters in a modern-dress production?

Structure and form

- What main differences do you notice between the openings of this scene and Act 1 Scene 1?

2 **generally**: He means 'severally' (one at a time), but says the opposite.
3 **scrip**: list
5 **interlude**: short play

7 **treats on**: is about
8 **grow to a point**: get to your conclusion
9 **Marry**: By the Virgin Mary (a mild oath)
    lamentable: sad
10 **Pyramus and Thisby**: They were tragic lovers, like Romeo and Juliet.

17 **A lover or a tyrant?**: These were two popular stage character-types.

21 **condole**: express grief
22 **my chief humour is for**: I'd mainly like to play
23 **tear a cat in**: rant and rave
    make all split: cause a commotion

Athens.

Enter QUINCE *the carpenter,* SNUG *the joiner,* BOTTOM *the weaver,* FLUTE *the bellows-mender,* SNOUT *the tinker, and* STARVELING *the tailor.*

QUINCE	Is all our company here?
BOTTOM	You were best to call them generally, man by man, according to the scrip.
QUINCE	Here is the scroll of every man's name which is thought fit, through all Athens, to play in our interlude before the Duke and the Duchess on his wedding-day at night.
BOTTOM	First, good Peter Quince, say what the play treats on. Then read the names of the actors – and so grow to a point.
QUINCE	Marry, our play is 'The most lamentable comedy and most cruel death of Pyramus and Thisby'.
BOTTOM	A very good piece of work, I assure you, and a merry. Now, good Peter Quince, call forth your actors by the scroll. Masters, spread yourselves.
QUINCE	Answer as I call you. Nick Bottom, the weaver.
BOTTOM	Ready. Name what part I am for, and proceed.
QUINCE	You, Nick Bottom, are set down for Pyramus.
BOTTOM	What is Pyramus? A lover or a tyrant?
QUINCE	A lover, that kills himself most gallant for love.
BOTTOM	That will ask some tears in the true performing of it. If I do it, let the audience look to their eyes. I will move storms! I will condole in some measure. To the rest – yet my chief humour is for a tyrant. I could play Ercles rarely, or a part to tear a cat in, to make all split:

> 'The raging rocks
> And shivering shocks
> Shall break the locks
> Of prison-gates –

5

10

15

20

25

Bottom decides he wants to play Thisby as well as Pyramus, but Peter Quince persuades him to be Pyramus while Flute plays Thisby. The other Mechanicals are given their parts. As soon as Bottom hears that Snug is to be the Lion, he wants to play that too.

THINK ABOUT for GCSE

Language

• What do you notice about the speech that Bottom quotes ('The raging rocks...', lines 24 to 31)? In what ways is it different from the verse spoken in Scene 1?

Context

• The women's parts are given to Flute and Starveling because women were not permitted to act on public stages in Shakespeare's time (or in ancient Athens where the story is set). What preparations would they have to make to play a woman successfully? Think about costume, gesture, voice and mannerisms, for example.

28   **Phibbus' car**: the chariot of the sun god, Phoebus Apollo

30   **mar**: ruin

31   **Fates**: In mythology, these three women decided each person's life span.

32   **lofty**: high-flown

33   **Ercles' vein**: The style of Hercules (a hero).

34   **vein**: style
      condoling: pathetic

37   **wandering knight**: knight errant (i.e. one who travels in search of adventure)

40   **That's all one**: No matter

41   **small**: high-pitched
      will: want / like

42   **An**: If

43   **monstrous**: amazingly

53   **fitted**: fully cast and organised

55   **of study**: at learning lines

56   **do it extempore**: improvise / make it up as you go along

	And Phibbus' car	
	Shall shine from far,	
	And make and mar	30
	The foolish Fates!'	

This was lofty! Now name the rest of the players. – This is
Ercles' vein, a tyrant's vein: a lover is more condoling.

QUINCE   Francis Flute, the bellows-mender.

FLUTE   Here, Peter Quince.   35

QUINCE   Flute, you must take Thisby on you.

FLUTE   What is Thisby? A wandering knight?

QUINCE   It is the lady that Pyramus must love.

FLUTE   Nay, faith, let not me play a woman! I have a beard coming.

QUINCE   That's all one. You shall play it in a mask, and you may   40
             speak as small as you will.

BOTTOM   An I may hide my face, let me play Thisby too. I'll
             speak in a monstrous little voice: 'Thisne, Thisne!' 'Ah
             Pyramus, my lover dear! Thy Thisby dear, and lady dear!'

QUINCE   No, no! You must play Pyramus – and Flute, you Thisby.   45

BOTTOM   Well, proceed.

QUINCE   Robin Starveling, the tailor.

STARVELING   Here, Peter Quince.

QUINCE   Robin Starveling, you must play Thisby's mother. – Tom
             Snout, the tinker.   50

SNOUT   Here, Peter Quince.

QUINCE   You, Pyramus' father – myself, Thisby's father – Snug the
             joiner, you, the lion's part. And I hope here is a play fitted.

SNUG   Have you the lion's part written? Pray you, if it be, give it
             me, for I am slow of study.   55

QUINCE   You may do it extempore, for it is nothing but roaring.

BOTTOM   Let me play the lion too. I will roar that I will do any
             man's heart good to hear me. I will roar that I will make

Peter Quince has to convince
Bottom that he is perfect to play
Pyramus. They discuss what
colour beard Pyramus should
wear, and agree to meet the
following night in the woods
outside the city where they can
rehearse in secret.

65 **discretion**: sound judgement
66 **aggravate**: He means the opposite:
    make softer.
    roar you: roar for you
67 **sucking**: He is confusing two
    expressions, 'the sitting dove' and 'the
    sucking lamb', both well known for
    their gentleness.
    an' t: as though it
70 **proper**: handsome

75 **what you will**: whichever you like
76 **discharge**: perform
77–8 **orange-tawny ... purple-in-grain ...
    French-crown-coloured**: brownish-
    yellow ... deep scarlet red ... gold (like
    a French coin)
79 **crowns**: heads
    no hair at all: Syphilis ('the French
    disease') was thought to cause
    baldness.
82 **con**: learn
83 **without**: outside
85 **dogged with**: followed around by
    devices: plans
86 **bill of properties**: list of props
88 **obscenely**: Perhaps he means the
    opposite: in a 'seemly' (fitting) way.
89 **perfect**: word-perfect
91 **Hold ... bow-strings**: Keep your word
    or you will be disgraced (based on the
    idea that if an archer was about to be
    captured, he would cut the string of
    his bow to prevent it being used by the
    enemy)

THINK ABOUT for GCSE

Characterisation

• What impression have you
  formed of Bottom from his
  first appearance?

Language

• What possibilities for
  comedy are there in the
  workmen's language? Look
  at: apparent contradictions,
  such as 'lamentable comedy'
  (line 9); odd pronunciations;
  malapropisms (mistakenly
  using a wrong word which
  sounds similar to the
  correct one); and tautology
  (unnecessary repetition).

	the Duke say, 'Let him roar again, let him roar again!'	
QUINCE	An you should do it too terribly, you would fright the Duchess and the ladies, that they would shriek – and that were enough to hang us all.	60
ALL	That would hang us, every mother's son!	
BOTTOM	I grant you, friends, if you should fright the ladies out of their wits they would have no more discretion but to hang us – but I will aggravate my voice so, that I will roar you as gently as any sucking dove. I will roar you an 't were any nightingale.	65
QUINCE	You can play no part but Pyramus! For Pyramus is a sweet-faced man, a proper man as one shall see in a summer's day, a most lovely, gentleman-like-man – therefore *you* must needs play Pyramus.	70
BOTTOM	Well, I will undertake it. What beard were I best to play it in?	
QUINCE	Why, what you will.	75
BOTTOM	I will discharge it in either your straw-colour beard, your orange-tawny beard, your purple-in-grain beard, or your French-crown-coloured beard – your perfect yellow.	
QUINCE	Some of your French crowns have no hair at all, and then you will play bare-faced. But, masters, here are your parts. And I am to entreat you, request you, and desire you, to con them by tomorrow night, and meet me in the palace wood, a mile without the town, by moonlight. There will we rehearse. For if we meet in the city we shall be dogged with company, and our devices known. In the meantime I will draw a bill of properties, such as our play wants. I pray you, fail me not.	80 85
BOTTOM	We will meet, and there we may rehearse most obscenely and courageously. Take pains; be perfect. Adieu!	
QUINCE	At the Duke's oak we meet.	90
BOTTOM	Enough. Hold, or cut bow-strings!	

They go off in different directions.

In this scene ...

- In the woods, Puck, Oberon's servant, tells a fairy that Oberon and his queen, Titania, are quarrelling.
- Oberon wants Titania to give him a little boy that she is looking after, but she refuses. He plots with Puck to gain his revenge. While Titania sleeps, Puck is to squeeze some juice from a flower onto Titania's eyes, which will make her fall in love with the first thing she sees on awakening.
- Oberon takes pity on Helena when he observes her being spurned by Demetrius and tells Puck to use the juice on Demetrius too.

In the wood a fairy meets Puck, a servant of Oberon, King of the Fairies. Puck warns the fairy that Oberon is angry because his queen, Titania, is refusing to hand over an Indian boy she is looking after.

THINK ABOUT for GCSE

Structure and form
- Think about the three worlds you have met so far: those of the court, the workmen and now the fairies. In what ways does the world of the fairies differ from the other two? Look at the characters, their language and their interests.

1 **Puck**: A 'puck' was a hobgoblin / mischievous countryside spirit.
 whither: where
3 **Thorough**: through
4 **park**: enclosed hunting ground
 pale: fenced-in land
7 **sphere**: orbit (People believed that the moon, planets and stars were fixed in transparent sphere orbiting the earth.)
9 **orbs**: fairy rings
10 **pensioners**: royal bodyguard
12 **favours**: gifts
13 **savours**: scent
16 **lob**: lout / country bumpkin
17 **anon**: straight away
18 **doth ... revels**: have his festivities
20 **passing ... wrath**: extremely bitter and angry
23 **changeling**: There was a belief that fairies stole beautiful human babies and left problematic fairy children in their place.
25 **trace**: range through
26 **perforce withholds**: keeps by force
29 **fountain**: spring
 spangled: glittering
 sheen: brightness
30 **square**: quarrel
32 **making**: build
33 **shrewd and knavish**: mischievous and trouble-making

The woods outside Athens: twilight.
Enter a FAIRY, *who meets* PUCK *coming from another direction.*

PUCK   How now, spirit, whither wander you?

FAIRY   Over hill, over dale,
Thorough bush, thorough briar,
Over park, over pale,
Thorough flood, thorough fire –   5
I do wander everywhere,
Swifter than the moon's sphere.
And I serve the Fairy Queen,
To dew her orbs upon the green.
The cowslips tall her pensioners be –   10
In their gold coats spots you see:
Those be rubies, fairy favours,
In those freckles live their savours.
I must go seek some dew-drops here,
And hang a pearl in every cowslip's ear.   15
Farewell, thou lob of spirits – I'll be gone.
Our Queen and all her elves come here anon.

PUCK   The King doth keep his revels here tonight.
Take heed the Queen come not within his sight.
For Oberon is passing fell and wrath,   20
Because that she as her attendant hath
A lovely boy, stol'n from an Indian King –
She never had so sweet a changeling.
And jealous Oberon would have the child
Knight of his train, to trace the forests wild.   25
But she perforce witholds the lovèd boy,
Crowns him with flowers, and makes him all her joy.
And now they never meet in grove or green,
By fountain clear, or spangled starlight sheen,
But they do square, that all their elves for fear   30
Creep into acorn cups and hide them there.

FAIRY   Either I mistake your shape and making quite,
Or else you are that shrewd and knavish sprite

The fairy tells Puck what she has heard about him and he describes some of his mischievous activities. Suddenly, Oberon and Titania enter and confront one another.

THINK ABOUT for GCSE

Characterisation

• A 'puck' is a pixie or hobgoblin. The fairy calls him by his real name at line 34, but most people think of him as Puck. What details might appear in a 'Wanted' poster for him? Think about his appearance, his various disguises (lines 46, 48 and 52), what he gets up to (lines 35 to 39, 44 and 47 to 54), the places he is known to visit and his different names (lines 34 and 40).

Performance and staging

• What directions would you give to the actors playing Oberon and Titania about how he might enter and how she might react?

35 **villagery**: country villages
36 **Skim milk**: steal the cream off milk
     labour in the quern: make it hard work to grind the corn
37 **bootless**: in vain (i.e. she churns, but the butter will not form)
38 **barm**: froth (i.e. the yeast won't ferment so the beer is flat)
41 **You ... work**: It was thought that, if treated kindly, Puck would do odd jobs during the night.

44 **jest**: joke
45 **beguile**: deceive
46 **filly**: female
47 **gossip's**: old woman's
48 **In very likeness of**: looking just like
     crab: crab apple
50 **dewlap**: loose skin round the neck
51 **aunt**: old woman

54 **'Tailor'**: 'O my bum!' ('Tail' was another word for 'bum'; a superstition for warding off the Devil like saying 'touch wood'.)
55 **choir**: company
56 **waxen ... mirth**: laugh even more
     sneeze: i.e. snort
58 **room**: make room

62 **forsworn**: sworn to avoid
63 **wanton**: wilful / irresponsible creature
66–8 **Corin ... Phillida**: These were usual names for a shepherd and shepherdess.

Called Robin Goodfellow. Are not you he,
That frights the maidens of the villagery,   35
Skim milk, and sometimes labour in the quern,
And bootless make the breathless housewife churn,
And sometimes make the drink to bear no barm,
Mislead night-wanderers, laughing at their harm?
Those that 'Hobgoblin' call you, and 'Sweet Puck',   40
You do their work, and they shall have good luck.
Are not you he?

PUCK   Thou speak'st aright –
I am that merry wanderer of the night.
I jest to Oberon, and make him smile,
When I a fat and bean-fed horse beguile,   45
Neighing in likeness of a filly foal.
And sometimes lurk I in a gossip's bowl,
In very likeness of a roasted crab –
And when she drinks, against her lips I bob,
And on her withered dewlap pour the ale.   50
The wisest aunt, telling the saddest tale,
Sometime for three-foot stool mistaketh me –
Then slip I from her bum, down topples she,
And 'Tailor' cries, and falls into a cough.
And then the whole choir hold their hips and laugh,   55
And waxen in their mirth, and sneeze, and swear
A merrier hour was never wasted there.
But room, fairy! Here comes Oberon.

FAIRY   And here my mistress! Would that he were gone!

Enter, from one direction, OBERON *King of the Fairies, with his*
followers. From another, enter TITANIA, *Queen of the Fairies,*
with hers.

OBERON   Ill met by moonlight, proud Titania!   60

TITANIA   What – jealous Oberon? Fairies, skip hence.
             I have forsworn his bed and company.

OBERON   Tarry, rash wanton! Am not I thy lord?

TITANIA   Then I must be thy lady. But I know
             When thou hast stol'n away from Fairyland,   65
             And in the shape of Corin sat all day

When Titania challenges Oberon about his affection for Hippolyta, he responds by accusing her of favouring Theseus. Titania complains that Oberon's quarrelling has repeatedly ruined her fairies' dances and has disturbed the natural pattern of the seasons.

THINK ABOUT for GCSE

Relationships
- What does this opening dialogue (lines 60 to 80) tell you about the relationship between Oberon and Titania?

Characterisation
- In some productions, the actors playing Oberon and Titania also play (or 'double') Theseus and Hippolyta. What similarities are there between the two couples?

67   **pipes of corn**: flutes made of straw
     versing love: writing love poems
69   **steep**: mountains
70   **forsooth**: indeed!
     bouncing: strapping
71   **buskined**: wearing hunting boots
75   **Glance … Hippolyta**: refer to / sneer at the fact that Hippolyta favours me
78–80   **Perigenia … Aegles … Ariadne and Antiopa**: Theseus had sexual relationships with all these women.
78   **ravishèd**: raped
81   **the forgeries of jealousy**: jealous fantasies
82   **spring**: beginning
83   **mead**: meadow
84   **pavèd fountain**: pebbly spring
85   **beachèd margent**: shore
86   **ringlets**: circular dances
87   **brawls**: quarrelling
91   **pelting**: small and insignificant
92   **overborne their continents**: broken their banks, flooded
93   **stretched**: strained at / pulled
94   **lost his sweat**: wasted his effort
95   **beard**: i.e. bristly growth of grain
96   **fold**: animal pen
97   **murrion**: diseased
98   **nine men's morris**: outdoor board game cut into the turf
99   **quaint … green**: intricate systems of paths cut into lush grass
100 **undistinguishable**: 1 overgrown; 2 invisible
101 **want**: lack, feel the loss of

103 **Therefore**: That is why (i.e. because of our dispute)
     governess of floods: controller of the tides
105 **rheumatic diseases**: colds and coughs

Playing on pipes of corn, and versing love
To amorous Phillida. Why art thou here,
Come from the farthest steep of India –
But that, forsooth, the bouncing Amazon,   70
Your buskined mistress and your warrior love,
To Theseus must be wedded; and you come
To give their bed joy and prosperity.

OBERON How canst thou thus, for shame, Titania,
Glance at my credit with Hippolyta,   75
Knowing I know thy love to Theseus?
Didst thou not lead him through the glimmering night
From Peregenia, whom he ravishèd?
And make him with fair Aegles break his faith,
With Ariadne, and Antiopa?   80

TITANIA These are the forgeries of jealousy! –
And never since the middle summer's spring
Met we on hill, in dale, forest, or mead,
By pavèd fountain or by rushy brook,
Or in the beachèd margent of the sea   85
To dance our ringlets to the whistling wind,
But with thy brawls thou hast disturbed our sport.
Therefore the winds, piping to us in vain,
As in revenge have sucked up from the sea
Contagious fogs – which, falling in the land,   90
Have every pelting river made so proud
That they have overborne their continents.
The ox hath therefore stretched his yoke in vain,
The ploughman lost his sweat, and the green corn
Hath rotted ere his youth attained a beard.   95
The fold stands empty in the drownèd field,
And crows are fatted with the murrion flock;
The nine men's morris is filled up with mud,
And the quaint mazes in the wanton green
For lack of tread are undistinguishable.   100
The human mortals want their winter cheer –
No night is now with hymn or carol blessed.
Therefore the moon, the governess of floods,
Pale in her anger, washes all the air,
That rheumatic diseases do abound –   105

35

Oberon offers to end the conflict if Titania will give him the 'changeling boy'. She refuses, explaining that she owes it to the child's dead mother to keep him.

106	**distemperature**: 1 bad weather; 2 disorder; 3 sickness
107	**hoary-headed**: white-haired
109	**Hiems**: the personification of winter
110	**odorous chaplet**: sweet-smelling garland
112	**childing**: fruitful / fertile
113	**wonted liveries**: usual uniforms (i.e. colours)
	mazèd: bewildered / confused
114	**increase**: produce / harvest
115–16	**this same … debate**: our quarrel has given birth to these evils
116	**dissension**: disagreement / dispute
117	**original**: origin
118	**Do *you* amend it**: You put it right
121	**henchman**: page / squire
123	**vot'ress of my order**: woman who had taken a vow to worship in Titania's sisterhood
126	**Neptune**: Roman god of the sea
127	**Marking**: watching
128	**conceive**: fill out, as though pregnant
129	**wanton**: lustful
130	**gait**: movement
133	**trifles**: little gifts
135	**of**: giving birth to
139	**Perchance**: Perhaps
140	**patiently**: peacefully
142	**shun**: avoid
	spare: avoid

THINK ABOUT for GCSE

Language
- How does the language of Titania's speech (lines 81 to 117) effectively convey a picture of a natural world in a state of disorder? Look, for example, at the use of adjectives ('contagious', 'drownèd') and images ('And on old Hiems… in mockery, set').

Context
- The argument between Oberon and Titania is not just a personal dispute. What does Titania's speech (lines 81 to 117) reveal about the power of the fairy world to influence the seasons?

And thorough this distemperature we see
The seasons alter: hoary-headed frosts
Fall in the fresh lap of the crimson rose,
And on old Hiems' thin and icy crown
An odorous chaplet of sweet summer buds   110
Is, as in mockery, set. The spring, the summer,
The childing autumn, angry winter, change
Their wonted liveries, and the mazèd world
By their increase now knows not which is which.
And this same progeny of evils comes   115
From our debate, from our dissension.
We are their parents and original.

OBERON   Do *you* amend it, then: it lies in you.
                Why should Titania cross her Oberon?
                I do but beg a little changeling boy   120
                To be my henchman.

TITANIA   Set your heart at rest.
                The fairy land buys not the child of me.
                His mother was a vot'ress of my order,
                And in the spicèd Indian air by night
                Full often hath she gossiped by my side,   125
                And sat with me on Neptune's yellow sands,
                Marking th' embarkèd traders on the flood –
                When we have laughed to see the sails conceive
                And grow big-bellied with the wanton wind –
                Which she with pretty and with swimming gait   130
                Following, her womb then rich with my young squire,
                Would imitate, and sail upon the land
                To fetch me trifles – and return again
                As from a voyage, rich with merchandise.
                But she, being mortal, of that boy did die: 135
                And for her sake do I rear up her boy.
                And for her sake I will not part with him.

OBERON   How long within this wood intend you stay?

TITANIA   Perchance till after Theseus' wedding-day.
                If you will patiently dance in our round,   140
                And see our moonlight revels, go with us.
                If not, shun me, and I will spare your haunts.

Oberon plans his revenge. He remembers a time when he saw a flower hit by Cupid's arrow, and tells Puck to fetch the flower for him. The juice of the flower has the power to make someone fall in love with the first thing they see upon wakening. Oberon plans to use it on Titania.

THINK ABOUT
for GCSE

Characterisation
- What do you think might be going through Oberon's mind as Titania leaves?

Themes and issues
- What does the story of Cupid and the 'fair vestal' (lines 155 to 164) tell us about the part played by accident and chance in the affairs of **love**? What part has been played so far by chance in the love affairs of Hermia, Helena, Lysander and Demetrius?

145 **chide downright**: quarrel openly

149 **Since**: the time when

151 **dulcet … breath**: sweet, melodious song
152 **rude**: 1 rough; 2 ill-mannered
     civil: 1 gentle; 2 polite

157 **all**: fully
     certain: sure
158 **vestal … west**: virgin enthroned / ruling in the west.
159 **shaft**: arrow
160 **As**: as if
161 **might**: could
162 **Quenched**: extinguished
     chaste: sexually pure
163 **imperial vot'ress**: queen dedicated to virginity (a reference to Queen Elizabeth I)
164 **fancy-free**: unaffected by love / love's power
165 **bolt**: arrow
168 **Love-in-idleness**: pansy or viola, also known as heartsease
171 **or man or**: either man or
     dote: be infatuated with
174 **Ere**: before
     leviathan: whale / sea-monster
     league: i.e. three miles

OBERON	Give me that boy, and I will go with thee.	
TITANIA	Not for thy fairy kingdom. Fairies, away!	
	We shall chide downright if I longer stay.	145

Exit TITANIA, ***with her followers.***

OBERON	Well, go thy way. Thou shalt not from this grove	
	Till I torment thee for this injury!	
	My gentle Puck, come hither. Thou rememb'rest	
	Since once I sat upon a promontory,	
	And heard a mermaid on a dolphin's back	150
	Uttering such dulcet and harmonious breath	
	That the rude sea grew civil at her song,	
	And certain stars shot madly from their spheres	
	To hear the sea-maid's music?	
PUCK	I remember.	
OBERON	That very time I saw, but thou couldst not,	155
	Flying between the cold moon and the earth,	
	Cupid, all armed. A certain aim he took	
	At a fair vestal thronèd by the west,	
	And loosed his love-shaft smartly from his bow	
	As it should pierce a hundred thousand hearts.	160
	But I might see young Cupid's fiery shaft	
	Quenched in the chaste beams of the watery moon –	
	And the imperial vot'ress passèd on,	
	In maiden meditation, fancy-free.	
	Yet marked I where the bolt of Cupid fell:	165
	It fell upon a little western flower –	
	Before, milk-white, now purple with love's wound,	
	And maidens call it 'Love-in-idleness'.	
	Fetch me that flower, the herb I showed thee once.	
	The juice of it on sleeping eye-lids laid	170
	Will make or man or woman madly dote	
	Upon the next live creature that it sees.	
	Fetch me this herb – and be thou here again	
	Ere the leviathan can swim a league.	
PUCK	I'll put a girdle round about the earth	175
	In forty minutes!	

Exit.

Oberon squeezes the flower's juice on Titania's eyes as she sleeps. When she awakes, and is distracted by falling in love with some hideous creature, he will get the child from her. Hearing people approaching, Oberon, being invisible, overhears Demetrius rejecting Helena.

185 **render**: give

190 **slayeth**: is killing
192 **and wood**: and mad

195 **draw**: attract
     adamant: 1 very hard substance; 2 magnet
197 **Leave you**: If you give up
199 **entice you**: try to attract you
     speak you fair: speak kindly to you

203 **spaniel**: breed of dog famous for its faithfulness
204 **fawn on**: show cringing affection to
205 **Use me but**: Just treat me
     spurn: 1 reject; 2 kick
206 **leave**: permission

211 **Tempt not ... spirit**: Don't push my hatred too far

THINK ABOUT for GCSE

Performance and staging
• As a director, would you want the audience to approve or disapprove of Oberon's plan (lines 177 to 185)? For example, should it be seen as an amusing practical joke or spiteful revenge?

Structure and form
• What do you think has happened between Helena and Demetrius since we last saw them in Act 1 Scene 1?

OBERON	Having once this juice,
	I'll watch Titania when she is asleep,
	And drop the liquor of it in her eyes.
	The next thing then she, waking, looks upon –

OBERON   Having once this juice,
I'll watch Titania when she is asleep,
And drop the liquor of it in her eyes.
The next thing then she, waking, looks upon –
Be it on lion, bear, or wolf, or bull,   **180**
On meddling monkey or on busy ape –
She shall pursue it with the soul of love.
And ere I take this charm from off her sight –
As I can take it with another herb –
I'll make her render up her page to me.   **185**
But who comes here? I am invisible,
And I will overhear their conference.

Enter DEMETRIUS, *followed by* HELENA.

DEMETRIUS   I love thee not, therefore pursue me not!
Where is Lysander, and fair Hermia?
The one I'll slay, the other slayeth me.   **190**
Thou told'st me they were stol'n unto this wood –
And here am I, and wood within this wood,
Because I cannot meet my Hermia.
Hence, get thee gone, and follow me no more!

HELENA   You draw me, you hard-hearted adamant!   **195**
But yet you draw not iron, for my heart
Is true as steel. Leave you your power to draw,
And I shall have no power to follow you.

DEMETRIUS   Do I entice you? Do I speak you fair?
Or rather do I not in plainest truth   **200**
Tell you I do not nor I cannot love you?

HELENA   And even for that do I love you the more.
I am your spaniel – and, Demetrius,
The more you beat me I will fawn on you.
Use me but as your spaniel: spurn me, strike me,   **205**
Neglect me, lose me – only give me leave,
Unworthy as I am, to follow you.
What worser place can I beg in your love,
And yet a place of high respect with me,
Than to be usèd as you use your dog?   **210**

DEMETRIUS   Tempt not too much the hatred of my spirit –

Demetrius rejects and threatens
Helena and runs off into the
woods.

214 **impeach your modesty**: discredit your
    chaste behaviour
215 **To leave**: by leaving
218 **ill ... place**: wicked thoughts (i.e. that I
    might have, being alone with you in a
    deserted spot)
220 **privilege**: safeguard
    for that: because

224 **in my respect**: to my mind

227 **brakes**: thickets

230–1 **the story ... chase**: In classical myth,
    Daphne was chased by the god Apollo;
    here, the woman chases the man.
232 **griffin**: ferocious mythical beast, part
    eagle, part lion
    hind: female deer
233 **bootless**: useless
235 **stay**: wait for
236–7 **do not believe but**: you'd better
    believe that
237 **mischief**: harm
239 **Fie**: You should be ashamed!
240 **set ... sex**: make me behave in a way
    that disgraces womankind

244 **upon**: by

THINK ABOUT for GCSE

Performance and staging

• While Oberon is invisible
  to them, what might he do
  during the exchange between
  Helena and Demetrius? Does
  he just stand out of the way,
  for example, or could he
  influence their behaviour in
  some way?

• If you were directing, what
  advice might you give to
  the actor playing Demetrius
  about how hard and
  unpleasant he should be to
  Helena? How would you
  want the audience to feel
  about him?

	For I am sick when I do look on thee.	
HELENA	And I am sick when I look *not* on you.	
DEMETRIUS	You do impeach your modesty too much,	
	To leave the city and commit yourself	215
	Into the hands of one that loves you not –	
	To trust the opportunity of night	
	And the ill counsel of a desert place	
	With the rich worth of your virginity.	
HELENA	Your virtue is my privilege – for that	220
	It is not night when I do see your face,	
	Therefore I think I am not in the night.	
	Nor doth this wood lack worlds of company,	
	For you, in my respect, are all the world.	
	Then how can it be said I am alone,	225
	When all the world is here to look on me?	
DEMETRIUS	I'll run from thee and hide me in the brakes,	
	And leave thee to the mercy of wild beasts!	
HELENA	The wildest hath not such a heart as you.	
	Run when you will, the story shall be changed:	230
	Apollo flies, and Daphne holds the chase;	
	The dove pursues the griffin; the mild hind	
	Makes speed to catch the tiger – bootless speed,	
	When cowardice pursues, and valour flies!	
DEMETRIUS	I will not stay thy questions. Let me go –	235
	Or, if thou follow me, do not believe	
	But I shall do thee mischief in the wood.	
HELENA	Ay, in the temple, in the town, the field	
	You do me mischief. Fie, Demetrius!	
	Your wrongs do set a scandal on my sex!	240
	We cannot fight for love, as men may do;	
	We should be wooed, and were not made to woo.	

Exit DEMETRIUS.

I'll follow thee, and make a heaven of hell,
To die upon the hand I love so well!

Exit HELENA, *following.*

Oberon vows to make Demetrius pursue Helena. Oberon explains to Puck how he plans to anoint Titania's eyes as she sleeps. He tells Puck to search the wood for a young man who is rejecting a sweet Athenian lady. Puck is to anoint the man's eyes so that he will fall in love with the lady when he awakes.

245 **nymph**: 1 mythological nature-spirit; 2 beautiful girl

249 **blows**: blooms
251 **Quite over-canopied**: completely roofed over
251–2 **luscious … eglantine**: luxuriant honeysuckle, rambling roses and sweetbriar
253 **sometime of**: at some time during
255 **throws**: sheds
256 **Weed**: cloth / a garment
257 **streak**: smear / anoint
258 **hateful fantasies**: horrible imaginings

THINK ABOUT for GCSE

Language
• How effective is the descriptive part of Oberon's speech to Puck)?

Structure and form
• Puck reassures Oberon by saying 'Fear not … do so' (line 268). What do you think could go wrong?

Context
• Look at Titania's speech (lines 81 to 117) and Oberon's instructions (lines 248 to 267). Shakespeare set this play in ancient Athens, but what details tell us that his audience might have recognised a description of England?

265 **Effect**: Do
    that: so that
266 **fond on**: infatuated with
267 **ere**: before

OBERON	Fare thee well, nymph! Ere he do leave this grove **245** Thou shalt fly *him*, and he shall seek *thy* love.

Re-enter PUCK.

– Hast thou the flower there? Welcome, wanderer.

PUCK	Ay, there it is.

OBERON	I pray thee give it me. I know a bank where the wild thyme blows, Where oxlips and the nodding violet grows – **250** Quite over-canopied with luscious woodbine, With sweet musk-roses, and with eglantine. There sleeps Titania sometime of the night, Lulled in those flowers with dances and delight – And there the snake throws her enamelled skin, **255** Weed wide enough to wrap a fairy in. And with the juice of this I'll streak her eyes, And make her full of hateful fantasies. Take thou some of it, and seek through this grove: A sweet Athenian lady is in love **260** With a disdainful youth. Anoint his eyes – But do it when the next thing he espies May be the lady. Thou shalt know the man By the Athenian garments he hath on. Effect it with some care, that he may prove **265** More fond on her than she upon her love. – And look thou meet me ere the first cock crow.

PUCK	Fear not, my lord. Your servant shall do so.

Exit OBERON.
PUCK *goes off in another direction.*

In this scene ...

- Oberon squeezes the magic juice onto Titania's eyes as she sleeps.
- Hermia and Lysander are lost and decide to sleep where they are for the night. Puck mistakenly squeezes the magic juice on Lysander's eyes and, when he awakes, he falls in love with Helena.
- Hermia wakes up to find herself alone and goes to look for Lysander.

Titania and her fairies arrive at her usual sleeping place. She falls asleep as the fairies sing a lullaby.

Line	Gloss
1	**roundel**: dance in a ring
3	**cankers**: caterpillars, grubs
4	**rere-mice**: bats
6	**clamorous**: noisy
7	**quaint**: beautiful, dainty and strange
8	**offices**: duties
9	**double**: forked
11	**blind-worms**: slow-worms (like newts, mistakenly believed poisonous)
13	**Philomel**: nightingale
19	**nigh**: near
24	**offence**: harm

THINK ABOUT for GCSE

Context

- What might Titania's words (lines 1 to 8) and the song (lines 9 to 24) tell us about fairies, as they were imagined by Shakespeare's audience?

Performance and staging

- There are songs in many Shakespeare plays. What kind of music might fit the fairies' words here?

Deeper in the woods: near Titania's wild-flower sleeping place.
Enter TITANIA, *with her* FAIRIES.

TITANIA   Come – now, a roundel and a fairy song.
                  Then, for the third part of a minute, hence –
                  Some to kill cankers in the musk-rose buds –
                  Some war with rere-mice for their leathern wings
                  To make my small elves coats – and some keep back   5
                  The clamorous owl that nightly hoots and wonders
                  At our quaint spirits. Sing me now asleep.
                  Then to your offices, and let me rest.

      As the FAIRIES *sing,* TITANIA *lies down to sleep.*

FIRST FAIRY   (*Sings*)
                  You spotted snakes with double tongue,
                  Thorny hedgehogs, be not seen.   10
                  Newts and blind-worms, do no wrong –
                  Come not near our Fairy Queen.

ALL   (*Chorus*)
                  Philomel with melody
                  Sing in our sweet lullaby:
                  Lulla lulla lullaby   15
                  Lulla lulla lullaby.
                  Never harm
                  Nor spell nor charm
                  Come our lovely lady nigh –
                  So good night, with lullaby.   20

SECOND FAIRY   (*Sings*)
                  Weaving spiders, come not here –
                  Hence, you long-legg'd spinners, hence!
                  Beetles black approach not near,
                  Worm nor snail do no offence.

Oberon squeezes the magic juice onto Titania's eyes. Lysander and Hermia arrive, lost and exhausted, and decide to stay put for the night. Hermia persuades Lysander to lie a proper distance away from her.

34 **aloof**: at a distance
sentinel: guard

37 **languish**: pine away
38 **ounce**: lynx
39 **Pard**: leopard

THINK ABOUT for GCSE

Performance and staging

- In what tone might Oberon utter his charm (lines 35 to 42)?

- What might Hermia and Lysander look like when they enter at line 43? How might Hermia react to Lysander's admission that he is lost?

46 **tarry**: wait

50 **one troth**: one promise / truth

ALL	(*Chorus*)	
	Philomel with melody	25
	Sing in our sweet lullaby:	
	Lulla lulla lullaby	
	Lulla lulla lullaby.	
	Never harm	
	Nor spell nor charm	30
	Come our lovely lady nigh –	
	So good night, with lullaby.	

TITANIA *sleeps.*

FIRST FAIRY	Hence – away! Now all is well.
	One aloof stand sentinel.

Exit, with the others.

Enter OBERON. *He approaches and squeezes the juice of the flower onto* TITANIA*'s eyelids.*

OBERON	What thou seest when thou dost wake,	35
	Do it for thy true love take –	
	Love and languish for his sake.	
	Be it ounce, or cat, or bear,	
	Pard, or boar with bristled hair	
	In thy eye that shall appear	40
	When thou wak'st, it is thy dear.	
	Wake when some vile thing is near!	

Exit.

Enter LYSANDER *and* HERMIA.

LYSANDER	Fair love, you faint with wandering in the wood,	
	And, to speak truth, I have forgot our way.	
	We'll rest us, Hermia, if you think it good,	45
	And tarry for the comfort of the day.	
HERMIA	Be it so, Lysander. Find you out a bed,	
	For I upon this bank will rest my head.	
LYSANDER	One turf shall serve as pillow for us both –	
	One heart, one bed, two bosoms, and one troth.	50
HERMIA	Nay, good Lysander. For my sake, my dear,	
	Lie further off yet: do not lie so near.	

As they sleep, Puck enters and, mistakenly assuming that these are the Athenian couple he has been sent to find, squeezes magic juice on Lysander's eyes.

53 take ... innocence!: interpret my meaning as innocent

54 Love ... conference: Love allows lovers to understand one another

57 bosoms: hearts / sets of feelings

60 lie: 1 deceive; 2 lie down

61 prettily: cleverly

62 beshrew: shame on

65 human: polite

67 Becomes: is fitting for

70 Amen: So be it

THINK ABOUT for GCSE

73 With ... pressed!: May you share the rest you have wished on me

Characterisation

• Hermia is not comfortable with the idea of lying down next to Lysander. Write down what each character might actually be thinking at lines 50, 52, 60, 68 and 72.

76 approve: test

Performance and staging

• Puck appears not to notice Hermia and Lysander immediately. Think of comic ways in which he might discover them. (In one production he actually mistook Lysander for a log and sat down on him.)

79 Weeds: Clothes

81 Despisèd: who despised (hated)

84 durst: dares

86 Churl: Rude scoundrel

87 owe: own

LYSANDER	O take the sense, sweet, of my innocence!
	Love takes the meaning in love's conference.
	I mean that my heart unto yours is knit, 55
	So that but one heart we can make of it –
	Two bosoms interchainèd with an oath,
	So then, two bosoms, and a single troth.
	Then by your side no bed-room me deny –
	For lying so, Hermia, I do not lie. 60

HERMIA	Lysander riddles very prettily.
	Now much beshrew my manners and my pride
	If Hermia meant to say Lysander lied.
	But, gentle friend, for love and courtesy
	Lie further off, in human modesty. 65
	Such separation as may well be said
	Becomes a virtuous bachelor and a maid,
	So far be distant – and good night, sweet friend:
	Thy love ne'er alter, till thy sweet life end!

LYSANDER	Amen, amen, to that fair prayer say I – 70
	And then end life when I end loyalty!
	Here is my bed. Sleep give thee all his rest.

HERMIA	With half that wish, the wisher's eyes be pressed!

They lie down separately, and sleep.
Enter PUCK.

PUCK	Through the forest have I gone,
	But Athenian found I none 75
	On whose eyes I might approve
	This flower's force in stirring love.
	Night and silence. – Who is here?
	Weeds of Athens he doth wear.
	This is he, my master said, 80
	Despisèd the Athenian maid –
	And here the maiden, sleeping sound,
	On the dank and dirty ground.
	Pretty soul, she durst not lie
	Near this lack-love, this kill-courtesy. 85
	Churl, upon thy eyes I throw
	All the power this charm doth owe!

Demetrius enters, still trying to get away from Helena. He runs off and Helena, too tired to keep chasing, stumbles across the sleeping Lysander. Awakening under the effects of the magic juice, Lysander immediately falls in love with Helena.

88–9 forbid ... eyelid: prevent you from getting any sleep

93 charge thee hence: command you to go away

94 darkling: in the dark

96 fond: 1 foolish; 2 infatuated

97 the lesser ... grace: the less my prayers are answered

98 wheresoe'er: wherever

THINK ABOUT *for* GCSE

Performance and staging

- What is your attitude to Helena at this point? If you were playing her, would you want the audience to feel sorry for her? Or would you want the audience to see why Demetrius is annoyed with her?
- Where might the actors find some comic moments after Lysander wakes up?

104 no marvel though: it's no wonder that

105 as: as though I were

106 dissembling glass: deceitful mirror

107 sphery eyne: starry eyes

112 Transparent: 1 Bright / Beautiful; 2 Open, without any deceit

shows art: gives me the skill

He squeezes juice from the flower onto LYSANDER's *eyelids.*

> When thou wak'st let love forbid
> Sleep his seat on thy eyelid.
> So awake when I am gone –   **90**
> For I must now to Oberon.

Exit.

Enter DEMETRIUS, *running, pursued by* HELENA.

HELENA   Stay – though thou kill me – sweet Demetrius!

DEMETRIUS   I charge thee hence, and do not haunt me thus.

HELENA   O wilt thou darkling leave me? Do not so!

DEMETRIUS   Stay on thy peril. I alone will go.   **95**

Exit.

HELENA   O – I am out of breath in this fond chase!
> The more my prayer, the lesser is my grace.
> Happy is Hermia, wheresoe'er she lies,
> For *she* hath blessèd and attractive eyes.
> How came her eyes so bright? Not with salt tears –   **100**
> If so, my eyes are oftener washed than hers.
> No, no, I am as ugly as a bear –
> For beasts that meet me run away for fear!
> Therefore no marvel though Demetrius
> Do as a monster fly my presence thus.   **105**
> What wicked and dissembling glass of mine
> Made me compare with Hermia's sphery eyne?
> But who is here? – Lysander, on the ground?
> Dead – or asleep? I see no blood, no wound.
> Lysander! If you live, good sir, awake!   **110**

LYSANDER   (*Waking and seeing her*)
> And run through fire I will for thy sweet sake!
> Transparent Helena! Nature shows art
> That through thy bosom makes me see thy heart.
> Where is Demetrius? O how fit a word
> Is that vile name, to perish on my sword!   **115**

Convinced that Lysander is making fun of her, Helena leaves him. Lysander bids farewell to the sleeping Hermia and goes off to devote himself to his new love, Helena.

THINK ABOUT *for* **GCSE**

Language

• Lysander finds a number of images to explain his change of heart (lines 119 to 130). Hermia is a 'raven' (dark and unattractive) compared with Helena's 'dove' (fair and beautiful); his own reason has only now 'ripened' like a fruit; and it now becomes the 'marshal' (or guide) to his wilder emotions. Finally, in Helena's eyes, he can read 'Love's stories, written in love's richest book'. Choose one of these images and think about the ways in which it helps us to understand what Lysander is trying to express.

117 **What though**: What of it if

123 **will**: inclination / desire
swayed: ruled

126 **ripe not to reason**: have only now fully developed my powers of reasoning
127 **touching … point**: reaching the peak
skill: discernment / intelligence
128 **marshal**: guide
129 **o'erlook**: read / look through
131 **Wherefore**: Why
keen: biting

136 **flout**: mock
insufficiency: inadequacy
137 **Good troth**: Truly
good sooth: indeed
139 **Perforce … confess**: I have to say
140 **lord … gentleness**: more of a gentleman
141 **of**: by
142 **abused**: mistreated

145 **as a surfeit**: just as eating too much
146 **The deepest … brings**: puts you off them completely
147 **heresies**: false beliefs
leave: reject / renounce
148 **of**: by

HELENA	Do not say so, Lysander – say not so.
	What though he love your Hermia? Lord, what
	though?
	Yet Hermia still loves you. Then be content.

LYSANDER	Content with Hermia? No! – I do repent
	The tedious minutes I with her have spent.	120
	Not Hermia but *Helena* I love.
	Who will not change a raven for a dove?
	The will of man is by his reason swayed,
	And reason says you are the worthier maid.
	Things growing are not ripe until their season –	125
	So I, being young, till now ripe not to reason.
	And touching now the point of human skill,
	Reason becomes the marshal to my will,
	And leads me to your eyes – where I o'erlook
	Love's stories, written in love's richest book!	130

HELENA	Wherefore was I to this keen mockery born?
	When at your hands did I deserve this scorn?
	Is 't not enough – is 't not enough, young man,
	That I did never – no – nor never can
	Deserve a sweet look from Demetrius' eye,	135
	But you must flout my insufficiency?
	Good troth, you do me wrong – good sooth, you do,
	In such disdainful manner me to woo!
	But fare you well. Perforce I must confess
	I thought you lord of more true gentleness.	140
	O, that a lady of one man refused
	Should of another therefore be abused!

Exit.

LYSANDER	She sees not Hermia. Hermia, sleep thou there –
	And never mayst thou come Lysander near.
	For, as a surfeit of the sweetest things	145
	The deepest loathing to the stomach brings,
	Or as the heresies that men do leave,
	Are hated most of those they did deceive,
	So thou, my surfeit and my heresy,
	Of all be hated, but the most of me!	150

Awakening from a nightmare only to find Lysander gone, Hermia runs off into the woods looking for him.

151 **address**: direct / apply

155 **Ay me, for pity!**: (expressions of distress)

158 **prey**: attack
159 **removed**: gone away

161 **Alack**: i.e. expression of dismay
     and if: if
162 **of all loves!**: for love's sake!
     swoon: faint

THINK ABOUT for GCSE

Context
- Dreams were of great significance to the Elizabethans. What unspoken fears about Lysander's love might Hermia's dream reveal (lines 153 to 158)?

Language
- Look at the concluding two speeches of this act (lines 143 to 164). What does Lysander's choice of nouns and verbs reveal about the strength of his feelings? Why do you think Hermia's speech is so full of exclamations and questions?

And, all my powers, address your love and might
To honour Helen, and to be her knight!

Exit.

HERMIA   (*Waking*)
Help me, Lysander, help me! – Do thy best
To pluck this crawling serpent from my breast!
Ay me, for pity! What a dream was here!   155
Lysander! – Look how I do quake with fear.
Methought a serpent ate my heart away,
And you sat smiling at his cruel prey.
Lysander! – What, removed? – Lysander! Lord!
What, out of hearing? – Gone? – No sound, no word?   160
Alack, where are you? Speak and if you hear.
Speak, of all loves! I swoon almost with fear.
No? Then I well perceive you are not nigh.
Either death or you I'll find immediately.

Exit.

In this scene ...

- The Mechanicals meet in the wood to rehearse their play. They discuss how to solve some of its problems and begin their rehearsal.
- When Puck fixes an ass's head on Bottom, the others are frightened and run off.
- Awaking at the sound of Bottom's voice, Titania falls in love with him and takes him off to her bower.

The Mechanicals decide to hold their rehearsal in the clearing where, unknown to them, Titania is sleeping. When Bottom suggests that the death of Pyramus in their play will upset the ladies, Peter Quince agrees to write an explanatory prologue.

THINK ABOUT for GCSE

Context
- The early audiences for *A Midsummer Night's Dream* must have contained some people who were new to the theatre but also many regulars. What tells us that Peter Quince and his friends have seen plays being performed? What do they seem to know about plays and the theatre?

2 **Pat**: Promptly
4 **brake**: thicket / clump of bushes
   tiring-house: dressing-room (in a playhouse)

7 **bully Bottom**: Bottom, old mate

10 **abide**: tolerate
12 **By 'r lakin**: By Our Lady (from lady-kin; a mild oath)
    parlous: terrible
13 **done**: said and done
14 **Not a whit**: Not at all
    device: plan
15 **prologue**: introductory speech

21 **in eight and six**: like a ballad with alternating lines of eight and six syllables

27 **fearful**: terrifying
    wildfowl: wild bird (he means 'wild beast')
28 **look to 't**: do something about it

The same place in the woods.

TITANIA *sleeps on, unseen, as before.*

Enter QUINCE, SNUG, BOTTOM, FLUTE, SNOUT *and* STARVELING.

BOTTOM	Are we all met?
QUINCE	Pat, pat. And here's a marvellous convenient place for our rehearsal. This green plot shall be our stage, this hawthorn-brake our tiring-house. And we will do it in action, as we will do it before the Duke.
BOTTOM	Peter Quince?
QUINCE	What sayest thou, bully Bottom?
BOTTOM	There are things in this comedy of Pyramus and Thisby that will never please. First, Pyramus must draw a sword to kill himself – which the ladies cannot abide. How answer you that?
SNOUT	By 'r lakin, a parlous fear!
STARVELING	I believe we must leave the killing out, when all is done.
BOTTOM	Not a whit. I have a device to make all well. Write me a prologue, and let the prologue seem to say we will do no harm with our swords, and that Pyramus is not killed indeed. And for the more better assurance, tell them that I, Pyramus, am not Pyramus, but Bottom the weaver. This will put them out of fear.
QUINCE	Well, we will have such a prologue – and it shall be written in eight and six.
BOTTOM	No, make it two more. Let it be written in eight and eight.
SNOUT	Will not the ladies be afeard of the lion?
STARVELING	I fear it, I promise you.
BOTTOM	Masters, you ought to consider with yourself. To bring in – God shield us! – a lion among ladies is a most dreadful thing. For there is not a more fearful wildfowl than your lion living – and we ought to look to 't.
SNOUT	Therefore, another prologue must tell he is not a lion.

5

10

15

20

25

The Mechanicals decide that, in order not to alarm people, Snug should explain that he is not actually a lion, and that one of them can represent the moon by entering with a thorn-bush and lantern. Bottom suggests that the wall that divides the lovers can be represented by a man in a wall-like costume.

THINK ABOUT for GCSE

Context

• What kind of audience is Bottom expecting at the Duke's court? How does he think they might react to the Pyramus and Thisby play?

• In Shakespeare's time, plays were staged with a minimum of scenery and much was left to the audience's imagination. What do Quince and his actors fail to realise about how theatre works when they raise the 'problems' of: the lion (Act 1 Scene 2, lines 60 to 68 and Act 3 Scene 1, lines 23 to 39); Pyramus killing himself (Act 3 Scene 1, lines 9 to 19); moonlight (Act 3 Scene 1, lines 40 to 52); and the wall (Act 3 Scene 1, lines 52 to 61)?

32 **defect**: imperfection (he means 'effect')

35 **my life for yours**: I swear you're safe (on my life)
36 **it were … life**: it would be a terrible thing (my life would be at risk)

44 **almanac**: calendar

47 **casement**: one side (of the window)

50–1 **bush … lantern**: i.e. objects thought to be carried by the Man in the Moon
51 **disfigure**: spoil / deface (he means 'figure': represent)

57 **present**: represent
58 **loam**: clay
     rough-cast: lime and gravel plaster
60 **cranny**: small opening

63 **rehearse**: recite
65 **according to his cue**: when it is his turn to speak

BOTTOM	Nay, you must name his name, and half his face must be seen through the lion's neck. And he himself must speak through, saying thus, or to the same defect: 'Ladies', or 'Fair ladies', 'I would wish you' or 'I would request you', or 'I would entreat you, not to fear, not to tremble: my life for yours. If you think I come hither as a lion, it were pity of my life. No, I am no such thing. I am a man as other men are.' And there indeed let him name his name, and tell them plainly he is Snug the joiner.
QUINCE	Well, it shall be so. But there is two hard things: that is, to bring the moonlight into a chamber – for, you know, Pyramus and Thisby meet by moonlight.
SNOUT	Doth the moon shine that night we play our play?
BOTTOM	A calendar, a calendar! Look in the almanac – find out moonshine, find out moonshine!
QUINCE	Yes, it doth shine that night.
BOTTOM	Why, then may you leave a casement of the great chamber window, where we play, open, and the moon may shine in at the casement.
QUINCE	Ay – or else one must come in with a bush of thorns and a lantern, and say he comes to disfigure, or to present, the person of Moonshine. Then there is another thing. We must have a wall in the great chamber – for Pyramus and Thisby, says the story, did talk through the chink of a wall.
SNOUT	You can never bring in a wall. What say you, Bottom?
BOTTOM	Some man or other must present Wall – and let him have some plaster, or some loam, or some rough-cast about him, to signify wall. Or let him hold his fingers thus – and through that cranny shall Pyramus and Thisby whisper.
QUINCE	If that may be, then all is well. Come, sit down, every mother's son, and rehearse your parts. Pyramus, you begin. When you have spoken your speech, enter into that brake – and so every one according to his cue.

30

35

40

45

50

55

60

65

As they begin their rehearsal, Puck enters and watches them. While Bottom is 'off-stage', Puck mischievously gives him an ass's head.

THINK ABOUT for GCSE

Context

- In Shakespeare's playhouse, actors were not given complete scripts, just their own speeches with one or two 'cue' lines of other characters to tell them when to speak. What in lines 77 to 90 shows that Flute doesn't know about cues and parts?

Performance and staging

- The *Pyramus and Thisby* playscript contains some terrible poetry (known as 'doggerel'). To fill out the six-beat lines with the right number of syllables, it features 'brisky' (rather than 'brisk'), 'Juvenal' (rather than 'youth'), 'eke' (rather than 'also'). In an attempt to find rhymes, 'Jew' rhymes with 'hue', and 'tire' with 'briar'. How might these lines be performed to bring out the comedy?

66 **hempen home-spuns**: yokels in rough hemp clothing
   swaggering: blustering / showing off
67 **cradle**: resting-place
68 **toward**: about to take place / in preparation
   auditor: audience member

71 **odious**: hateful (he should say 'odorous': sweet-smelling)

83 **brisky juvenal**: lively young man
   eke: also
   most lovely jew: Possibly Flute's mistake for 'jewel' or put in just to make a rhyme.
85 **Ninny**: fool (he means 'Ninus')

88 **cues**: last words of the previous actor's speech

Enter PUCK, *unseen, behind the rehearsal.*

PUCK	(*Aside*) What hempen home-spuns have we
	swaggering here,
	So near the cradle of the Fairy Queen?
	What, a play toward? I'll be an auditor –
	An actor too, perhaps, if I see cause.

QUINCE	Speak, Pyramus! Thisby, stand forth!	**70**

BOTTOM (*as* PYRAMUS)	Thisby, the flowers of odious savours sweet!

QUINCE	'Odorous!' – 'Odours!'

BOTTOM (*as* PYRAMUS)	– *odours* savours sweet.	
	So hath thy breath, my dearest Thisby dear.	
	But hark, a voice! Stay thou but here a while,	
	And by and by I will to thee appear.	**75**

Exit into the bushes.

PUCK	(*Aside*) A stranger Pyramus than e'er played here!

He goes after BOTTOM.

FLUTE	Must I speak now?

QUINCE	Ay, marry, must you. For you must understand he	
	goes but to see a noise that he heard, and is to come	
	again.	**80**

FLUTE (*as* THISBY)	Most radiant Pyramus, most lily-white of hue,	
	Of colour like the red rose on triumphant briar,	
	Most brisky juvenal, and eke most lovely Jew,	
	As true as truest horse, that yet would never tire –	
	I'll meet thee, Pyramus, at Ninny's tomb.	**85**

QUINCE	'Ninus' tomb', man! – Why, you must not speak that
	yet. That you answer to Pyramus! You speak all your
	part at once – cues and all. Pyramus, enter! Your
	cue is past – it is 'never tire'.

FLUTE (*as* THISBY)	O – As true as truest horse, that yet would never tire.	**90**

When Bottom returns, unaware of his changed appearance, the others are terrified and run off. Convinced that his friends are playing a trick to try to frighten him, Bottom sings to show that he isn't scared.

91 fair: handsome

94 about a round: a merry dance

97 fire: Hobgoblins were linked with will-o'-the-wisp, the ghostly flame caused by marsh gas.

THINK ABOUT for GCSE

Language

• Bottom and Quince occasionally use malapropisms (mistakenly using a wrong word which sounds similar to the correct one). Look at these examples: 'aggravate' (Act 1 Scene 2, line 66), 'obscenely' (Act 1 Scene 2, line 88), 'defect' (Act 3 Scene 1, line 32), 'disfigure' (Act 3 Scene 1, line 51), 'odious' (Act 3 Scene 1, line 71) and 'Ninny' (Act 3 Scene 1, line 85). What meaning were they trying to get across? How does each example add to the comedy?

100 knavery: dirty trick

105 translated: transformed

110 ousel-cock: male blackbird

Re-enter BOTTOM (*transformed by* PUCK): *he now has an ass's head.*

BOTTOM (*as* PYRAMUS)	If I were fair, fair Thisby, I were only thine –
QUINCE	O monstrous! O strange! We are haunted! Pray, masters – fly, masters. Help!

All rush off in panic.

BOTTOM *and* PUCK *remain.*

PUCK	(*Aside, looking after the runaways*) I'll follow you – I'll lead you about a round, Through bog, through bush, through brake, through briar!	95
	Sometime a horse I'll be, sometime a hound, A hog, a headless bear, sometime a fire – And neigh, and bark, and grunt, and roar, and burn, Like horse, hound, hog, bear, fire, at every turn.	

Exit.

BOTTOM	Why do they run away? This is a knavery of them to make me afeard.	100

Re-enter SNOUT.

SNOUT	O Bottom, thou art changed! What do I see on thee?
BOTTOM	What do you see? You see an ass-head of your own, do you?

SNOUT *runs off again.*

Re-enter QUINCE.

QUINCE	Bless thee Bottom, bless thee! Thou art translated!	105

He runs away again.

BOTTOM	I see their knavery. This is to make an ass of me – to fright me, if they could. But I will not stir from this place, do what they can. I will walk up and down here, and I will sing, that they shall hear I am not afraid.

(*He sings.*)
	The ousel-cock so black of hue With orange-tawny bill,	110

Titania awakes at the sound and, under the influence of the magic flower, immediately declares her love for Bottom.

112 **throstle**: thrush
113 **quill**: 1 shrill voice; 2 throat

116 **plain-song**: simple melody
119 **set his wit**: use his intelligence (Bottom is thinking of the proverb: it's a waste of time using your intelligence to answer a fool.)
120 **give a *bird* the lie**: tell a bird it was a liar
     though … never so: however much he might
122 **is much enamoured of**: has fallen in love with
123 **enthrallèd to thy shape**: captivated by your appearance
124 **perforce … me**: forces me

130 **gleek**: make a joke / be witty

133 **turn**: needs / purposes

135 **thou wilt or no**: you want to or not
136 **rate**: rank / worth
137 **still**: always
     doth … state: attends upon me because I am Queen
142 **purge … grossness**: purify you out of your human body
144 **Peaseblossom**: flower of the pea plant
     Moth: speck of dust (and therefore tiny); pronounced 'mote'.
     Mustardseed: tiny seed of the mustard plant

THINK ABOUT for GCSE

Performance and staging
- What might the actor do to make Bottom move and sound like an ass? Which words might easily turn into a donkey's bray? Is it more effective for Bottom to wear a complete ass's head or one that allows his own face to be seen?

Context
- The sound 'cuckoo' reminded Shakespeare's audience of the word 'cuckold' (a man whose wife is unfaithful). According to Bottom's song, many men would hear the cuckoo and not be able to deny that he was a cuckold (lines 115 to 120). How could this meaning be brought out in performance?

	The throstle with his note so true,	
	The wren with little quill –	
TITANIA	(*Waking*)	
	What angel wakes me from my flowery bed?	

BOTTOM   (*Singing*)
  The finch, the sparrow, and the lark,   **115**
    The plain-song cuckoo grey
  Whose note full many a man doth mark,
    And dares not answer nay –
  For indeed, who would set his wit to so foolish a bird? Who
  would give a *bird* the lie, though he cry 'cuckoo' never so? **120**

TITANIA   I pray thee, gentle mortal, sing again!
  Mine ear is much enamoured of thy note –
  So is mine eye enthrallèd to thy shape.
  And thy fair virtue's force perforce doth move me
  On the first view to say – to swear – I love thee!   **125**

BOTTOM   Methinks, mistress, you should have little reason for
  that. And yet, to say the truth, reason and love keep little
  company together nowadays. The more the pity that
  some honest neighbours will not make them friends.
  Nay – I can gleek upon occasion.   **130**

TITANIA   Thou art as wise as thou art beautiful!

BOTTOM   Not so, neither. But if I had wit enough to get out of this
  wood, I have enough to serve mine own turn.

TITANIA   Out of this wood do not desire to go:
  Thou shalt remain here, whether thou wilt or no.   **135**
  I am a spirit of no common rate –
  The summer still doth tend upon my state,
  And I do love thee. Therefore go with me.
  I'll give thee fairies to attend on thee,
  And they shall fetch thee jewels from the deep,   **140**
  And sing, while thou on pressèd flowers dost sleep.
  And I will purge thy mortal grossness so
  That thou shalt like an airy spirit go.
  Peaseblossom, Cobweb, Moth, and Mustardseed!

Enter four FAIRIES.

Titania refuses to let Bottom leave the wood, and calls her fairies – Peaseblossom, Cobweb, Moth and Mustardseed – to be his attendants.

147 **gambol**: skip
    eyes: sight
148 **dewberries**: blackberries

151 **night-tapers ... thighs**: collect wax from the bees' thighs to make night-lights

156 **courtesies**: honour / curtsies

158 **I cry ... mercy**: (a polite greeting)
    beseech: beg / ask

Performance and staging
- Bottom addresses the four fairies as 'Master' (lines 161 to 174) and on Shakespeare's stage they would have been played by boys or men. Would you prefer to see them played by males or females, or by adults or children?

161 **shall ... acquaintance**: would like to get to know you better
162 **cut my finger**: Spiders' webs were wrapped around cuts to stop bleeding.
    make bold: take advantage / use
165 **commend me**: give my regards
    Squash: unripe pea-pod
166 **Peascod**: ripe pea-pod

FIRST FAIRY	Ready!	
SECOND FAIRY	And I.	
THIRD FAIRY	And I.	
FOURTH FAIRY	And I.	
ALL	Where shall we go?	145

TITANIA   Be kind and courteous to this gentleman –
Hop in his walks, and gambol in his eyes.
Feed him with apricots and dewberries,
With purple grapes, green figs, and mulberries.
The honey-bags steal from the humble-bees,   150
And for night-tapers crop their waxen thighs
And light them at the fiery glow-worms' eyes,
To have my love to bed – and to arise.
And pluck the wings from painted butterflies
To fan the moonbeams from his sleeping eyes.   155
Nod to him, elves, and do him courtesies!

FIRST FAIRY	Hail, mortal!
SECOND FAIRY	Hail!
THIRD FAIRY	Hail!
FOURTH FAIRY	Hail!

BOTTOM   I cry your worships mercy heartily. I beseech your
worship's name?

FIRST FAIRY   Cobweb.   160

BOTTOM   I shall desire you of more acquaintance, good Master
Cobweb. If I cut my finger, I shall make bold with you.
– Your name, honest gentleman?

SECOND FAIRY   Peaseblossom.

BOTTOM   I pray you, commend me to Mistress Squash, your   165
mother, and to Master Peascod, your father. Good Master
Peaseblossom, I shall desire you of more acquaintance
too. – Your name, I beseech you, sir?

THIRD FAIRY   Mustardseed.

Bottom meets the fairies and Titania orders them to lead her and Bottom to her bower.

170 **your patience**: what you put up with

172–3 **house … kindred**: family

176–7 **The moon … flower**: Some people believed that dew came from the moon.

178 **Lamenting**: feeling sad about **enforcèd chastity**: chaste woman who has been raped

---

THINK ABOUT *for* GCSE

Performance and staging
- As a director, would you want the audience to be sympathetic towards Titania by the end of this scene, or laughing at her?

Themes and issues
- In what ways do the events of this scene contribute to the theme of **change and transformation**?
- Bottom talks about 'reason and love' (lines 127 to 128). What has happened in the play so far to show that **love** is an irrational business?

BOTTOM   Good Master Mustardseed, I know your patience well.   **170**
That same cowardly, giant-like ox-beef hath devoured
many a gentleman of your house. I promise you, your
kindred hath made my eyes water ere now. I desire you
of more acquaintance, good Master Mustardseed.

TITANIA   Come, wait upon him – lead him to my bower.   **175**
The moon, methinks, looks with a watery eye,
And when she weeps, weeps every little flower,
Lamenting some enforcèd chastity.
Tie up my love's tongue – bring him silently.

Exit.
The FAIRIES *lead* BOTTOM *after her.*

In this scene ...

- Demetrius, under the influence of the magic juice, falls in love with Helena. Both he and Lysander now claim to be in love with Helena, who thinks they are mocking her.
- Hermia turns on Helena for having stolen Lysander, and the two men prepare to fight it out.
- Puck keeps the lovers apart and each falls into exhausted asleep.

Puck tells Oberon what he did to Bottom and how the other Mechanicals reacted.

THINK ABOUT for GCSE

Performance and staging

- If you were making a film, what could you show in a flashback to illustrate Puck's report (lines 6 to 34)?

Language

- Puck calls the workmen 'rude mechanicals' (line 9), and this is how people now often refer to them. How does Puck's extended image of startled birds (lines 20 to 24) help us to imagine the Mechanicals' reactions to Bottom's transformation?

---

3   **in extremity**: desperately

5   **night-rule**: night activity / disorder
    haunted: busy / crowded with spirits

7   **close**: secret
    consecrated: sacred

8   **dull**: drowsy

9   **patches**: clowns
    rude mechanicals: uneducated workmen

10   **work for bread**: earn their living

12   **nuptial day**: wedding day

13   **shallowest thick-skin**: dimmest idiot
     barren sort: stupid gang

15   **Forsook his scene**: left the stage

17   **nole**: head

18   **Anon**: Very soon

19   **mimic**: actor

20   **As**: like
     fowler: bird hunter
     eye: spot / see

21   **russet-pated choughs**: dark-headed jackdaws
     sort: flock

23   **Sever**: divide

25   **at our stamp**: here where we stand

26   **He**: one of them

30   **from yielders ... catch**: From a proverb: everybody will steal from cowards.

32   **translated**: transformed

Another part of the woods.

Enter OBERON.

OBERON
I wonder if Titania be awaked –
Then, what it was that next came in her eye,
Which she must dote on in extremity.

Enter PUCK.

Here comes my messenger. How now, mad spirit!
What night-rule now about this haunted grove? 5

PUCK
My mistress with a monster is in love!
Near to her close and consecrated bower,
While she was in her dull and sleeping hour,
A crew of patches, rude mechanicals,
That work for bread upon Athenian stalls, 10
Were met together to rehearse a play
Intended for great Theseus' nuptial day.
The shallowest thick-skin of that barren sort,
Who Pyramus presented, in their sport
Forsook his scene and entered in a brake. 15
When I did him at this advantage take,
An ass's nole I fixèd on his head.
Anon his Thisby must be answerèd,
And forth my mimic comes. When they him spy,
As wild geese that the creeping fowler eye, 20
Or russet-pated choughs, many in sort,
Rising and cawing at the gun's report,
Sever themselves and madly sweep the sky –
So at his sight, away his fellows fly.
And at our stamp here o'er and o'er one falls – 25
He 'Murder!' cries, and help from Athens calls.
Their sense thus weak, lost with their fears thus strong,
Made senseless things begin to do them wrong,
For briars and thorns at their apparel snatch –
Some sleeves, some hats: from yielders all things catch. 30
I led them on in this distracted fear,
And left sweet 'Pyramus' translated there –

Puck explains that Titania has woken up and has fallen in love with Bottom. Oberon is delighted. When Hermia enters, pursued by Demetrius, Puck admits that he made a mistake. He and Oberon watch as Hermia accuses Demetrius of having murdered Lysander.

THINK ABOUT for GCSE

Performance and staging

• How might Puck say 'but not this the man' (line 42)? Nervous, because Oberon might punish him? Amused? Confused?

Language

• Hermia refuses to believe that Lysander could have been untrue to her (lines 52 to 55). What is the link between that image and Titania's description in Act 2 Scene 1, lines 88 to 117?

36 **latched**: moistened

40 **That**: so that
    of force ... eyed: he cannot avoid seeing her

41 **Stand close!**: Stand aside!

43 **rebuke**: scold
44 **breath**: words
45 **but chide**: only scold
    use: treat

48 **o'er shoes**: ankle-deep

50 **true**: faithful

53 **whole**: solid
55 **Her brother's**: i.e. the sun's
    Antipodes: opposite side of the earth
57 **dead**: deadly

61 **glimmering sphere**: shining orbit

65 **cur**: dog / mongrel

When in that moment, so it came to pass,
Titania waked – and straightway loved an ass.

OBERON   This falls out better than I could devise.   **35**
But hast thou yet latched the Athenian's eyes
With the love-juice, as I did bid thee do?

PUCK   I took him sleeping – that is finished too –
And the Athenian woman by his side –
That, when he waked, of force she must be eyed.   **40**

Enter DEMETRIUS *and* HERMIA.
(OBERON *and* PUCK *are invisible to them.*)

OBERON   Stand close! This is the same Athenian.

PUCK   This is the woman, but not this the man.

DEMETRIUS   O, why rebuke you him that loves you so?
Lay breath so bitter on your bitter *foe.*

HERMIA   Now I but chide – but I should use thee worse,   **45**
For thou, I fear, hast given me cause to curse.
If thou hast slain Lysander in his sleep,
Being o'er shoes in blood, plunge in the deep,
And kill me too.
The sun was not so true unto the day   **50**
As he to me. Would he have stol'n away
From sleeping Hermia? I'll believe as soon
This whole earth may be bored, and that the moon
May through the centre creep, and so displease
Her brother's noontide with th' Antipodes.   **55**
It cannot be but thou hast murdered him!
So should a murderer look – so dead, so grim.

DEMETRIUS   So should the murdered look – and so should I,
Pierced through the heart with your stern cruelty.
Yet you, the murderer, look as bright, as clear   **60**
As yonder Venus in her glimmering sphere.

HERMIA   What's this to my Lysander? Where is he?
Ah, good Demetrius, wilt thou give him me?

DEMETRIUS   I had rather give his carcass to my hounds.

HERMIA   Out, dog! Out, cur! – Thou driv'st me past the bounds   **65**

Hermia angrily runs off and the exhausted Demetrius lies down and sleeps. Telling off Puck for his mistake, Oberon orders him to search through the wood and find Helena.

67 **numbered among men**: considered a man
69 **Durst thou**: Would you have dared
70 **O brave touch!**: A fine thing to do!
71 **worm**: snake
72 **doubler**: 1 more forked; 2 more deceitful

74 **spend your passion**: waste your feelings
   misprised mood: mistaken anger
76 **aught**: anything
78 **And if**: If
   therefore: for it, as a reward
82 **vein**: mood

Performance and staging
• Does Demetrius just fall asleep or does he get some help from Oberon? Think what stage 'business' (movements or gestures) Oberon might perform to make him sleepy.

Relationships
• Which of the following kinds of relationship have you seen so far between Oberon and Puck, and where: king and important subject; king and lowly subject; master and servant; father and son; brothers; friends; professional colleagues?

84–5 **So sorrow's ... owe**: The combination of sorrow and lack of sleep is exhausting me
86–7 **Which ... stay**: If I lie down, I might get some of the sleep I am owed
87 **his tender**: sleep's offer (i.e. to 'repay' him)
88 **quite**: utterly / completely
90 **Of thy ... ensue**: From your mistake there must follow
91 **turned**: changed / misdirected
92 **o'er-rules**: takes charge
   holding troth: staying faithful
93 **confounding ... oath**: breaking one promise after another
95 **look**: make sure
96 **fancy-sick**: love-sick
   of cheer: in the face
97 **costs ... blood**: There was a belief that you would lose a drop of blood every time you sighed.
98 **illusion**: trick / deception

	Of maiden's patience. Hast thou slain him, then?	
	Henceforth be never numbered among men!	
	O, once tell true! – Tell true, even for my sake.	
	Durst thou have looked upon him, being awake?	
	And hast thou killed him sleeping? O brave touch!	70
	Could not a worm, an adder do so much?	
	An adder did it – for with doubler tongue	
	Than thine, thou serpent, never adder stung!	
DEMETRIUS	You spend your passion on a misprised mood:	
	I am not guilty of Lysander's blood.	75
	Nor is he dead, for aught that I can tell.	
HERMIA	I pray thee tell me then that he is well.	
DEMETRIUS	And if I could, what should I get therefore?	
HERMIA	A privilege never to see me more.	
	And from thy hated presence part I so –	80
	See me no more, whether he be dead or no!	

Exit.

DEMETRIUS	There is no following her in this fierce vein.	
	Here therefore, for a while, I will remain.	
	So sorrow's heaviness doth heavier grow	
	For debt that bankrupt sleep doth sorrow owe –	85
	Which now in some slight measure it will pay,	
	If for his tender here I make some stay.	

He lies down and sleeps.

OBERON	What hast thou done? Thou hast mistaken quite,	
	And laid the love-joice on some true-love's sight!	
	Of thy misprision must perforce ensue	90
	Some true love turned, and not a false turned true.	
PUCK	Then fate o'er-rules – that, one man holding troth,	
	A million fail, confounding oath on oath.	
OBERON	About the wood go swifter than the wind,	
	And Helena of Athens look thou find.	95
	All fancy-sick she is and pale of cheer	
	With sighs of love that costs the fresh blood dear.	
	By some illusion see thou bring her here;	

As Oberon is squeezing the magic juice onto Demetrius's eyes so that he will fall in love with Helena when he wakes up, she arrives, pursued by Lysander (now under the influence of the same magic and in love with her).

THINK ABOUT for GCSE

Characterisation

- How far would you agree with each of these descriptions of Puck: mischievous, irresponsible, malicious, child-like, all-powerful? What other words could describe him?

Language

- Up to line 101, the verse is iambic pentameter (lines of five stresses) in rhymed couplets. Oberon's charm (lines 102 to 109) is in four-stress lines with all eight lines rhyming; his exchange with Puck (lines 110 to 121) is also in four-stressed lines but in rhymed couplets. When Lysander enters, the verse reverts to iambic pentameter. What effects do these changes in verse forms have?

99 **against**: ready for when

101 **Tartar's bow**: The Tartars from Central Asia were famous archers.

103 **Cupid's archery**: arrow of love (see also Act 2 Scene 1, lines 155 to 168)
104 **apple**: pupil

109 **remedy**: relief

113 **fee**: reward
114 **fond pageant**: foolish drama / spectacle

121 **befall preposterously**: happen in an abnormal and absurd way

122 **scorn**: mockery
124 **Look when**: Whenever
    so born: i.e. born from tears
125 **nativity**: birth
127 **badge**: outward sign

I'll charm his eyes against she do appear.

PUCK   I go, I go – look how I go! –   **100**
                Swifter than arrow from the Tartar's bow.

                                                          Exit.

OBERON   (*Squeezing the juice of the flower onto* DEMETRIUS*'s
                eyelids.*)
                Flower of this purple dye,
                Hit with Cupid's archery,
                Sink in apple of his eye.
                When his love he doth espy,   **105**
                Let her shine as gloriously
                As the Venus of the sky.
                When thou wak'st, if she be by,
                Beg of her for remedy.

        Re-enter PUCK.

PUCK   Captain of our fairy band,   **110**
                Helena is here at hand,
                And the youth, mistook by me,
                Pleading for a lover's fee.
                Shall we their fond pageant see?
                Lord, what fools these mortals be!   **115**

OBERON   Stand aside. The noise they make
                Will cause Demetrius to awake.

PUCK   Then will two at once woo one.
                That must needs be sport alone –
                And those things do best please me   **120**
                That befall preposterously.

        They stand aside (*invisible*).
        Enter LYSANDER *and* HELENA.

LYSANDER   Why should you think that I should woo in scorn?
                Scorn and derision never come in tears.
                Look when I vow I weep – and vows so born,
                In their nativity all truth appears.   **125**
                How can these things in me seem scorn to you,
                Bearing the badge of faith to prove them true?

In the middle of Lysander's unsuccessful wooing of Helena, Demetrius wakes up and immediately declares his love for her. She now believes that both the men are making fun of her.

128 **advance**: show / increase
129 **truth kills truth**: a promise to one person destroys a promise to another
devilish-holy fray: complete conflict involving falsehood and truth
130 **o'er**: up
133 **even weigh**: weigh the same
light as tales: false as lies

138 **thine eyne**: your eyes

141 **congealèd white**: pale fair skin
Taurus: mountain range in Turkey
142 **turns to a crow**: seems black in comparison
144 **seal**: promise
145 **bent**: determined

THINK ABOUT *for* GCSE

Characterisation
• Five characters are on stage. What might each one be thinking by the end of Demetrius's waking-up speech (line 144)?

Performance and staging
• Demetrius wakes up. By this point the men are under a spell but the women are not. Is this distinction reflected in what the men and women say and do?

148 **do me ... injury**: insult me so much

150 **join in souls**: unite

152 **use**: treat
153 **super-praise**: over-exaggeratedly praise
parts: qualities

157 **trim**: fine
158 **conjure**: raise

160 **extort**: torture
161 **to make you sport**: for fun

HELENA	You do advance your cunning more and more.
	When truth kills truth, O devilish-holy fray!
	These vows are Hermia's. Will you give her o'er? 130
	Weigh oath with oath, and you will nothing weigh.
	Your vows to her and me, put in two scales,
	Will even weigh – and both as light as tales.
LYSANDER	I had no judgement when to her I swore.
HELENA	Nor none, in my mind, now you give her o'er. 135
LYSANDER	Demetrius loves her, and he loves not you.
DEMETRIUS	(Waking)
	O Helen, goddess, nymph, perfect, divine!
	To what, my love, shall I compare thine eyne?
	Crystal is muddy! O how ripe in show
	Thy lips, those kissing cherries, tempting grow! 140
	That pure congealèd white, high Taurus' snow,
	Fanned with the eastern wind, turns to a crow
	When thou hold'st up thy hand. O let me kiss
	This princess of pure white, this seal of bliss!
HELENA	O spite! O hell! I see you all are bent 145
	To set against me for your merriment!
	If you were civil, and knew courtesy,
	You would not do me thus much injury.
	Can you not hate me, as I know you do,
	But you must join in souls to mock me too? 150
	If you were men, as men you are in show,
	You would not use a gentle lady so –
	To vow, and swear, and super-praise my parts,
	When I am sure you hate me with your hearts.
	You both are rivals, and love Hermia – 155
	And now both rivals to mock Helena.
	A trim exploit, a manly enterprise,
	To conjure tears up in a poor maid's eyes
	With your derision! None of noble sort
	Would so offend a virgin, and extort 160
	A poor soul's patience, all to make you sport.
LYSANDER	You are unkind, Demetrius. Be not so.
	For you love Hermia – this you know I know.

When Hermia finds Lysander,
she cannot understand why he
had left her, and she is shocked
and upset when he says he
hates her. Helena now decides
that Hermia must be in on the
men's plot to have a joke at her
expense.

166 **bequeath**: hand over

169 **will none**: want nothing to do with her

171 **as guest-wise sojourned**: stayed like a
     visitor

174 **Disparage not**: Don't criticise
175 **aby it dear**: pay dearly for it

177 **his**: its
178 **more quick of apprehension**: sharper

180 **pays ... recompense**: compensates by
     making hearing doubly sensitive

THINK ABOUT for GCSE

Language
- Find an example from each
  of the four lovers' speeches
  that shows the effectiveness
  of the rhyme in conveying
  the power of their emotions.

Characterisation
- How far do Lysander's words
  to Hermia (lines 184 to 190)
  affect our attitude to him?

186 **bide**: stay
187 **engilds**: brightens with gold
188 **yon**: up there
     oes: silver spangles (i.e. the stars)

192 **confederacy**: alliance

194 **in spite of me**: to vex me
195 **Injurious**: 1 Unjust; 2 Harmful

	And here with all good will, with all my heart,	
	In Hermia's love I yield you up my part:	165
	And yours of Helena to me bequeath,	
	Whom I do love, and will do till my death.	

HELENA   (*In tears*) Never did mockers waste more idle breath.

DEMETRIUS   Lysander, keep thy Hermia: I will none.
            If e'er I loved her, all that love is gone.   170
            My heart to her but as guest-wise sojourned,
            And now to Helen is it home returned,
            There to remain.

LYSANDER   Helen, it is not so.

DEMETRIUS   Disparage not the faith thou dost not know,
            Lest to thy peril thou aby it dear!   175
            Look where thy love comes – yonder is thy dear.

    Enter HERMIA.

HERMIA   Dark night, that from the eye his function takes,
            The ear more quick of apprehension makes;
            Wherein it doth impair the seeing sense,
            It pays the hearing double recompense.   180
            Thou art not by mine eye, Lysander, found –
            Mine ear, I thank it, brought me to thy sound.
            But why unkindly didst thou leave me so?

LYSANDER   Why should he stay whom love doth press to go?

HERMIA   What love could press Lysander from my side?   185

LYSANDER   Lysander's love, that would not let him bide –
            Fair Helena – who more engilds the night
            Than all yon fiery oes and eyes of light.
            Why seek'st thou me? Could not this make thee know
            The hate I bare thee made me leave thee so?   190

HERMIA   You speak not as you think – it cannot be!

HELENA   Lo, she is one of this confederacy!
            Now I perceive they have conjoined, all three,
            To fashion this false sport in spite of me.
            Injurious Hermia, most ungrateful maid!   195
            Have you conspired, have you with these contrived

Helena reminds Hermia that they used to be close friends and tells her how upset she is that Hermia has joined with the men in mocking and teasing her.

197 **bait**: torment / persecute
198 **counsel**: inmost thoughts / secrets

200 **chid**: complained at

203 **artificial**: creative / skilful

205 **sampler**: piece of embroidery

208 **incorporate**: in one body

210 **an union in partition**: united, even though two individuals

213 **Two of the first**: A term from heraldry: two of the first things mentioned, i.e. their two bodies.
coats in heraldry: coats of arms
214 **Due but to one**: belonging to one person
crest: the design above a heraldic shield
215 **rent ... asunder**: tear apart
ancient: long-standing
218 **Our sex**: Women in general
chide: rebuke

225 **even but now**: only recently
spurn: kick aside
227 **celestial**: heavenly
Wherefore: Why

230 **tender**: offer
231 **But by**: Unless it's by
setting on: putting him up to it
232 **grace**: favour

THINK ABOUT for GCSE

Performance and staging

• What advice would you give the actor playing Helena? For example, where might she show that she is: making an unpleasant discovery; angry; disappointed; and happily remembering the past?

To bait me with this foul derision?
Is all the counsel that we two have shared,
The sisters' vows, the hours that we have spent,
When we have chid the hasty-footed time   **200**
For parting us – O, is all forgot?
All school-days' friendship, childhood innocence?
We, Hermia, like two artificial gods,
Have with our needles created both one flower,
Both on one sampler, sitting on one cushion,   **205**
Both warbling of one song, both in one key –
As if our hands, our sides, voices, and minds
Had been incorporate. So we grew together,
Like to a double cherry, seeming parted,
But yet an union in partition,   **210**
Two lovely berries, moulded on one stem –
So, with two seeming bodies but one heart,
Two of the first, like coats in heraldry,
Due but to one and crownèd with one crest.
And will you rent our ancient love asunder,   **215**
To join with men in scorning your poor friend?
It is not friendly. 'Tis not maidenly.
Our sex, as well as I, may chide you for it,
Though I alone do feel the injury.

HERMIA   I am amazèd at your passionate words.   **220**
              I scorn you not. It seems that *you* scorn me.

HELENA   Have you not set Lysander, as in scorn,
              To follow me, and praise my eyes and face?
              And made your other love, Demetrius,
              Who even but now did spurn me with his foot,   **225**
              To call me goddess, nymph, divine, and rare,
              Precious, celestial? Wherefore speaks he this
              To her he hates? And wherefore doth Lysander
              Deny your love, so rich within his soul,
              And tender *me* – forsooth! – affection,   **230**
              But by your setting on, by your consent?
              What though I be not so in grace as you,
              So hung upon with love, so fortunate –
              But miserable most, to love unloved?
              This you should pity rather than despise.   **235**

Convinced that the other three are joining together to make fun of her, Helena tries to leave, but is stopped by Demetrius and Lysander, who continue to declare their love for her.

237 **Ay, do! Persever**: OK, go on, keep it up
      counterfeit: put on / fake
      sad: serious, solemn
238 **mouths upon**: faces at
240 **chronicled**: put on record
242 **argument**: butt of your joke

248 **she cannot entreat**: her requests don't work
      compel: use force

252 **that ... lose**: i.e. his life, in a duel

255 **withdraw**: leave with me (i.e. to fight)

256 **whereto ... this?**: what's this all about?

258 **Seem ... loose**: pretend to be trying to break away (from her)
      take on as: you behave as if
259 **tame man**: coward
260 **Hang off**: Let go
      burr: prickly seed-case which sticks to clothes
262 **rude**: harsh / unkind

THINK ABOUT *for* GCSE

Language

• 'Ethiope' (line 257) is Shakespeare's word for anyone with a black skin. How would you respond to the argument that the word is racist and ought to be changed or cut altogether?

Performance and staging

• In most stage productions there is some very active and physical stage 'business' in this part of the scene, with actors struggling with and holding onto each other. What might the actors do at lines 245, 248 to 255 and 260, for example?

HERMIA	I understand not what you mean by this.
HELENA	Ay, do! Persever – counterfeit sad looks! Make mouths upon me when I turn my back! Wink each at other, hold the sweet jest up! This sport, well carried, shall be chronicled.　　　**240** If you have any pity, grace, or manners, You would not make me such an argument. But fare ye well. 'Tis partly mine own fault – Which death or absence soon shall remedy.
LYSANDER	Stay, gentle Helena, hear my excuse –　　　**245** My love, my life, my soul, fair Helena!
HELENA	O, excellent!
HERMIA	(*To* LYSANDER) Sweet, do not scorn her so.
DEMETRIUS	If she cannot entreat, I can compel.
LYSANDER	Thou canst compel no more than she entreat. Thy threats have no more strength than her weak prayers.　**250** Helen, I love thee – by my life I do! I swear by that which I will lose for thee To prove him false that says I love thee not.
DEMETRIUS	I say I love thee more than he can do.
LYSANDER	If thou say so, withdraw and prove it too.　　　**255**
DEMETRIUS	Quick, come!
HERMIA	Lysander, whereto tends all this?
LYSANDER	Away, you Ethiope!
DEMETRIUS	No, no, sir – Seem to break loose – take on as you would follow, But yet come not. You are a tame man, go!
LYSANDER	(***Struggling with*** HERMIA, ***who tries to stop him going to fight***) Hang off, thou cat, thou burr! – Vile thing, let loose! –　**260** Or I will shake thee from me like a serpent!
HERMIA	(***Clinging on***) Why are you grown so rude? What change is this, Sweet love?

Finally convinced that Lysander really has rejected her, Hermia turns on Helena, accusing her of stealing Lysander's love. The two women begin to argue.

263 **tawny**: dark-skinned
    Tartar: (see line 101)
264 **medicine**: poison

265 **sooth**: for sure

267 **would**: wish
268 **weak bond**: 1 promise; 2 Hermia

272 **what news**: what's the matter?

274 **erewhile**: before / earlier

277 **In earnest**: Intentionally

THINK ABOUT for GCSE

Characterisation

- Look at what Hermia says between lines 262 and 277. She speaks mainly in questions, with just a few exclamations. What does that tell you about her state of mind?

Performance and staging

- What might the actor playing Hermia do to bring out the comedy as she reacts to being called a 'puppet' (lines 289 to 298)?

282 **juggler**: trickster
    canker-blossom: flower-eating maggot
284 **Fine, i'faith!**: O, very nice!

288 **Fie, fie**: Shame on you!
    counterfeit: fake
    puppet: 1 someone acting falsely; 2 small person
289 **why so?**: So that's how it is!
291 **urged**: brought into the argument
292 **personage**: appearance / figure
293 **prevail'd with him**: won him over

LYSANDER	Thy love? Out, tawny Tartar – out!
	Out, loathèd medicine! – O hated potion – hence!
HERMIA	Do you not jest?
HELENA	Yes, sooth, and so do you.
LYSANDER	Demetrius, I will keep my word with thee.
DEMETRIUS	I would I had your bond – for I perceive
	A weak bond holds you. I'll not trust your word.
LYSANDER	What, should I hurt her, strike her, kill her dead?
	Although I hate her, I'll not harm her so.
HERMIA	What, can you do me greater harm than hate?
	Hate me? Wherefore? – O me, what news, my love!
	Am not I Hermia? Are not you Lysander?
	I am as fair now as I was erewhile.
	Since night you loved me – yet since night you left me.
	Why then, you left me – O, the gods forbid! –
	In earnest, shall I say?
LYSANDER	Ay, by my life! –
	And never did desire to see thee more.
	Therefore be out of hope, of question, of doubt –
	Be certain, nothing truer – 'tis no jest
	That I do hate thee, and love Helena.
HERMIA	(*To* HELENA) O me! You juggler, you canker-blossom!
	You thief of love! What, have you come by night
	And stol'n my love's heart from him?
HELENA	Fine, i' faith!
	Have you no modesty, no maiden shame,
	No touch of bashfulness? What, will you tear
	Impatient answers from my gentle tongue?
	Fie, fie, you counterfeit! – You puppet, you!
HERMIA	'Puppet'? Why so? – Ay, that way goes the game.
	Now I perceive that she hath made compare
	Between our statures! She hath urged her height –
	And with her personage – her *tall* personage –
	Her *height*, forsooth! – she hath prevailed with him.
	And are you grown so *high* in his esteem

265

270

275

280

285

290

Insulting each other over their heights – Hermia is shorter, Helena taller – the women nearly fight.

295 **low**: short (in stature)
296 **painted**: i.e. wearing make-up
  maypole: i.e. tall, skinny person

300 **curst**: bad-tempered / quarrelsome
301 **shrewishness**: 1 bad temper; 2 sharpness of tongue
302 **right**: real / typical
304 **something lower**: somewhat shorter

307 **evermore**: always

310 **stealth**: secret escape
312 **chid me hence**: told me angrily to go away

314 **so**: if / so long as

317 **fond**: foolish

THINK ABOUT for GCSE

Characterisation
• What do you think is in Helena's mind during the speech that ends on line 317? Is she genuinely trying to calm Hermia down?

Performance and staging
• How might Helena say line 317?

322 **part**: side
323 **keen and shrewd**: bitter and bad-tempered
324 **vixen**: she-fox (i.e. ferocious female)

327 **flout**: mock / insult

	Because I am so dwarfish and so low?	295
	How low am I, thou painted maypole? Speak!	
	How low am I? I am not yet so low	
	But that my nails can reach unto thine eyes.	

HELENA I pray you, though you mock me, gentlemen,
Let her not hurt me. I was never curst –   300
I have no gift at all in shrewishness.
I am a right maid for my cowardice –
Let her not strike me. You perhaps may think,
Because she is something lower than myself,
That I can match her.

HERMIA   'Lower'! Hark – again!   305

HELENA Good Hermia, do not be so bitter with me.
I evermore did love you, Hermia,
Did ever keep your counsels, never wronged you –
Save that, in love unto Demetrius,
I told him of your stealth unto this wood.   310
He followed you. For love I followed *him* –
But he hath chid me hence and threatened me
To strike me, spurn me, nay, to kill me too.
And now, so you will let me quiet go,
To Athens will I bear my folly back,   315
And follow you no further. Let me go.
You see how simple and how fond I am.

HERMIA Why, get you gone! Who is 't that hinders you?

HELENA A foolish heart, that I leave here behind.

HERMIA What, with Lysander?

HELENA   With Demetrius.   320

LYSANDER Be not afraid: she shall not harm thee, Helena.

DEMETRIUS No, sir, she shall not, though you take her part.

HELENA O, when she's angry, she is keen and shrewd!
She was a vixen when she went to school –
And though she be but little, she is fierce.   325

HERMIA 'Little' again! – Nothing but 'low' and 'little'!
Why will you suffer her to flout me thus?

Hermia has had enough of being insulted and Helena runs off. Meanwhile the men stride off together to settle their differences by fighting. After Hermia has left, Oberon tells Puck off for having caused the problem.

329   **minimus**: tiny, insignificant thing
      knot-grass: smothering weed (thought to stunt growth)

330–1 **officious … behalf**: over keen to offer help to her

335   **aby it**: pay for it dearly

336–7 **whose … most in**: which of us has the greater right to

338   **cheek by jowl**: side by side

339   **coil**: trouble
      'long of: caused by / because of

342   **fray**: fight

345   **Still**: Always
346   **wilfully**: deliberately

350   **so far**: to this extent
351   **'nointed**: anointed (i.e. sprinkled with the juice)
352   **so did sort**: turned out like this
353   **jangling**: squabbling / quarrelling
      I esteem a sport: is my idea of fun

THINK ABOUT *for* GCSE

Context

- It seems certain that the original boy actor who played Helena was tall, while the one who played Hermia was shorter. Hermia draws attention to this in lines 290 to 291. Which parts of the dialogue in lines 260 to 343 clearly refer to the differences in height? What opportunities for comedy are there in casting a tall Helena and a shorter Hermia?

Characterisation

- What are Oberon's and Puck's moods at lines 345 to 353? Is Oberon angry, for example, or amused? Is Puck apologetic or delighted?

	(*Struggling with* LYSANDER) Let me come to her!	
LYSANDER	(*Pushing her away*) Get you gone, you dwarf – You minimus, of hindering knot-grass made – You bead, you acorn!	
DEMETRIUS	You are too officious In her behalf that scorns your services. Let her alone. Speak not of Helena: Take not her part. For if thou dost intend Never so little show of love to her, Thou shalt aby it.	330
LYSANDER	Now she holds me not. Now follow, if thou dar'st, to try whose right, Of thine or mine, is most in Helena.	335
DEMETRIUS	Follow? – Nay, I'll go with thee, cheek by jowl!	

Exit, with LYSANDER (*intending to fight*).

| HERMIA | You, mistress – all this coil is 'long of you!
Nay – go not back. | |
| HELENA | I will not trust you, I,
Nor longer stay in your curst company.
Your hands than mine are quicker for a fray –
My legs are longer, though, to run away! | 340 |

Exit.

| HERMIA | I am amazed, and know not what to say. | |

Exit.

OBERON *and* PUCK *come forward.*

| OBERON | This is *thy* negligence! Still thou mistak'st –
Or else committ'st thy knaveries wilfully. | 345 |
| PUCK | Believe me, King of Shadows, I mistook.
Did not you tell me I should know the man
By the Athenian garments he had on?
And so far blameless proves my enterprise
That I have 'nointed an Athenian's eyes –
And so far am I glad it so did sort,
As this their jangling I esteem a sport. | 350 |

Oberon orders Puck to ensure that Lysander and Demetrius lose each other in the wood. When they fall asleep, Puck is to use the magic juice on Lysander's eyes. Meanwhile Oberon will get the changeling boy from Titania and then release her from the charm. Puck urges haste as morning approaches.

THINK ABOUT for GCSE

Structure and form
- How do the ends of Oberon's speech (lines 370 to 377) and Puck's (lines 378 to 387) help to change the mood of this scene and also return us to the world of the fairies and the supernatural?

Themes and issues
- Oberon tells Puck that, when the lovers awake, 'all this derision / Shall seem a dream and fruitless vision' (lines 370 to 371). How much of the story has had a **dream-like** quality? Which characters or events might have come straight out of a dream? Which visions created by the language have seemed particularly dream-like or surreal?

355   **Hie**: Hurry
356   **welkin**: sky
357   **drooping**: falling
       Acheron: a river in the Underworld
358   **testy**: bad-tempered
359   **As**: so that
360   **frame thy tongue**: disguise your voice
361   **wrong**: insults
362   **rail**: speak insultingly
363   **look**: make sure
364   **death-counterfeiting**: that looks like death
365   **batty**: bat-like
367   **virtuous**: powerful / good

369   **wonted**: accustomed / usual
370   **derision**: ridiculousness

372   **wend**: make their way
373   **league**: friendship / alliance
       date: duration

376   **charmèd**: bewitched

380   **Aurora's harbinger**: the morning star (Venus) that shows that dawn is approaching
382   **Damnèd spirits**: Ghosts of the wicked
383   **crossways**: i.e. where suicides were buried

387   **aye**: ever

391   **eastern gate**: dawn sun
392   **Neptune**: the sea (Roman god)

OBERON	Thou seest these lovers seek a place to fight.	
	Hie, therefore, Robin – overcast the night.	355
	The starry welkin cover thou anon	
	With drooping fog as black as Acheron –	
	And lead these testy rivals so astray	
	As one come not within another's way.	
	Like to Lysander sometime frame thy tongue,	360
	Then stir Demetrius up with bitter wrong;	
	And sometime rail thou like Demetrius –	
	And from each other look thou lead them thus,	
	Till o'er their brows death-counterfeiting sleep	
	With leaden legs and batty wings doth creep.	365
	Then crush this herb into Lysander's eye –	
	Whose liquor hath this virtuous property,	
	To take from thence all error with his might	
	And make his eyeballs roll with wonted sight.	
	When they next wake, all this derision	370
	Shall seem a dream, and fruitless vision –	
	And back to Athens shall the lovers wend,	
	With league whose date till death shall never end.	
	Whiles I in this affair do thee employ,	
	I'll to my Queen, and beg her Indian boy.	375
	And then I will her charmèd eye release	
	From monster's view, and all things shall be peace.	
PUCK	My fairy lord, this must be done with haste,	
	For night's swift dragons cut the clouds full fast,	
	And yonder shines Aurora's harbinger –	380
	At whose approach ghosts, wandering here and there,	
	Troop home to churchyards. Damnèd spirits all,	
	That in crossways and floods have burial,	
	Already to their wormy beds are gone.	
	For fear lest day should look their shames upon,	385
	They wilfully themselves exile from light,	
	And must for aye consort with black-browed night.	
OBERON	But we are spirits of another sort.	
	I with the morning's love have oft made sport,	
	And like a forester the groves may tread	390
	Even till the eastern gate, all fiery-red,	
	Opening on Neptune with fair blessèd beams,	

Puck keeps Lysander and Demetrius apart by imitating their voices and leading them astray.

394 **notwithstanding**: despite that / nevertheless

395 **ere**: before

402 **drawn**: with my sword drawn

403 **straight**: immediately

404 **plainer**: 1 flatter; 2 more open

THINK ABOUT for GCSE

Context
• It is easy for modern audiences to forget that the hobgoblin was once 'feared in field and town' (line 398). What might Shakespeare's audience have found disturbing about Puck?

Performance and staging
• How could this quality be brought out in performance?

408 **look'st for wars**: are looking for a fight
409 **recreant**: coward / traitor

410 **defiled**: disgraced

412 **try**: put to the test (i.e. by fighting)

	Turns into yellow gold his salt green streams.	
	But notwithstanding, haste – make no delay!	
	We may effect this business yet ere day.	395

Exit.

PUCK   Up and down, up and down,
I will lead them up and down!
I am feared in field and town –
Goblin, lead them up and down!
– Here comes one.   400

Enter LYSANDER.

LYSANDER   Where art thou, proud Demetrius? Speak thou now.

PUCK   (*Invisible – imitating Demetrius's voice*)
Here villain, drawn and ready! Where art thou?

LYSANDER   I will be with thee straight.

PUCK   (*Demetrius's voice*)   Follow me, then,
To plainer ground.

Exit LYSANDER.

Enter DEMETRIUS.

DEMETRIUS   Lysander, speak again!
Thou runaway – thou coward! Art thou fled?   405
Speak! In some bush? – Where dost thou hide thy
head?

PUCK   (*Imitating Lysander's voice*)
Thou coward, art thou bragging to the stars?
Telling the bushes that thou look'st for wars,
And wilt not come? Come, recreant – come, thou
child!
I'll whip thee with a rod. He is defiled   410
That draws a sword on thee!

DEMETRIUS   Yea, art thou there?

PUCK   (*Lysander's voice*) Follow my voice. We'll try no
manhood here.

Exit, calling so that
DEMETRIUS *follows him.*

Tired out by running around the forest, Lysander and Demetrius are led in by Puck and lie down, separately, to sleep.
An exhausted Helena arrives, followed by Hermia, untidy and miserable.

417   That: so that

420   spite: vexation

422   Abide: Stay and fight
wot: know

426   buy this dear: pay dearly for this

428   constraineth: forces
429   measure ... length: lie down
430   look: expect

432   Abate: shorten

THINK ABOUT for GCSE

Performance and staging
• Lysander is the first of the lovers to collapse in exhaustion. Do you think his tiredness should appear natural or as though inflicted upon him by one of Puck's spells?

Re-enter LYSANDER.

LYSANDER   He goes before me, and still dares me on:
                When I come where he calls, then he is gone.
                The villain is much lighter-heeled than I.   **415**
                I followed fast, but faster he did fly,
                That fallen am I in dark uneven way,
                And here will rest me.

He lies down.

                                        Come, thou gentle day –
                For if but once thou show me thy grey light,
                I'll find Demetrius, and revenge this spite.   **420**

He sleeps.

Re-enter PUCK, *with* DEMETRIUS *following.*

PUCK   (*Lysander's voice*) Ho, ho, ho! – Coward, why com'st
                    thou not?

DEMETRIUS   Abide me if thou dar'st! For well I wot
                Thou runn'st before me, shifting every place,
                And dar'st not stand nor look me in the face.
                Where art thou now?

PUCK   (*Lysander's voice*)   Come hither! – I am here.   **425**

DEMETRIUS   Nay then, thou mock'st me. Thou shalt buy this dear
                If ever I thy face by daylight see.
                Now, go thy way – faintness constraineth me
                To measure out my length on this cold bed.
                By day's approach look to be visited.   **430**

He lies down and sleeps.

Re-enter HELENA.

HELENA   O weary night, O long and tedious night,
                Abate thy hours. Shine comforts from the east –
                That I may back to Athens by daylight
                From these that my poor company detest.
                And sleep, that sometimes shuts up sorrow's eye,   **435**
                Steal me awhile from mine own company.

She lies down and sleeps.

Unaware of each other, or of Lysander and Demetrius already there, Helena and Hermia lie down and fall asleep. Puck squeezes the antidote onto Lysander's eyes so that he will regain his love for Hermia when he awakes. Puck predicts a happy ending.

440 knavish: mischievous

443 Bedabbled: splashed

THINK ABOUT for GCSE

Performance and staging
- The lovers have to remain asleep on stage, unnoticed, during the following scene with Titania and Bottom. Where do you think they might be on the stage?

Language
- How does the rhythm of Puck's speech at the end of the scene help to convey the feeling that 'all shall be well'?

462 Nought: nothing

PUCK Yet but three? Come one more –
Two of both kinds makes up four.
Here she comes, curst and sad –

Enter HERMIA.

 Cupid is a knavish lad   440
Thus to make poor females mad.

HERMIA Never so weary, never so in woe,
Bedabbled with the dew and torn with briars,
I can no further crawl, no further go –
My legs can keep no pace with my desires. 445
Here will I rest me till the break of day.
Heavens shield Lysander, if they mean a fray!

She lies down and sleeps, not seeing the others.

PUCK On the ground
Sleep sound.
I'll apply   450
To your eye,
Gentle lover, remedy.

He squeezes the juice of the healing herb onto LYSANDER'*s eyelids.*

 – When thou wak'st
Thou tak'st
True delight   455
In the sight
Of thy former lady's eye –
And the country proverb known,
That every man should take his own,
In your waking shall be shown. 460
Jack shall have Jill –
Nought shall go ill –
The man shall have his mare again, and all shall
 be well.

        Exit.

The lovers remain, asleep.

In this scene ...

- Oberon releases Titania from the spell and Puck removes Bottom's ass's head. The King and Queen of the fairies have ended their quarrel.
- Theseus discovers the four lovers asleep. He decides to overrule Egeus and allow the two pairs of lovers to marry.
- Bottom wakes up and expresses wonder at his amazing dream.

Bottom is caressed and pampered by Titania and the fairies.

2 **amiable**: lovable
   coy: caress

7 **Monsieur**: Mister

THINK ABOUT for GCSE

Relationships
- What, in your opinion, is now the relationship between Bottom and Titania? (For example, some productions have made it seem very sexual.)

Performance and staging
- How might Bottom and Titania enter? What do they look like? How are they behaving with each other?

15 **loath**: unwilling
    overflown: drenched
16 **signior**: sir

19 **neaf**: hand
20 **leave your curtsy**: stop bowing

The same place in the woods.

The human lovers, (HERMIA, HELENA, DEMETRIUS *and* LYSANDER) *all sleep on.*

Enter TITANIA *and* BOTTOM (*with ass's head*), *attended by* PEASEBLOSSOM, COBWEB, MUSTARDSEED, *and other Fairies.*

OBERON *enters behind, unseen, and watches them.*

TITANIA	Come, sit thee down upon this flowery bed, While I thy amiable cheeks do coy, And stick musk-roses in thy sleek smooth head, And kiss thy fair large ears, my gentle joy.	
BOTTOM	Where's Peaseblossom?	5
PEASE-BLOSSOM	Ready.	
BOTTOM	Scratch my head, Peaseblossom. Where's Monsieur Cobweb?	
COBWEB	Ready.	
BOTTOM	Monsieur Cobweb, good Monsieur, get you your weapons in your hand and kill me a red-hipped humble-bee on the top of a thistle – and, good Monsieur, bring me the honey-bag. Do not fret yourself too much in the action, Monsieur – and, good Monsieur, have a care the honey-bag break not. I would be loath to have you overflown with a honey-bag, signior.	10 15

Exit COBWEB.

	– Where's Monsieur Mustardseed?	
MUSTARDSEED	Ready.	
BOTTOM	Give me your neaf, Monsieur Mustardseed. Pray you, leave your curtsy, good Monsieur.	20
MUSTARDSEED	What's your will?	

Bottom makes some final requests of his fairy attendants and falls asleep. Oberon has been watching Titania asleep with Bottom in her arms.

23 Cavalery: Soldier

25 marvellous: amazingly

30 the tongs and the bones: basic musical instruments; tongs were struck like a triangle, bones were clicked together in pairs.
32 peck: a large bucketful
provender: fodder / animal feed
33 bottle: bundle
34 fellow: equal
35 venturous: daring

38 stir: wake / rouse
39 exposition: explanation (he means 'disposition': inclination)
41 all ways: in all directions

THINK ABOUT for GCSE

Performance and staging

- In what ways has Bottom changed since we saw him last? How would you account for these changes? How might the audience notice the changes in the way he talks and behaves?

- Oberon has entered unseen at the beginning of the scene. How might he behave/react as he watches Titania with Bottom?

Themes and issues

- **Change and transformation**: What does Bottom say and do to bring out the joke that he has been transformed into an ass but doesn't realise it?

44 Enrings: encircles

47 dotage: infatuation
49 favours: love tokens
hateful: repulsive
50 upbraid: scold / rebuke

BOTTOM	Nothing, good Monsieur, but to help Cavalery Peaseblossom to scratch. I must to the barber's, Monsieur, for methinks I am marvellous hairy about the face. And I am such a tender ass – if my hair do but tickle me, I must scratch.
TITANIA	What, wilt thou hear some music, my sweet love?
BOTTOM	I have a reasonable good ear in music. Let's have the tongs and the bones.
TITANIA	Or say, sweet love, what thou desir'st to eat.
BOTTOM	Truly, a peck of provender! I could munch your good dry oats. Methinks I have a great desire to a bottle of hay. Good hay, sweet hay, hath no fellow.
TITANIA	I have a venturous fairy that shall seek The squirrel's hoard, and fetch thee new nuts.
BOTTOM	I had rather have a handful or two of dried peas. But I pray you, let none of your people stir me. I have an exposition of sleep come upon me.
TITANIA	Sleep thou – and I will wind thee in my arms! Fairies, be gone, and be all ways away.

25

30

35

40

Exit PEASEBLOSSOM, *with* MUSTARDSEED.
Other Fairies go off in different directions.

(*Embracing* BOTTOM)
– So doth the woodbine the sweet honeysuckle
Gently entwist – the female ivy so
Enrings the barky fingers of the elm.
O, how I love thee! How I dote on thee!

45

They go to sleep, BOTTOM *cradled in* TITANIA*'s arms.*
Enter PUCK.
OBERON *comes forward to meet him.*

OBERON	Welcome, good Robin. Seest thou this sweet sight? Her dotage now I do begin to pity – For meeting her of late behind the wood, Seeking sweet favours for this hateful fool, I did upbraid her and fall out with her. For she his hairy temples then had rounded

50

Oberon informs Puck that Titania has handed over her changeling boy and that he now feels sorry for her. He lifts the charm and awakens her.

54 **Was wont**: used
    orient: 1 lustrous; 2 from the East
55 **Stood**: hung
56 **bewail**: weep for
57 **at my pleasure**: as much as I liked

59 **changeling child**: (see Act 2 Scene 1, lines 20 to 27, and 120 to 145)
60 **straight**: straight away
63 **hateful imperfection**: i.e. the effect of the juice
64 **scalp**: head
65 **swain**: young country lover
66 **other**: others
67 **repair**: return
68 **accidents**: incidents
69 **fierce vexation**: wild agitation

THINK ABOUT *for* GCSE

Language
• Look at the language Oberon uses (lines 46 to 70). In what ways does it help to show that he is now more calm and contented than he was in his confrontation with Titania (in Act 2 Scene 1)?

Context
• Releasing Titania from the charm, Oberon says 'Dian's bud ... blessed power' (lines 73 to 74). What does Oberon mean by this statement? What does it tell us about the contest between sexual love and chastity?

71 **thou wast wont**: you used
73 **Dian's bud**: i.e. the antidote herb; Diana was the goddess of chastity.
    Cupid's flower: (see Act 2 Scene 1, lines 165–9)

77 **enamoured of**: in love with

79 **visage**: face

83 **charmeth**: brings about by magic

With coronet of fresh and fragrant flowers –
And that same dew, which sometime on the buds
Was wont to swell like round and orient pearls,
Stood now within the pretty flowerets' eyes   55
Like tears that did their own disgrace bewail.
When I had at my pleasure taunted her,
And she in mild terms begged my patience,
I then did ask of her her changeling child –
Which straight she gave me, and her fairy sent   60
To bear him to my bower in Fairyland.
And now I have the boy, I will undo
This hateful imperfection of her eyes.
And, gentle Puck, take this transformèd scalp
From off the head of this Athenian swain –   65
That he awaking when the other do,
May all to Athens back again repair,
And think no more of this night's accidents
But as the fierce vexation of a dream.
– But first I will release the Fairy Queen.   70

He squeezes the healing herb onto TITANIA*'s eyelids.*

Be as thou wast wont to be –
See as thou wast wont to see.
Dian's bud o'er Cupid's flower
Hath such force and blessed power.
Now, my Titania, wake you, my sweet Queen!   75

TITANIA	(*Starting out of her sleep*)
	My Oberon! What visions have I seen!
	Methought I was enamoured of an ass.

| OBERON | There lies your love. |

| TITANIA | How came these things to pass? |
| | O, how mine eyes do loathe his visage now! |

OBERON	Silence awhile. (*To* PUCK) Robin, take off this head. 80
	Titania, music call – and strike more dead
	Than common sleep of all these five the sense.

| TITANIA | Music, ho! Music such as charmeth sleep! |

Soft music plays through the woods.

As Puck takes the ass's head off Bottom, the King and Queen of the fairies have made up.
The fairies leave as Theseus enters, out hunting with Hippolyta and Egeus.

87 **new in amity**: friends once again
88 **solemnly**: ceremoniously
89 **triumphantly**: festively / with great celebration

93 **attend and mark**: listen!

95 **sad**: sober / serious
96 **Trip**: move swiftly
97 **compass**: circle

THINK ABOUT for GCSE

Performance and staging
• If you were playing Titania, what tone might you give lines 99 to 102?

Structure and form
• In what ways does the mood of the scene change when Theseus, Hippolyta and Egeus enter (line 103)?

104 **observation**: observance (i.e. of May morning ceremonies)
105 **va'ward**: early part
107 **Uncouple**: Unleash (his hounds)
108 **Dispatch**: Hurry!

PUCK	(*Removing the ass's head from* BOTTOM)
	Now, when thou wak'st, with thine own fool's eyes
	peep.
OBERON	Sound, music! Come, my Queen, take hands with me 85
	And rock the ground whereon these sleepers be.

They dance.

    – Now thou and I are new in amity,
    And will tomorrow midnight solemnly
    Dance in Duke Theseus' house triumphantly,
    And bless it to all fair prosperity.   90
    There shall the pairs of faithful lovers be
    Wedded, with Theseus, all in jollity.

PUCK	Fairy King, attend and mark –
	I do hear the morning lark.
OBERON	Then, my Queen, in silence sad, 95
	Trip we after night's shade.
	We the globe can compass soon,
	Swifter than the wandering moon.
TITANIA	Come, my lord – and in our flight
	Tell me how it came this night 100
	That I sleeping here was found,
	With these mortals on the ground.

          Exit OBERON *with* TITANIA, *followed by* PUCK.

The lovers, and BOTTOM, *still lie asleep.*

Hunting horns are heard.

Enter DUKE THESEUS *and* HIPPOLYTA, *with* EGEUS *and followers.*

THESEUS	Go one of you – find out the forester,
	For now our observation is performed.
	And since we have the va'ward of the day, 105
	My love shall hear the music of my hounds.
	Uncouple in the western valley – let them go!
	Dispatch, I say, and find the forester.

          Exit an Attendant.

We will, fair queen, up to the mountain's top,

As Theseus and Hippolyta are discussing the benefits of his hunting dogs, Theseus discovers the lovers asleep on the ground. He recalls that this is the day when Hermia is required to make her decision and orders them to be woken up.

110–11 musical … conjunction: the combined sounds of the hounds and the echo

112 Hercules and Cadmus: Greek heroes

113 bayed: cornered

114 hounds of Sparta: They were famed for their hunting skill.

115 gallant chiding: fine barking / baying (of hounds)

117 mutual: common / shared

119 kind: strain, lineage

120 So flewed: with the same hanging cheek-folds
sanded: sandy coloured

122 dewlapped: with loose flaps of skin on their necks
Thessalian: from Thessaly, a region in north-eastern Greece

123–4 matched … each: their barks in tune, like a peal of bells

124 tuneable: melodious

125 holla'd … cheered: cheered on

127 soft!: wait!

131 of: at

134 grace: honour
solemnity: ceremony

139 Saint Valentine: 14 February (when birds were believed to choose their mates)

140 couple: pair off

THINK ABOUT for GCSE

Relationships
• Look back at the Think About questions on pages 8 and 14 concerning the relationship between Theseus and Hippolyta. Then look at their discussion about hounds in this scene (lines 105 to 127). Do you think they are genuinely fascinated by the quality of the dogs? Or is Theseus determined to go one better than Hippolyta?

	And mark the musical confusion	110
	Of hounds and echo in conjunction.	

HIPPOLYTA   I was with Hercules and Cadmus once,
            When in a wood of Crete they bayed the bear
            With hounds of Sparta. Never did I hear
            Such gallant chiding – for besides the groves,   115
            The skies, the fountains, every region near
            Seemed all one mutual cry. I never heard
            So musical a discord, such sweet thunder.

THESEUS   My hounds are bred out of the Spartan kind –
            So flewed, so sanded. And their heads are hung   120
            With ears that sweep away the morning dew,
            Crook-kneed and dewlapped, like Thessalian bulls –
            Slow in pursuit, but matched in mouth like bells,
            Each under each. A cry more tuneable
            Was never holla'd to nor cheered with horn,   125
            In Crete, in Sparta, nor in Thessaly.
            Judge when you hear. But soft! (*Noticing the
            sleeping lovers*) – What nymphs are these?

EGEUS   My lord – this is my daughter here asleep!
            – And this Lysander! – This Demetrius is –
            This Helena – old Nedar's Helena!   130
            I wonder of their being here together.

THESEUS   No doubt they rose up early to observe
            The rite of May, and hearing our intent
            Came here in grace of our solemnity.
            But speak, Egeus – is not this the day   135
            That Hermia should give answer of her choice?

EGEUS   It is, my lord.

THESEUS   Go bid the huntsmen wake them with their horns.

Shouted commands: hunting horns sound.

The lovers start out of their sleep.

            – Good morrow, friends! Saint Valentine is past –
            Begin these wood-birds but to couple now?   140

The lovers kneel before the DUKE.

When Lysander admits that he
and Hermia had planned to
elope, Egeus demands that he
should be punished. But then
Demetrius declares that he again
loves Helena.

143 **gentle concord**: state of peaceful
agreement
144 **jealousy**: suspicion / mistrust
145 **enmity**: hostility / opposition

149 **truly would I speak**: I want to tell the
truth
150 **bethink me**: realise

THINK ABOUT for GCSE

Characterisation
• What different thoughts
might go through Hermia's
head from the moment she
wakes up (line 139) to the
end of Egeus's speech
(line 159)?

Performance and staging
• How might the four lovers
react during Egeus's speech
(lines 154 to 159)?

Themes and issues
• How accurate is Demetrius's
account of his changing
feelings for Hermia (line
167). How accurate is
Demetrius's account of his
changing feelings (lines 160
to 176)? What do we know
that he doesn't?

157 **Thereby**: in that way
defeated: defrauded / falsely deprived

160 **stealth**: secret escape
161 **hither**: in coming here
163 **in fancy**: motivated by love
164 **wot not**: do not know

167 **idle gaud**: worthless toy / trinket

172 **was I betroth'd ere**: I had agreed to be
married before
173 **like a sickness**: just as when you are ill
174 **come to**: having regained
natural: normal
175 **it**: i.e. the 'food' that is Helena

LYSANDER	Pardon, my lord.

THESEUS
       I pray you all, stand up.
(*To* LYSANDER *and* DEMETRIUS)
I know you two are rival enemies:
How comes this gentle concord in the world,
That hatred is so far from jealousy
To sleep by hate, and fear no enmity?   **145**

LYSANDER
My lord, I shall reply amazèdly –
Half sleep, half waking. But as yet, I swear,
I cannot truly say how I came here.
But as I think – for truly would I speak –
And now I do bethink me, so it is –   **150**
I came with Hermia hither. Our intent
Was to be gone from Athens, where we might,
Without the peril of the Athenian law –

EGEUS
Enough, enough, my lord! You have enough.
I beg the law – the law upon his head!   **155**
They would have stolen away. They would, Demetrius,
Thereby to have defeated you and me –
You of your wife, and me of my consent –
Of my consent that she should be your wife.

DEMETRIUS
My lord, fair Helena told me of their stealth,   **160**
Of this their purpose hither to this wood,
And I in fury hither followed them –
Fair Helena in fancy following me.
But, my good lord, I wot not by what power,
But by some power it is, my love to Hermia – **165**
Melted as doth the snow – seems to me now
As the remembrance of an idle gaud
Which in my childhood I did dote upon.
And all the faith, the virtue of my heart,
The object and the pleasure of mine eye,   **170**
Is only Helena. – To her, my lord,
Was I betrothed ere I saw Hermia –
But like a sickness did I loathe this food.
But as in health, come to my natural taste,
Now I do wish it, love it, long for it –   **175**
And will for evermore be true to it.

Theseus decides to override Egeus's wishes and declares that the two pairs of lovers can marry on the day he marries Hippolyta. Before following Theseus back to Athens, the four lovers try to make some sense of their strange experience, and wonder if they have been dreaming.

178 **discourse**: account of events
179 **overbear your will**: overrule your wishes
180 **by and by**: soon
181 **knit**: married
182 **for**: since
    something worn: partly over

185 **in great solemnity**: very ceremoniously

187 **undistinguishable**: unrecognisable

189 **Methinks**: It seems to me
    parted eye: eyes out of focus

194 **yet**: still

199 **by**: on

THINK ABOUT for GCSE

Performance and staging
• Imagine you are Egeus. Theseus overrides your wishes and allows Hermia to marry Lysander (line 179). Without speaking, how might you show that you either (a) accept the situation or (b) are not happy with it?

Themes and issues
• **Love**: Helena describes Demetrius as 'Mine own, and not mine own' (line 192), perhaps because she has 'found' him 'like a jewel' (line 191) and it is uncertain to whom he belongs. Think about the magic juice. In what way might Helena's impression be true?

114

THESEUS	Fair lovers, you are fortunately met.
	Of this discourse we more will hear anon.
	Egeus, I will overbear your will –
	For in the temple by and by, with us, 180
	These couples shall eternally be knit.
	And, for the morning now is something worn,
	Our purposed hunting shall be set aside.
	Away with us to Athens. Three and three,
	We'll hold a feast in great solemnity. 185
	Come, Hippolyta.

Exit, with HIPPOLYTA, EGEUS, *and attendants.*

The lovers – and BOTTOM *(still asleep) – remain.*

DEMETRIUS	These things seem small and undistinguishable,
	Like far-off mountains turnèd into clouds.
HERMIA	Methinks I see these things with parted eye,
	When everything seems double.
HELENA	So methinks – 190
	And I have found Demetrius, like a jewel,
	Mine own, and not mine own!
DEMETRIUS	Are you sure
	That we are awake? It seems to me
	That yet we sleep – we dream. Do not you think
	The Duke was here, and bid us follow him? 195
HERMIA	Yea – and my father.
HELENA	And Hippolyta.
LYSANDER	And he did bid us follow to the temple.
DEMETRIUS	Why then, we are awake. Let's follow him,
	And by the way let us recount our dreams.

Exit, with the others.

Bottom wakes up and recalls the most extraordinary dream.

203 **God's my life**: Good lord!
hence: away

205 **wit**: understanding

206 **go about**: attempt
but: no more than

207 **expound**: explain

209 **patched fool**: jester (wearing a patchwork costume)
offer: venture

212 **conceive**: imagine

214 **ballad**: poem or song telling a story

215 **it hath no bottom**: you can't get to the bottom of it

216 **in the latter end**: towards the end

217 **Peradventure**: Perhaps
gracious: appealing / elegant

218 **her**: i.e. Thisby's

THINK ABOUT for GCSE

Performance and staging
- How would you direct an actor playing Bottom to perform this speech (lines 200 to 218)? Which parts of it might be funny and which touching?

BOTTOM   (*Suddenly waking*) When my cue comes, call me, and   **200**
I will answer. My next is 'Most fair Pyramus' – (*Yawning*)
Hey-ho! Peter Quince! Flute the bellows-mender! Snout
the tinker? Starveling? – God's my life! – Stolen hence,
and left me asleep! I have had a most rare vision. I
have had a dream, past the wit of man to say what   **205**
dream it was. Man is but an *ass* if he go about to
expound this dream. Methought I was – there is no
man can tell what. Methought I was – and methought
I had – but man is but a patched fool, if he will offer
to say what methought I had. The eye of man hath not   **210**
heard – the ear of man hath not seen – man's hand is
not able to taste, his tongue to conceive, nor his heart
to report, what my dream was! I will get Peter Quince
to write a ballad of this dream. It shall be called
'Bottom's Dream', because it hath no bottom – and I   **215**
will sing it in the latter end of a play, before the Duke.
Peradventure, to make it the more gracious, I shall sing
it at her death.

Exit.

In this scene ...

• The Mechanicals gloomily discuss the loss of Bottom and the money they could have earned. But he arrives with news that their play has been shortlisted as possible entertainment for the Duke's wedding.

The other Mechanicals are depressed by Bottom's continued absence; without him, their play cannot go on. As they are complaining about the loss of the money the Duke might have given them, Bottom enters.

THINK ABOUT for GCSE

Context
• From what you have learned of the Mechanicals and their way of life, and from what you gain from their conversation here, think about why they might be depressed by Bottom's continued absence.

Performance and staging
• How might Bottom make his entrance? Should he appear suddenly, for example, or creep up unnoticed?

2   **transported**: carried off (i.e. by magic or the fairies)
3   **marred**: ruined

6   **discharge**: perform
7   **wit**: talent
9   **person**: appearance / bearing
    paramour: cheating lover (he means 'paragon')

11 **paragon**: example of perfection / model of excellence
12 **thing of naught**: immoral person

15 **we ... men**: our fortunes would have been made
16 **sweet bully Bottom!**: dear, good old Bottom!
17 **'scaped**: avoided
17–18 **sixpence a day**: i.e. the pension from the Duke; roughly a day's wages for a craftsman at that time.
18 **An**: If
20 **in**: for
21 **hearts**: fine friends
22 **courageous**: wonderful
23 **discourse**: tell you / recount
25 **right**: just / exactly
    fell out: happened

Athens.

Enter Quince, Flute, Snout, *and* Starveling.

Quince	Have you sent to Bottom's house? Is he come home yet?
Starveling	He cannot be heard of. Out of doubt he is transported.
Flute	If he come not, then the play is marred. It goes not forward – doth it?
Quince	It is not possible. You have not a man in all Athens able to discharge Pyramus but he.
Flute	No – he hath simply the best wit of any handicraft man in Athens.
Quince	Yea, and the best person too – and he is a very paramour for a sweet voice.
Flute	You must say 'paragon'. A paramour is – God bless us! – a thing of naught.

Enter Snug.

Snug	Masters! The Duke is coming from the temple, and there is two or three lords and ladies more married. If our sport had gone forward, we had all been made men.
Flute	O sweet bully Bottom! Thus hath he lost sixpence a day during his life – he could not have 'scaped sixpence a day. An the Duke had not given him sixpence a day for playing Pyramus, I'll be hanged! He would have deserved it. Sixpence a day in Pyramus, or nothing.

Enter Bottom.

Bottom	Where are these lads? Where are these hearts?
Quince	Bottom! – O most courageous day! O, most happy hour!
Bottom	Masters, I am to discourse wonders! But ask me not what – for if I tell you, I am no true Athenian. I will tell you everything, right as it fell out.

5

10

15

20

25

The Mechanicals are delighted to see Bottom, who refuses to tell them what has happened to him. But he tells them to get all their costumes together and prepare themselves – their play has been shortlisted as a possible entertainment for the Duke's wedding.

27 **of**: out of

28 **apparel**: costumes

29 **strings**: i.e. to tie on their false beards
    ribbons: decorative laces
    pumps: light shoes (plimsolls)

30 **presently**: immediately

31 **preferred**: shortlisted (i.e. as one of the entertainments from which Theseus will choose)

33 **pare**: trim

THINK ABOUT for GCSE

Characterisation

- Twice Bottom promises to tell his friends what happened and each time he fails to do so (lines 23 to 32). Is he deliberately keeping them in suspense? Is he genuinely unable to recall what happened? Or is he incapable of putting it into words?

QUINCE   Let us hear, sweet Bottom!

BOTTOM   Not a word of me. All that I will tell you is – that the
            Duke hath dined. Get your apparel together, good
            strings to your beards, new ribbons to your pumps. Meet
            presently at the palace. Every man look o'er his part –   30
            for the short and the long is, our play is preferred! In any
            case, let Thisby have clean linen – and let not him that
            plays the lion pare his nails, for they shall hang out for
            the lion's claws. And, most dear actors, eat no onions
            nor garlic – for we are to utter sweet breath, and I do   35
            not doubt but to hear them say it is a sweet comedy. No
            more words. Away! Go – away!

                                    Exit, the others following.

In this scene ...

- Theseus discusses the lovers' experience with Hippolyta and then selects the Mechanicals' 'Pyramus and Thisby' as the wedding-night performance.
- The Mechanicals perform their play and end with a dance.
- Oberon and Titania bless the married couples and Puck asks the audience to applaud.

It is the wedding night. Theseus and Hippolyta discuss the lovers' strange story and the power of the imagination.

THINK ABOUT for GCSE

Relationships
- What difference of opinion do Theseus and Hippolyta have about the lovers' stories?

Themes and issues
- **Imagination, dreaming and fantasy:** Could Theseus's description of a poet (lines 12 to 17) be applied to Shakespeare himself? Which parts of his account, and Hippolyta's answer (lines 23 to 27), could describe what Shakespeare has done in this play?

1 **that**: what
3 **antique**: 1 old; 2 ridiculous
   fairy toys: silly fairy tales
4 **seething**: frantic
5 **shaping fantasies**: creative imaginations
   apprehend: grasp / understand
6 **comprehends**: takes in / understands
8 **all compact**: composed entirely
11 **Sees ... Egypt**: thinks an unattractive woman is beautiful
   Helen: the beautiful Helen of Troy
   brow of Egypt: unattractive face (Dark-skinned women were not considered attractive at that time.)
12 **fine frenzy**: noble burst of inspiration
14 **bodies forth**: gives shape to
16 **airy nothing**: pure imagination
17 **local habitation**: 1 reality; 2 place in which to live
18 **strong imagination**: (could mean madness)
19 **would but**: merely wishes to
20 **comprehends**: creates and includes
21 **some fear**: something frightening
24 **transfigured so together**: changed in the same way and at the same time
25 **More witnesseth**: is stronger evidence
   fancy's: the imagination's
26 **grows to**: arrives at / becomes
   constancy: consistent truth
27 **But howsoever**: even though still / in any case
   admirable: wondrous / extraordinary

Athens: Duke Theseus's palace.

Enter THESEUS *and* HIPPOLYTA, *with* PHILOSTRATE
and other attendants.

HIPPOLYTA   'Tis strange, my Theseus, that these lovers speak of.

THESEUS   More strange than true. I never may believe
These antique fables nor these fairy toys.
Lovers and madmen have such seething brains,
Such shaping fantasies, that apprehend   5
More than cool reason ever comprehends.
The lunatic, the lover, and the poet
Are of imagination all compact.
One sees more devils than vast hell can hold –
That is the madman. The lover, all as frantic,   10
Sees Helen's beauty in a brow of Egypt.
The poet's eye, in a fine frenzy rolling,
Doth glance from heaven to earth, from earth to heaven,
And as imagination bodies forth
The forms of things unknown, the poet's pen   15
Turns them to shapes, and gives to airy nothing
A local habitation and a name.
Such tricks hath strong imagination
That, if it would but apprehend some joy,
It comprehends some bringer of that joy.   20
– Or in the night, imagining some fear,
How easy is a bush supposed a bear!

HIPPOLYTA   But all the story of the night told over,
And all their minds transfigured so together,
More witnesseth than fancy's images,   25
And grows to something of great constancy –
But howsoever, strange and admirable.

Enter LYSANDER, DEMETRIUS, HERMIA *and* HELENA.

THESEUS   Here come the lovers, full of joy and mirth.
Joy, gentle friends – joy and fresh days of love
Accompany your hearts!

Philostrate, in charge of court entertainments, gives Theseus a list of all the performances on offer. Theseus rejects the first three, but he chooses the Mechanicals' play.

THINK ABOUT for GCSE

Context
• Theseus reads the list of entertainments on offer (lines 44 to 60). In what ways might each of these have been unsuitable for a wedding celebration?

Performance and staging
• How might the actor playing Theseus read out this list? Think about how he might react to each item.

---

31   board: dining table

32   masques: entertainments with music and dance

34   after-supper: the time after the meal

39   abridgement: 1 pastime (to make the time go quickly); 2 shortened entertainment

40–1   beguile … time: deceive slow time into passing more quickly

42   brief: summary
sports: entertainments
ripe: fully prepared / ready to be performed

44   battle … Centaurs: The centaurs (half horse, half man) were fought off by the Lapiths (people who lived in the region of Lapithae) and Theseus when they attempted to carry off the bride at the wedding of Theseus's friend, Pirithous.

45   eunuch: castrated male who sang in a high voice

48   tipsy Bacchanals: These were women who tore Orpheus ('the Thracian singer') apart while they were drunkenly worshipping Bacchus, Roman god of wine.

50   device: show

52   thrice three Muses: Each of the nine Muses in Greek myth was responsible for a different branch of the arts.

52–3   mourning … beggary: Poets, playwrights and scholars in Shakespeare's time often complained that they were starving for lack of money.

54   satire: play or poem written to expose some wrong or foolishness
keen: sharp / biting

55   sorting … ceremony: appropriate for a wedding

60   concord of: harmony in

LYSANDER	More than to us $\qquad$ 30
	Wait in your royal walks, your board, your bed!
THESEUS	Come now: what masques, what dances shall we have
	To wear away this long age of three hours
	Between our after-supper, and bed-time?
	Where is our usual manager of mirth? $\qquad$ 35
	What revels are in hand? – Is there no play
	To ease the anguish of a torturing hour?
	Call Philostrate.
PHILOSTRATE	Here, mighty Theseus.
THESEUS	Say, what abridgement have you for this evening?
	What masque? What music? How shall we beguile $\qquad$ 40
	The lazy time, if not with some delight?
PHILOSTRATE	(*Giving him a paper*) There is a brief how many
	$\qquad$ sports are ripe:
	Make choice of which your Highness will see first.
THESEUS	(*Reading from the list*)
	'The battle with the Centaurs, to be sung
	By an Athenian eunuch, to the harp' – $\qquad$ 45
	We'll none of that. That have I told my love
	In glory of my kinsman Hercules.
	(*Reads*) 'The riot of the tipsy Bacchanals,
	Tearing the Thracian singer in their rage'.
	That is an old device, and it was played $\qquad$ 50
	When I from Thebes came last a conqueror.
	(*Reads*) 'The thrice three Muses, mourning for the
	$\qquad$ death
	Of Learning, late deceased in beggary' –
	That is some satire, keen and critical,
	Not sorting with a nuptial ceremony. $\qquad$ 55
	(*Reads*) 'A tedious brief scene of young Pyramus
	And his love Thisby: very tragical mirth'.
	Merry and tragical? Tedious and brief?
	That is hot ice, and wondrous strange snow!
	How shall we find the concord of this discord? $\qquad$ 60
PHILOSTRATE	A play there is, my lord, some ten words long,
	Which is as brief as I have known a play –

Philostrate explains that the
Mechanicals' play is laughably
bad, but Theseus insists on
seeing it as it is always the
thought that counts.

THINK ABOUT *for* GCSE

Themes and issues
- In what ways has the concept of **authority** been explored? Look at the ways Egeus and Theseus exercised their authority in Act 1 Scene 1, for example, Theseus's overruling of Egeus in Act 4 Scene 1 and his responses to Philostrate here.

Characterisation
- Why is Hippolyta reluctant to see the Mechanicals' play? How does Theseus answer her concerns? What does this exchange (lines 85 to 105) reveal about each of them?

65 **fitted**: suited to his part / appropriately cast

70 **passion**: strong emotion
71 **What**: What kind of men

74 **toiled ... memories**: exhausted their little-used powers of memory (i.e. in learning the lines)
75 **against your nuptial**: in preparation for your wedding
79 **find ... intents**: get a laugh out of their attempts
80 **Extremely ... pain**: they have stretched their abilities to the limit and tormented themselves learning the lines
82 **amiss**: wrong
83 **tender**: offer

85 **wretchedness o'ercharged**: humble people overburdened
86 **duty ... perishing**: people attempting to offer loyal service and failing
88 **in this kind**: of this sort (i.e. performing a play)
90 **sport**: pleasure
take ... mistake: accept / understand what they get wrong
91–2 **noble ... merit**: a generous, considerate person values their intentions, rather than what they achieve
93 **clerks**: scholars

But by ten words, my lord, it is *too* long,
Which makes it tedious. For in all the play
There is not one word apt, one player fitted.   65
And tragical, my noble lord, it is,
For Pyramus therein doth kill himself –
Which when I saw rehearsed, I must confess,
Made mine eyes water: but more merry tears
The passion of loud laughter never shed.   70

THESEUS   What are they that do play it?

PHILOSTRATE   Hard-handed men that work in Athens here,
Which never laboured in their minds till now –
And now have toiled their unbreathed memories
With this same play, against your nuptial.   75

THESEUS   And we will hear it.

PHILOSTRATE   No, my noble lord –
It is not for you. I have heard it over,
And it is nothing, nothing in the world –
Unless you can find sport in their intents,
Extremely stretched and conned with cruel pain,   80
To do you service.

THESEUS   I will hear that play.
For never anything can be amiss
When simpleness and duty tender it.
Go, bring them in – and take your places, ladies.

                              Exit PHILOSTRATE.

All take their places as 'audience' for the play.

HIPPOLYTA   I love not to see wretchedness o'ercharged,   85
And duty in his service perishing.

THESEUS   Why, gentle sweet, you shall see no such thing.

HIPPOLYTA   He says they can do nothing in this kind.

THESEUS   The kinder we, to give them thanks for nothing.
Our sport shall be take what they mistake –   90
And what poor duty cannot do, noble respect
Takes it in might, not merit.
Where I have come, great clerks have purposèd

127

Peter Quince stumbles through the opening speech as Prologue.

94 **premeditated welcomes**: pre-planned welcome speeches
96 **Make periods**: pause
97 **Throttle ... accent**: choke on their rehearsed speech

100 **picked**: extracted
103 **saucy ... eloquence**: over-confident smooth-talking
104 **simplicity**: sincerity
105 **In least speak most**: express most in fewest words
to my capacity: as I understand it (i.e. in my judgement)
106 **addressed**: ready to begin

THINK ABOUT for GCSE

Language

• Here is a re-punctuated version of what Quince might have intended to say (lines 108 to 117): 'If we offend, it is with our good will that you should think we come – not to offend – but with good will to show our simple skill. That is the true beginning of our end. Consider then, we come – but in despite we do not come – as minding to content you. Our true intent is all for your delight. We are not here that you should here repent you. The actors are at hand, and, by their show, you shall know all that you are like to know.' What *unintended* meanings does he get across by ignoring the punctuation?

111 **end**: aim / purpose
112 **in despite**: maliciously / to irritate you
113 **as minding**: intending
114 **All**: Exclusively / Totally
115 **repent you**: regret what you have done

118 **not stand upon points**: 1 is not a stickler for detail; 2 does not bother about punctuation
119 **rid**: ridden
rough colt: unbroken horse
120 **stop**: 1 the sudden pulling up of a horse; 2 full stop
121 **true**: 1 the truth; 2 correctly
123 **in government**: under control
124–5 **nothing impaired**: not broken at all

To greet me with premeditated welcomes –
Where I have seen them shiver and look pale,   95
Make periods in the midst of sentences,
Throttle their practised accent in their fears,
And in conclusion dumbly have broke off,
Not paying me a welcome. Trust me, sweet –
Out of this silence yet I picked a welcome.   100
And in the modesty of fearful duty
I read as much as from the rattling tongue
Of saucy and audacious eloquence.
Love, therefore, and tongue-tied simplicity,
In least speak most, to my capacity.   105

Re-enter PHILOSTRATE.

PHILOSTRATE   So please your Grace, the Prologue is addressed.

THESEUS   Let him approach.

A trumpet sounds.

Enter QUINCE.

QUINCE   If we offend, it is with our good will.
(*as* PROLOGUE) That you should think, we come not to offend,
But with good will. To show our simple skill,   110
That is the true beginning of our end.
Consider then, we come but in despite.
We do not come as minding to content you,
Our true intent is. All for your delight,
We are not here. That you should here repent you,   115
The actors are at hand – and by their show
You shall know all that you are like to know.

THESEUS   This fellow doth not stand upon points.

LYSANDER   He hath rid his prologue like a rough colt: he
knows not the stop. A good moral, my lord – it is   120
not enough to speak, but to speak true.

HIPPOLYTA   Indeed he hath played on his prologue like a child
on a recorder – a sound, but not in government.

THESEUS   His speech was like a tangled chain – nothing
impaired, but all disordered. Who is next?   125

Peter Quince introduces the characters and gives an outline of the story. All the Mechanicals leave the stage except Snout.

126 **perchance**: perhaps

131 **sunder**: keep apart

THINK ABOUT
for GCSE

Performance and staging

• In performance, the Mechanicals have to act in front of two audiences: the court and us – the theatre audience. How would you stage the scene? Which way might the Mechanicals face? Where might the court sit?

Context

• The story of Pyramus and Thisby comes from _Metamorphoses_ ('Shape Changes') by the Roman poet Ovid, often described as Shakespeare's favourite book and the source of most of the classical references in _A Midsummer Night's Dream_. In what ways have changes of physical shape, or changes of feeling, been central to this play?

136 **think no scorn**: consider it no disgrace

138 **hight**: is called

141 **mantle**: loose cloak
     fall: drop (i.e. let fall)
143 **Anon**: Immediately
     tall: brave

146 **broached**: pierced

149 **twain**: two
150 **At large discourse**: tell / explain at length

152 **No wonder**: I wouldn't be surprised

153 **interlude**: short play

156 **crannied**: with a narrow opening

Trumpet sounds again.   .

Enter the actors in procession: BOTTOM *(as* PYRAMUS*)*,
FLUTE *(as* THISBY*)*, SNOUT *(as* WALL*)*, STARVELING *(as* MOONSHINE*)*
and SNUG *(as* LION*)*.

They stand in line while QUINCE *presents them.*

QUINCE	Gentles, perchance you wonder at this show –
(as PROLOGUE*)*	But wonder on, till truth make all things plain.

This man is Pyramus, if you would know –
This beauteous lady Thisby is, certain.
This man with lime and rough-cast doth present   **130**
Wall, that vile Wall, which did these lovers sunder:
And through Wall's chink, poor souls, they are content
To whisper – at the which let no man wonder.
This man, with lantern, dog, and bush of thorn,
Presenteth Moonshine – for, if you will know,   **135**
By moonshine did these lovers think no scorn
To meet at Ninus' tomb, there, there to woo.
This grisly beast, which Lion hight by name,
The trusty Thisby, coming first by night,
Did scare away, or rather did affright: **140**
And as she fled, her mantle she did fall,
Which Lion vile with bloody mouth did stain.
Anon comes Pyramus, sweet youth and tall,
And finds his trusty Thisby's mantle slain –
Whereat with blade, with bloody blameful blade,   **145**
He bravely broached his boiling bloody breast.
And Thisby, tarrying in mulberry shade,
His dagger drew, and died. For all the rest,
Let Lion, Moonshine, Wall, and Lovers twain,
At large discourse, while here they do remain.   **150**

Exit, followed by all the actors except SNOUT *(*WALL*)*.

THESEUS	I wonder if the lion be to speak.
DEMETRIUS	No wonder, my lord: one lion may, when many asses do.
SNOUT	In this same interlude it doth befall
(as WALL*)*	That I, one Snout by name, present a wall:
	And such a wall, as I would have you think, **155**
	That had in it a crannied hole or chink,

Snout explains that he represents the wall that kept the lovers apart. Pyramus approaches and peeps through the wall's chink. Unable to spy Thisby, he curses the wall, and then explains to the court audience what is about to happen.

161 **right and sinister**: running right to left (i.e. horizontal)

163 **lime and hair**: i.e. the ingredients of plaster

164 **wittiest partition**: most intelligent wall

166 **grim-looked**: grim-looking
hue: colour

168 **alack**: alas (an expression of misery)

173 **eyne**: eyes

174 **Jove**: Jupiter, supreme god of the Romans

178 **sensible**: able to feel / sensitive
again: back

181 **fall pat**: happen exactly
yonder: there

THINK ABOUT for GCSE

Language
- What is particularly bad about the language of Bottom's speech (lines 166 to 173)?

Performance and staging
- Which parts of Bottom's performance might suggest that he is totally absorbed in the role, living the part of Pyramus, and which suggest he is aware that he is performing a play?

Through which the lovers, Pyramus and Thisby,
Did whisper often, very secretly.
This loam, this rough-cast, and this stone doth show
That I am that same Wall – the truth is so.   160
And this the cranny is (*showing parted fingers*), right
   and sinister,
Through which the fearful lovers are to whisper.

THESEUS Would you desire lime and hair to speak better?

DEMETRIUS It is the wittiest partition that ever I heard discourse, my
lord.

Enter BOTTOM (*as* PYRAMUS).

THESEUS Pyramus draws near the wall. Silence!   165

BOTTOM O grim-looked night! O night with hue so black!
(*as* PYRAMUS) O night, which ever art when day is not!
O night, O night – alack, alack, alack,
I fear my Thisby's promise is forgot!
And thou O wall, O sweet, O lovely wall,   170
That stand'st between her father's ground and mine,
Thou wall, O wall, O sweet and lovely wall! –
Show me thy chink, to blink through with mine eyne.

SNOUT (*as* WALL) **holds out his fingers.**

– Thanks, courteous wall! Jove shield thee well for this!
But what see I? No Thisby do I see.   175
O wicked wall, through whom I see no bliss,
Cursed be thy stones for thus deceiving me!

THESEUS The wall, methinks, being sensible, should curse again

BOTTOM No, in truth sir, he should not. 'Deceiving me' is Thisby's
cue. She is to enter now, and I am to spy her through the   180
wall. You shall see it will fall pat as I told you – yonder
she comes.

133

Thisby enters and the lovers talk through the chink in the wall. They declare their everlasting love, agree to meet at 'Ninny's' tomb and depart. Wall politely excuses himself and exits after them.

THINK ABOUT
for GCSE

Language

• 'Stones' (line 185) can mean 'testicles' and there are sexual connotations in 'chink' (line 156), 'lime', ('limb' could mean 'penis') (line 163), 'hair' (lines 163 and 186) and 'I kiss the wall's hole' (line 197). What comic moments can be found if it is clear that the Mechanicals are unaware of the double meanings?

Performance and staging

• What might Wall do while Pyramus and Thisby are declaring their love (lines 187 to 199)?

185 **stones**: This can mean 'testicles'.

188 **an:** if

192 **Limander**: He means Leander, who swam the Hellespont to visit his lover, Hero.

193 **Helen**: He means Hero; an unfortunate mistake as Helen of Troy was not faithful.
      Fates: In Greek myth the three sister goddesses who decided a person's life-span.

194 **Shafalus ... Procrus**: These are mispronunciations: Cephalus remained faithful to his wife Procris when he was abducted by the goddess Aurora.

199 **'Tide life, 'tide death**: Come life, come death

202 **mural**: wall

Enter FLUTE (THISBY).

FLUTE (*as* THISBY)	O wall, full often hast thou heard my moans, For parting my fair Pyramus and me. My cherry lips have often kissed thy stones, 185 Thy stones with lime and hair knit up in thee.
BOTTOM (*as* PYRAMUS)	I see a voice! Now will I to the chink, To spy an I can hear my Thisby's face. Thisby!
FLUTE (*as* THISBY)	My love! Thou art my love, I think. 190
BOTTOM (*as* PYRAMUS)	Think what thou wilt, I am thy lover's grace, And like Limander am I trusty still.
FLUTE (*as* THISBY)	And I like Helen, till the Fates me kill.
BOTTOM (*as* PYRAMUS)	Not Shafalus to Procrus was so true.
FLUTE (*as* THISBY)	As Shafalus to Procrus, I to you. 195
BOTTOM (*as* PYRAMUS)	O kiss me through the hole of this vile wall!
FLUTE (*as* THISBY)	I kiss the wall's hole, not your lips at all.
BOTTOM (*as* PYRAMUS)	Wilt thou at Ninny's tomb meet me straightway?
FLUTE (*as* THISBY)	'Tide life, 'tide death, I come without delay.

Exit.

BOTTOM (PYRAMUS) *goes off in another direction.*

SNOUT (*as* WALL)	Thus have I, Wall, my part dischargèd so – 200 And being done, thus Wall away doth go.

Exit.

THESEUS	Now is the mural down between the two neighbours.

The court audience joke about the performance and then Snug enters. He reassures them that he is not really a lion.

203 wilful: 1 willing; 2 perverse (referring to the proverb 'walls have ears')

206 kind: type of person / actors
but shadows: no more than representations of reality ('shadow' could mean actor)
207 amend: improve

THINK ABOUT *for* GCSE

Themes and issues
- **Imagination, dreaming and Fantasy**: Theseus's reply to Hippolyta (lines 206 to 207) might mean 'even the best actors are no more than representations of real life; and the worst actors can be improved by imagination'. What might we learn from *A Midsummer Night's Dream* about the powers of the imagination?

Context
- The lion was famous in fables for its bravery and kingly qualities; the fox for its cunning and the goose for its cowardice and stupidity. What is the court audience suggesting about Snug's Lion (lines 220 to 228)?

213 smallest monstrous: very small but like a terrifying monster to the ladies

216–7 I as Snug … fell: it is only as Snug (playing a part) that I am a fierce lion
217 nor else … dam: in no way am I a lion's mother
218 in strife: aggressively
220 of a good conscience: thoughtful / considerate
221 at: at playing
222 very … valour: more crafty than courageous
223 a goose … discretion: more foolish than crafty (referring to Aesop's fable)
discretion: 1 judgement; 2 instinct for self-preservation

229 lanthorn: lantern (the sides were often made of horn)

230 horns on his head: Cuckolds – men whose wives were unfaithful – were said to grow horns.

DEMETRIUS	No remedy, my lord, when walls are so wilful, to hear without warning.	
HIPPOLYTA	This is the silliest stuff that ever I heard.	205
THESEUS	The best in this kind are but shadows, and the worst are no worse, if imagination amend them.	
HIPPOLYTA	It must be your imagination then, and not theirs.	
THESEUS	If we imagine no worse of them than they of themselves, they may pass for excellent men. Here come two noble beasts in, a man and a lion.	210

Enter SNUG (as the LION) and STARVELING (as MOONSHINE).

SNUG (as LION)	You, ladies, you whose gentle hearts do fear The smallest monstrous mouse that creeps on floor, May now, perchance, both quake and tremble here When Lion rough in wildest rage doth roar. Then know that I as Snug the joiner am A lion fell – nor else no lion's dam. For if I should as Lion come in strife Into this place, 'twere pity on my life.	215
THESEUS	A very gentle beast, and of a good conscience.	220
DEMETRIUS	The very best at a beast, my lord, that e'er I saw.	
LYSANDER	This lion is a very fox for his valour.	
THESEUS	True – and a goose for his discretion.	
DEMETRIUS	Not so, my lord – for his valour cannot carry his discretion, and the fox carries the goose.	225
THESEUS	His discretion, I am sure, cannot carry his valour – for the goose carries not the fox. It is well. Leave it to his discretion, and let us listen to the Moon.	
STARVELING (as MOONSHINE)	This lanthorn doth the hornèd moon present –	
DEMETRIUS	He should have worn the horns on his head.	230

Starveling tries to explain his role as Moonshine, but he is constantly interrupted. When Thisby reappears, Lion roars and she flees, dropping her mantle. Lion tears at Thisby's mantle and runs off.

231 **is no crescent**: 1 has no 'horns'; 2 is not fat (he is called Starveling)

238 **for the**: because of the
239 **in snuff**: 1 in need of trimming; 2 offended

242 **reason**: reasonable behaviour
243 **stay the time**: wait patiently

THINK ABOUT for GCSE

Themes and issues
- **Authority and power**: How do you react to the court's interruptions during and after Starveling's speech (lines 230 to 249)? Do you find them amusing or impolite and unfair?

Performance and staging
- Might Theseus's observation ('It appears … on the wane', lines 241 to 242) suggest that Starveling is losing his patience? If you were playing him, how might you deliver his final speech (lines 245 to 247)?

s.d. **mantle**: shawl

THESEUS	He is no crescent, and his horns are invisible within the circumference.
STARVELING (*as* **MOONSHINE**)	This lanthorn doth the hornèd moon present: Myself the Man i' th' Moon do seem to be –
THESEUS	This is the greatest error of all the rest. The man should 235 be put *into* the lantern. How is it else the Man i' th' Moon?
DEMETRIUS	He dares not come there for the candle – for you see it is already in snuff.
HIPPOLYTA	I am a-weary of this Moon. Would he would change! 240
THESEUS	It appears, by his small light of discretion, that he is in the wane – but yet in courtesy, in all reason, we must stay the time.
LYSANDER	Proceed, Moon.
STARVELING (*as* **MOONSHINE**)	All that I have to say is to tell you that the lanthorn is 245 the moon – I the Man i' th' Moon – this thorn-bush my thorn-bush, and this dog my dog.
DEMETRIUS	Why, all these should be in the lantern – for all these are in the moon. But silence: here comes Thisby.

Re-enter **FLUTE** (*as* **THISBY**).

FLUTE (*as* **THISBY**)	This is old Ninny's tomb. Where is my love?	250
SNUG (*as* **LION**)	(*Roaring*) Oo – ow…!	

FLUTE (*as* **THISBY**) *runs away* (*dropping her mantle*).

DEMETRIUS	Well roared, Lion!	
THESEUS	Well run, Thisby!	
HIPPOLYTA	Well shone, Moon! Truly, the Moon shines with a good grace.	255

SNUG (*as* **LION**) *chews and tears at* **THISBY**'*s mantle, then runs off.*

When Pyramus enters, he is shocked to see the bloodstained clothing. Assuming that she has been killed by a lion, he gives a tragic speech and stabs himself.

256 **moused**: The Lion savaging the mantle looked like a cat shaking a mouse.

265 **dole**: sorrowful sight
268 **duck**: darling
271 **Furies**: These were snake-haired goddesses who punished the guilty.
      fell: fierce / terrible
273 **cut thread and thrum**: destroy me completely (i.e. he is calling upon the Fates – see line 193 – to cut his thread of life)
      thrum: the loose ends in weaving
274 **Quail**: Overpower
      quell: kill
275 **passion**: fit of grief / suffering
      friend: This could mean a lover.
277 **Beshrew**: Shame on
278 **frame**: create
279 **deflowered my dear**: taken my darling's virginity (he means 'devoured')
281 **cheer**: cheerful face
284 **pap**: breast

THINK ABOUT for GCSE

Performance and staging
- How might an actor bring out the comic effects in Bottom's speeches (lines 259 to 293)? Look, for example, at the repeated sounds in lines 261, 262 and 274; the rhythm of lines 263 to 268; and the ending of line 268.

Characterisation
- What difference can you find in Theseus's and Hippolyta's reactions to the play (lines 275 to 277)?

Re-enter BOTTOM (*as* PYRAMUS).

THESEUS	Well moused, Lion!
DEMETRIUS	And then came Pyramus –
LYSANDER	And so the lion vanished.

BOTTOM
(*as* PYRAMUS)

Sweet Moon, I thank thee for thy sunny beams:
I thank thee, Moon, for shining now so bright –   260
For by thy gracious, golden, glittering gleams
I trust to take of truest Thisby sight.
But stay – O spite!
But mark, poor knight,
What dreadful dole is here!   265
Eyes, do you see?
How can it be?
O dainty duck! – O dear!
Thy mantle good –
What, stained with blood?   270
Approach, ye Furies fell!
O Fates! – Come, come,
Cut thread and thrum,
Quail, crush, conclude, and quell!

THESEUS   This passion, and the death of a dear friend, would   275
go near to make a man look sad.

HIPPOLYTA   Beshrew my heart, but I pity the man.

BOTTOM
(*as* PYRAMUS)

O wherefore, Nature, didst thou lions frame –
Since lion vile hath here deflowered my dear
Which is – no, no, which *was* – the fairest dame   280
That lived, that loved, that liked, that looked with cheer.
Come tears, confound!
Out sword, and wound
The pap of Pyramus! –
Ay, that left pap   285
Where heart doth hop –
Thus die I – (*stabbing himself*) thus, thus, thus!
– Now am I dead,
Now am I fled –
My soul is in the sky.   290
Tongue, lose thy light!

Pyramus 'dies' and, after some comments from the court audience, Thisby enters and finds her lover's body.

294   **No 'die' … one**: he is not a whole die (i.e. one of a pair of dice) but merely a single spot on one of the faces
295   **Less … nothing**: i.e. less than one equals nothing
297   **ass**: (A pun – it sounds like 'ace'.)

304   **mote**: a speck of dust / tiny particle
305   **warrant**: preserve

THINK ABOUT
for GCSE

Performance and staging
- How might Bottom perform Pyramus's suicide (lines 282 to 293) to make it as funny as possible? What comic effects might occur?
- After Flute enters, the onstage audience exchanges several comments (line 300 to 308). Does Flute hear them, or not? Decide what he might do during their speeches if (a) he hears them and (b) he doesn't.

308   **moans**: laments for the dead
      videlicet: that is to say (Latin) / as follows

321   **Sisters Three**: i.e. the Fates (see lines 193 and 272)

Moon, take thy flight –

Exit STARVELING (*as* MOONSHINE).

Now die! – Die, die, die, die.

PYRAMUS *dies.*

DEMETRIUS	No 'die' but an ace for him – for he is but one.
LYSANDER	Less than an ace, man – for he is dead: he is nothing.	295
THESEUS	With the help of a surgeon he might yet recover – and yet prove an ass.
HIPPOLYTA	How chance Moonshine is gone before Thisby comes back and finds her lover?

Re-enter FLUTE (*as* THISBY).

THESEUS	She will find him by starlight. Here she comes, and her passion ends the play.	300
HIPPOLYTA	Methinks she should not use a long one for such a Pyramus. I hope she will be brief.
DEMETRIUS	A mote will turn the balance which Pyramus, which Thisby, is the better – he for a man, God warrant us – she for a woman, God bless us!	305
LYSANDER	She hath spied him already with those sweet eyes.
DEMETRIUS	– And thus she moans, *videlicet* –

FLUTE
(*as* THISBY)

Asleep, my love?
What, dead, my dove?   310
O Pyramus, arise!
Speak, speak! Quite dumb?
Dead, dead? A tomb
Must cover thy sweet eyes.
These lily lips,   315
This cherry nose,
These yellow cowslip cheeks
Are gone, are gone.
Lovers, make moan:
His eyes were green as leeks.   320
O Sisters Three,

Distraught at Pyramus's death, Thisby takes his sword and kills herself. The Mechanicals' play has ended and Bottom leaps up to offer either an epilogue or a dance. Theseus says their play does not need an epilogue, and two of the Mechanicals dance instead. Theseus, Hippolyta and the lovers go off to bed.

324 **gore**: blood
325 **shore**: cut / shorn

329 **imbrue**: 1 pierce / stab; 2 stain with blood

337 **Epilogue**: speech delivered at the end of a play (like Puck's in this play)
Bergomask dance: A rough country dance from Italy, thought funny in England.

344 **notably discharged**: well / unusually performed

346 **iron tongue**: i.e. clapper of a bell

349 **overwatched**: stayed up too long
350 **palpable gross**: obviously crude
beguiled: whiled away
351 **heavy gait**: slow, steady passage
352 **this solemnity**: these celebrations

THINK ABOUT for GCSE

Performance and staging
- In some productions, Flute plays Thisby's final moments seriously, as though he were acting in a genuine Shakespearean tragedy. What effect might a serious performance have on (a) the onstage audience and (b) the theatre audience?

Themes and issues
- **Love; imagination, dreaming and fantasy**: What has *Pyramus and Thisby* added to the exploration of love in *A Midsummer Night's Dream*?

Come, come to me,
With hands as pale as milk!
Lay them in gore,
Since you have shore   325
With shears his thread of silk.
Tongue, not a word!
Come, trusty sword!
Come blade, my breast imbrue –
(*Stabbing herself*) – And farewell, friends,   330
Thus Thisby ends.
Adieu, adieu, adieu.

Thisby *dies.*

THESEUS   Moonshine and Lion are left to bury the dead.

DEMETRIUS   Ay, and Wall too.

BOTTOM   (*Jumping to his feet*) No, I assure you – the wall is   335
down that parted their fathers. Will it please you to see
the Epilogue, or to hear a Bergomask dance between
two of our company?

THESEUS   No epilogue, I pray you – for your play needs no
excuse. Never excuse: for when the players are all   340
dead there need none to be blamed. Marry, if he that
writ it had played Pyramus, and hanged himself in
Thisby's garter, it would have been a fine tragedy – and
so it is truly, and very notably discharged. But come,
your Bergomask: let your epilogue alone.   345

The actors return, and two of them dance a country jig.
As the dancing ends, a bell strikes the hour.

– The iron tongue of midnight hath told twelve.
Lovers, to bed. 'Tis almost fairy-time.
I fear we shall out-sleep the coming morn
As much as we this night have overwatched.
This palpable gross play hath well beguiled   350
The heavy gait of night. Sweet friends, to bed.
A fortnight hold we this solemnity,
In nightly revels and new jollity.

Exit, with HIPPOLYTA, *followed by all the others.*

Puck appears, followed by Oberon, Titania and the fairies. The fairies sing and dance.

355 **behowls**: howls at
356 **heavy**: weary
357 **fordone**: exhausted
358 **wasted brands**: burnt-out logs

361 **shroud**: sheet wound round a corpse for burial

364 **sprite**: spirit / ghost

367 **triple**: Hecate was the moon goddess in heaven (known by several names including Cynthia and Phoebe), Diana or Artemis on earth, and Proserpina or Persephone in the underworld.
Hecate's team: The team of dragons that drew the chariot of the goddess of the underworld.
370 **frolic**: high-spirited
371 **hallowed**: blessed
372 **with broom**: Pucks were sometimes believed to keep the house clean.
373 **behind**: 1 out from behind; 2 out of sight
378 **ditty**: song
379 **trippingly**: lightly
380 **rehearse**: repeat
by rote: from memory

THINK ABOUT for GCSE

Language
• Imagine you were filming the play and had decided to have Puck's speech (lines 354 to 373) heard in 'voice over' while the pictures he describes are actually seen. Which images would you focus on?

Context
• Puck introduces his speech here with a description of night. *A Midsummer Night's Dream*, however, would originally have been staged in daylight. How does the language inform the audience that a scene takes place at night? Look, for example, at the opening of Act 2 Scene 2, Act 2 Scene 2, line 78 and Act 3 Scene 2, line 177.

Enter PUCK, *with a broom.*

PUCK   Now the hungry lion roars
And the wolf behowls the moon,   355
Whilst the heavy ploughman snores,
All with weary task fordone.
Now the wasted brands do glow,
Whilst the screech-owl, screeching loud,
Puts the wretch that lies in woe   360
In remembrance of a shroud.
Now it is the time of night
That the graves, all gaping wide,
Every one lets forth his sprite
In the church-way paths to glide.   365
And we fairies, that do run
By the triple Hecate's team
From the presence of the sun,
Following darkness like a dream,
Now are frolic. Not a mouse   370
Shall disturb this hallowed house.
I am sent with broom before,
To sweep the dust behind the door.

Enter OBERON *and* TITANIA, *King and Queen of Fairies, with all their followers (some holding candles).*

OBERON   Through the house give glimmering light,
By the dead and drowsy fire.   375
Every elf and fairy sprite
Hop as light as bird from briar:
And this ditty after me
Sing, and dance it trippingly.

TITANIA   First rehearse your song by rote,   380
To each word a warbling note.
Hand in hand, with fairy grace,
Will we sing and bless this place.

The Fairies sing together (following OBERON), *and dance in a ring.*

OBERON   — Now until the break of day
Through this house each fairy stray.   385

Oberon and Titania tell the fairies to bless the three couples and the children who will be born to them. As Oberon, Titania and the fairies leave, Puck stays behind and speaks to the audience. He asks them to forgive the actors for any shortcomings, and to think of the play as nothing more than a dream. He ends by asking for applause.

388 **issue**: children

392 **blots of Nature's hand**: birth defects

394 **hare lip**: cleft lip
395 **prodigious**: unlucky
396 **Despisèd in nativity**: considered bad / unlucky at birth
398 **consecrate**: blessed
399 **take his gait**: go his own way
400 **several chamber**: individual bedroom

404 **stay**: delay

406 **shadows**: 1 fairies; 2 actors (see line 206)

410 **idle theme**: trivial story
411 **No more yielding but**: offering up nothing more meaningful than
412 **Gentles**: ladies and gentlemen
reprehend: find fault
413 **mend**: do better next time
416 **the serpent's tongue**: the audience's hisses
417 **ere**: before
420 **Give me your hands**: 1 Applaud; 2 Shake hands (as friends)
421 **restore amends**: put things right in return

THINK ABOUT for GCSE

Language

- The word order in lines 410 to 412 is tricky. Speak line 412 first and then say the earlier two lines (cutting 'And'). What is he asking?

- In what ways does the language of Puck's epilogue contribute to the idea that the events we have witnessed may have been a dream?

To the best bride-bed will we,
Which by us shall blessèd be –
And the issue there create
Ever shall be fortunate.
So shall all the couples three   390
Ever true in loving be,
And the blots of Nature's hand
Shall not in their issue stand.
Never mole, hare-lip, nor scar,
Nor mark prodigious, such as are   395
Despisèd in nativity,
Shall upon their children be.
With this field-dew consecrate,
Every fairy take his gait,
And each several chamber bless   400
Through this palace, with sweet peace.
And the owner of it, blessèd,
Ever shall in safety rest.
Trip away, make no stay!
Meet me all by break of day.   405

Exit, with TITANIA.
The Fairies go off in different directions (through the palace).

PUCK *remains, alone, and speaks to the audience.*

PUCK   If we shadows have offended,
Think but this, and all is mended –
That you have but slumbered here,
While these visions did appear.
And this weak and idle theme,   410
No more yielding but a dream,
Gentles, do not reprehend:
If you pardon, we will mend.
And, as I am an honest Puck,
If we have unearnèd luck   415
Now to 'scape the serpent's tongue,
We will make amends ere long –
Else the Puck a liar call.
So, good night unto you all.
Give me your hands, if we be friends,   420
And Robin shall restore amends.

Exit.

FAIRIES AND MAGIC

Fairies have not always been imagined as small girls with pretty see-through wings. In Shakespeare's time they were regarded very differently and many people still believed in them and feared them. Ten years or so before Shakespeare wrote *A Midsummer Night's Dream*, Reginald Scot published a book called *The Discovery of Witchcraft*, in which he stated that, according to old beliefs, fairies 'made strange apparitions ... being like men and women, soldiers, kings and ladies, children and horsemen, clothed in green ...' It was believed that they would play with household servants at night, 'pinching them black and blue'. Most terrifyingly, many people were said to have experienced what we might call alien abductions, having been 'taken away by the said spirits for a fortnight or a month together ... till at last they have been found lying in some meadow or mountain, bereaved of their senses' – having sometimes lost an arm or a leg as well!

Reginald Scot was writing about people fifty years before Shakespeare's time. He also tells us: 'Indeed your grandams' [grandmothers'] maids were wont [accustomed] to set a bowl of milk before ... Robin Goodfellow, for grinding of malt or mustard.' He goes on to say that 'Robin Goodfellow and Hobgoblin were as terrible and also as credible to the people, as hags and witches be now.'

Robin Goodfellow is the name given in folklore to a supernatural spirit known for shape-shifting and misleading travellers. A puck was a name for a hobgoblin ('Hob' is a shortened form of 'Robin' or 'Robert' and is another name for the devil). Puck was fond of playing practical jokes on humans, especially at night, but, if treated well, would secretly perform household chores. There are Puck equivalents in many countries, including Wales, where he is called Pwca, and Ireland where he can be Phouka, Pooka or Puca.

CLASSICAL MYTHOLOGY IN THE PLAY

A *Midsummer Night's Dream* is packed with references to Greek and Roman mythology. As the play opens we are introduced to Theseus, who was famous for having killed the Minotaur in the Labyrinth, and Hippolyta, the queen of the Amazons, a tribe of warrior women. Throughout the play there are references to Venus, the Roman goddess of love, and her archer-son Cupid (Act 1 Scene 1, line 169; Act 2 Scene 1, lines 155 to 168; Act 3 Scene 2, line 103). Known to the Greeks as Eros, Cupid was often depicted as a little boy carrying a bow and arrows. Sometimes he would be represented blindfolded – unable to see, he would fire his arrows randomly, demonstrating that love often depends on chance.

Diana, the Roman goddess of chastity, hunting and the moon is another important mythological figure in this play. As Diana represents chastity, it is fitting that Hermia will be required to make a vow 'on Diana's altar' if she becomes a nun (Act 1 Scene 1, line 89) and that the antidote to the magic flower is referred to as 'Dian's bud' (Act 4 Scene 1, line 73).

Many of the mythological references in the play are taken from a book that has been called Shakespeare's favourite, the *Metamorphoses* by the Roman poet, Ovid. *Metamorphoses* is a long narrative poem in fifteen books, telling stories from classical mythology. In many of the episodes a human is transformed by the gods into something else, such as an animal, tree or fountain. The story of the Mechanicals' *Pyramus and Thisby* can be found in Ovid, as can the tales about Daphne, changed into a laurel tree when she fled from the god Apollo (Act 2 Scene 1, line 231), Philomela, turned into a nightingale (Act 2 Scene 2, lines 13 and 25), and Procris, who was accidentally killed by her husband, Cephalus, when he was hunting and mistook her for an animal (Act 5 Scene 1, lines 194 to 195).

FESTIVALS AND TRADITIONS

Midsummer Eve was celebrated on June 23, when people would drink, dance and light bonfires to bring good luck. The festival was a celebration of fertility, and it was also believed that on that night young girls would dream of the man who would be their true love. Midsummer Eve was a time when spirits might roam about, and men and women, affected by 'midsummer madness', would behave in unpredictable and wild ways.

Despite the play's title, Shakespeare makes no mention of Midsummer Eve in the play itself, but there are references to two other festivals, May Day and Saint Valentine's Day. Lysander recalls a May Day meeting with Hermia (Act 1 Scene 1, lines 165 to 168) to identify the place in the wood where they will meet; and later in the play Theseus, discovering the four lovers asleep together, suggests: 'No doubt they rose up early / To observe the rite of May' (Act 4 Scene 1, lines 132 to 133). May Day was another ancient fertility festival celebrating spring and the rebirth of the land after winter. Young men and women would collect flowers and greenery to decorate the house in a tradition known as 'bringing in the May' or 'bringing home of May'. To this day children dance around that ancient fertility symbol, the maypole.

After his reference to 'the rite of May', Theseus asks: 'Saint Valentine is past – / Begin these wood-birds but to couple now?' (Act 4 Scene 1, lines 139 to 140). He refers to the tradition that on Saint Valentine's Day (14 February), birds were supposed to choose their mates. Saint Valentine's Day is another festival that has remained popular in modern times. Today it consists largely in sending cards, but we still recall earlier centuries when, on Valentine's Day, women were allowed to propose to men. There was also once a Valentine's Day belief that whoever you saw on waking would be your true love – a tradition Shakespeare's audience might well have recalled when they observed the effect of the magic juice sprinkled by Robin Goodfellow.

THEATRES, STAGES AND WEDDINGS

A Midsummer Night's Dream probably dates from 1595–96. Because the play is relatively short, and directed so much towards wedding celebrations, it has been suggested that Shakespeare may have written it for performance at an Elizabethan high-society wedding – perhaps even one where Queen Elizabeth may have been present. There is, however, no real evidence for this. The first stage performances probably took place in the playhouse called 'The Theatre', in Shoreditch, on what was then the north-east edge of London. This playhouse was of the same familiar type as the more famous Globe. The Theatre was pulled down in 1598 and its timbers re-used for building the Globe, so the size of the stage and the yard and galleries round it were probably much the same.

What we know about the early staging of *A Midsummer Night's Dream* comes mainly from the action of the play and its stage directions. Most important is the continuous and varying use of the large main-stage platform on which all the action of the play takes place. This was clearly big enough for characters to appear in separate groups, and to watch or overhear others (as Puck and Oberon often do). The number of actors on stage reaches a maximum in Act 4 Scene 1. Titania and Bottom fall asleep together in Titania's 'bower', unaware that the stage is already occupied by the four separated lovers (Lysander, Demetrius, Helena and Hermia), each sleeping exhausted and 'alone' in the woods. Oberon then 'heals' Titania's eyes with his magic juice, waking her and dancing with her before they depart reunited. Once Duke Theseus and his company have entered, woken the lovers, and signalled a return to Athens, only Bottom (turned back into normal shape by Puck) remains, to wake up alone and amazed about his wonderful 'dream'. All this has relied on the wide imaginative 'space' of the main-stage platform.

ACTION, SETTINGS AND COSTUMES

The action of the play in an Elizabethan theatre would have been fast and continuous, with no intervals between Acts or Scenes, and new scenes often marked simply by the entrance of new characters. When Peter Quince and his fellow 'mechanicals' appear for Act 1 Scene 2, it is clear that a new scene is beginning in a new setting: Theseus's palace has been replaced, perhaps by Quince's humble house or workshop. No scenery or stage lighting, as we think of them, was used. The play's language and activity were enough to suggest places and settings to the audience.

In this theatre, buildings were represented only by the rising wall behind the stage, with its raised gallery (used only by musicians in *A Midsummer Night's Dream*) and two main doors. Action 'in Theseus's palace' might well stay closer to this rear-stage wall, while scenes in the woods would more probably be played out on the open fore-stage. This, symbolically, was open ground, more distant from 'civilisation' and normality. The use of the two stage doors is clear in Act 2 Scene 1, where an old direction reads 'Enter a Fairy at one door, and Robin Goodfellow [Puck] at another.' Oberon and Titania then make entrances in the same way, with their fairy followers, and confront each other. Between the stage doors of the Theatre (as at the Globe) would have been a third central opening, usually curtained off. This was known as the 'discovery' space, because special props (such as beds or tombs) could be pushed out from it or revealed ('discovered') inside it. This recess may have been used for Titania's 'bower' during the fairy scenes of the play. Even without scenery, the stage would not necessarily have been bare. Stage hands might have brought out props, such as seats for the on-stage audience of *Pyramus and Thisby* in Act 5.

The two great columns that held up the canopy over the stage would also have served as the trunks of imagined 'trees'. However, the 'woods' of *A Midsummer Night's Dream* are mainly suggested by the language of the play. Shakespeare's poetry makes Oberon and Titania powerful nature-spirits, and the fairies of the play speak constantly of their 'green' world, of 'bush' and 'briar', 'grove' and 'forests wild'. They are also 'shadows', creatures of night, and the three central acts of the comedy take place almost entirely in the imagined twilight or moonlit darkness of a single night in the woods. Night-time scenes in the real afternoon daylight of an open Elizabethan theatre were usually suggested by actors carrying burning torches or candles, but the fairies need no torches. Titania sends her fairies for night-lights, in Act 3 Scene 1, because Bottom, being merely human as well as an ass, cannot see in the dark.

The fairies carry candles to bless Theseus's palace in Act 5, but again it is the language of the play ('Ill met by moonlight'; 'spangled starlight sheen') that creates the night and the absence of the sun.

Costumes were the most valuable possessions of Elizabethan theatre companies, serving as strong signs of rank, character and location. In *A Midsummer Night's Dream*, there would have been a huge contrast between the luxurious dress of Duke Theseus and his court, and the rough 'working' clothes of Peter Quince and his company of amateur actors. There would have been a further sharp contrast with the fairies of the play. We cannot be sure how these were dressed, but green (the fairy colour) would probably have been dominant. No expense would have been spared on spectacular costumes or fairy crowns for Oberon and Titania. The very few illustrations of fairies or similar 'spirits' that survive from Shakespeare's time show long hair, coronets and plumes, and decorated green robes. The fairies would have looked clearly 'other than human'.

'SPIRITS OF ANOTHER SORT': FAIRIES AND MAGIC

Male actors, almost always the highly trained 'apprentice' boys of the company, played the female parts in Shakespeare's theatre. Audiences were therefore used to expert female impersonation: Hippolyta, Titania, Hermia and Helena would all have been played by boys. Shakespeare jokes with this convention when Flute (who plays Thisby in Act 5) worries that he cannot take the part because he has 'a beard coming'. It also becomes part of the fun in the woods that the boy who played Helena was clearly taller than the one who played Hermia. Shakespeare was writing for performers he knew well: Bottom, for instance, was a part written for his company's famous leading comedian, Will Kemp.

Fairies, however, raise further questions. If we imagine that they may also have been played by boy actors (so as to be 'smaller than humans'), Shakespeare's company would have needed an unusual number of extra boys. It is more likely that Oberon, and probably Puck, were played by adults and that other fairies were played by both men and boys, as far as the 'doubling' of parts (actors playing more than one role) allowed.

The fairies also bring music and dancing to the comedy. They are visible to human characters only when they choose to be, as when Titania declares her passion for Bottom. More usually, as Oberon says when he sees Demetrius and Helena coming (Act 2 Scene 1), 'I am invisible, and I will overhear their conference.' Words like these, and further 'invisible' action (as when Puck leads Demetrius and Lysander astray and apart at the end of Act 3), may have been enough to establish the fairies' invisibility. Other methods were sometimes used, however; the costume-list of another Elizabethan acting company included a 'cloak for to go invisible'. The 'magic' of the play is otherwise simple in performance. Bottom is out of an audience's sight when Puck transforms him with a donkey's head, for instance. Other magic tricks are only a matter of anointing sleeping eyes with magic flowers and herbs. The 'magic' is more a matter of language and atmosphere than of sophisticated stage-trickery.

In the end, *A Midsummer Night's Dream* invites its audience to compare *Pyramus* and *Thisby* with Shakespeare's own play, and the whole play with enchantments and dreams: 'Think … you have but slumbered here, while these visions did appear.' The play remains one of Shakespeare's most popular comedies. Its staging in the Elizabethan theatre may seem simple by modern standards, but it was extremely effective in playing to the imaginations and emotions of its audiences.

A play in performance at the reconstruction of Shakespeare's Globe

Recent productions of *A Midsummer Night's Dream* have been relatively dark explorations of sexual jealousy and the dangerous night in the woods. Ever since 1970, when **Peter Brook** stripped back the play to a minimalist, bare white box, in which his brightly costumed actors swung from trapezes, directors have looked for ways to express the mix of bright and dark, comic and serious that the play contains. Designers sometimes take the text's description of Puck as a 'hobgoblin' and Oberon's 'fierce vexation of a dream' to emphasise the 'otherness' or alien nature of the fairy world. Recent stage interpretations of the fairies have ranged from mischievous St Trinian's urchins to quirky alter egos of the Athenian court and an Oberon who removed the lovers' eyeballs to administer the love drug. Shakespeare sets the plot in motion with a death threat that leads to Hermia and Lysander to flee Athens and although we never are seriously worried for Hermia's life, the sense of danger creates enjoyment for the audience.

PERFORMING *PYRAMUS* AND *THISBY*

As 'quick bright things come to confusion' for the lovers, so do they in *Pyramus* and *Thisby*. The 'tragical mirth' of the Mechanicals' amateur dramatics is always funny, but some productions have chosen to emphasise the tragedy of the story over the unbelievable script and the actors' delivery. In the 1981 BBC production, directed by **Elijah Moshinsky**, Thisby (played by a boy actor) wept over Pyramus's body and hushed the courtiers' jokes about the play with the force of his acting.

The role of Bottom has long been a prize to gifted comic actors, but it, too, can be played to create sympathy. In **Michael Hoffman**'s 1999 film, Kevin Kline plays Bottom as a dreamer, a would-be gentleman of leisure, for whom acting the role of Pyramus satisfies a need for romance and adventure in his life. Although Puck still has the final speech in the film, the lasting image is that of Bottom in the scene immediately before it. After his triumphant performance at the royal wedding, he returns home and thoughtfully gazes out of his bedroom window as fairies (tiny dots of light) dash across the night sky.

In most productions, however, Bottom is far more comical than tragic. In a 1989 RSC production (directed by John Caird), which quickly became iconic for its inventive irreverence, strong group acting and humour, David Troughton's Bottom wore a cuddly donkey head with waggling ears and fluttering eyelashes.

ATHENS AND THE FOREST

Elijah Moshinsky's version for the BBC was inspired by Old Master Paintings. Acts 1 and 5 took place in slightly claustrophobic Jacobean interiors and the characters' costumes made them resemble portraits by Rubens and Vermeer. The forest, built in a set, was dark, disorienting and full of pitfalls – the lovers tripped over tree roots and waded through ponds before finally collapsing in exhaustion.

Two RSC productions that emphasised dreamlike parallels between the Athenian world and the fairies' world in the woods were **Adrian Noble**'s 1994 interpretation and **Michael Boyd**'s in 1999. Noble's vision drew on studies of dreams and the subconscious, suggesting that Hippolyta and Theseus's anxieties about their upcoming wedding were acted out through Titania and Oberon's quarrel and reconciliation. As he repaired the exhausted lovers, Puck wrapped them up in sheets and suspended them, cocoon-like, from the ceiling. The slightly surreal set, a red box scattered with doors coming from and leading to nowhere (unless it was to another level of consciousness), allowed the action to move easily from court to woods and back again.

Michael Boyd's 1999 RSC production made the transition between court and forest with a frenzy of kisses and torn clothing. The design for Athens was a cold world of grey-coated men in an austere setting. Philostrate and a female courtier remained on the stage, picking bright-coloured flowers that suddenly popped through the floor. The two actors freed themselves from the world of the court by ripping off much of one another's clothing and, transforming themselves into Puck and the First Fairy, played their scene as a sexually charged power struggle that matched the one between the fairy king and queen. Oberon and Titania, doubled with Theseus and Hippolyta, wore 'distressed' versions of the costumes of their courtier counterparts and the whole cast ended the show with a physically demanding dance that blended the play's multiple realms. In addition to the flowers, boards on the set shifted aside as hiding places for fairies to suggest that another level of reality is always lurking, waiting to be revealed.

MAGIC AND THE FAIRY REALM

In 1989, **John Caird** dressed the fairies in pointy ears and white ballet tutus, but with black Doc Marten boots and droopy stockings, undercutting the traditional image of Victorian magical beings. The gum-snapping young fairies clumped their way through the 'roundel and a fairy song' and Puck was a prank-loving schoolboy.

In **Elijah Moshinsky**'s 1981 BBC production, Helen Mirren's Titania, a stately goddess in a knee-length blonde wig, with her troop of child fairies (she even carried the little Indian boy) in wings and seventeenth-century costumes, visually contrasted with Peter McEnery's piratical Oberon and Phil Daniels's slightly vampiric-looking Puck. The camera helped to create a sense of the magical, with Puck jumping into tightly framed shots as if suddenly appearing.

In 1996, when **Adrian Noble** filmed his stage production, he added to the cast a little boy in his pyjamas, suggesting that the whole story was like a dream. Titania and Bottom's romp in her bower, which was an enormous pillow-strewn pink umbrella, was unmistakably sexual. Desmond Barrit (Bottom) remembered some shocked reactions from audiences of the stage production, but he saw this as a key moment that fed directly into Bottom's relishing of his life-changing dream.

An extremely popular 2005 RSC production directed by **Greg Doran** combined elements of the natural world with magic tricks and puppetry in the costuming, set and staging. Oberon wore a golden-brown cloak with a wood-like texture, as if he were a spirit of the forest, and he made the magic flower 'float' between his hands. When Puck returned with the magic flower, what initially looked like a shooting star heralded his crash-landing to earth. There were three different representations of fairies: shadow projections, human actors in punk black-and-white net and leather, and dolls with wings, carried by the actors, who clustered around Bottom to 'do him courtesies'. The fairies stood in 'tree' poses, raising and lowering their arms like vines dropping from branches to hide the sleeping Hermia and mischievously echoed her panicky calls to Lysander. When they helped Puck round up the lovers, they formed obstacle courses with their bodies through which Demetrius and Lysander had to fight. The fairies' pranks increased the lovers' frustration to boiling point (at one point they made off with Hermia's luggage and strewed her clothing all over the place), but there was an innocence in their tricks.

However the fairy world has been represented in the theatre, directors, designers and actors have always relied to a large extent on the audiences themselves to create much of the magic – 'Such tricks hath strong imagination' (Act 5 Scene 1, line 18).

Assessment of Shakespeare in your English Literature GCSE

All students studying GCSE English Literature have to study at least six texts, three of which are from the English, Welsh or Irish literary heritage. These texts must include prose, poetry and drama, and in England this must include a play by Shakespeare.

The four major exam boards: AQA, Edexcel, WJEC and OCR, include Shakespeare as part of their specifications for English Literature. All the exam boards offer controlled assessment to assess their students' understanding of Shakespeare, although some offer a traditional examination as an alternative option, or as one element of the assessment.

This section of the book offers guidance and support to help you prepare for your GCSE assessment on Shakespeare. The first part (pages 162–4) is relevant to all students, whichever exam board's course you are taking. The second part (pages 165–78) is board-specific, and you should turn to those pages that are relevant to your exam board. Your teacher will advise you if you are unsure which board you are working with.

What you will be assessed on

In your English Literature GCSE you will be marked on various Assessment Objectives (AOs). These assess your ability to:

- **AO1: respond to texts critically and imaginatively; select and evaluate relevant textual detail to illustrate and support interpretations**
  This means that you should show insight and imagination when writing about the text, showing understanding of what the author is saying and how he or she is saying it; and use quotations or direct references to the text to support your ideas and point of view.

- **AO2: explain how language, structure and form contribute to writers' presentation of ideas, themes and settings**
  This means that you need to explain how writers use language (vocabulary, imagery and other literary features), structure and form (the 'shape' of the text) to present ideas, themes and settings (where the action takes place).

- **AO3: make comparisons and explain links between texts, evaluating writers' different ways of expressing meaning and achieving effects**
  This means that you compare and link texts, identifying what they have in common and looking at how different writers express meaning and create specific effects for the reader/audience.

- **AO4: relate texts to their social, cultural and historical contexts; explain how texts have been influential and significant to self and other readers in different contexts and at different times**
  This means that, where it is relevant, you need to show awareness of the social, cultural and historical background of the texts; explain the influence of texts on yourself and other readers in different places and times.

You will also be assessed on the **Quality of your Written Communication**. This means you need to ensure that: your text is legible and your spelling, punctuation and grammar are accurate so that the meaning is clear; you choose a style of writing that is suitable for the task; you organise information clearly and logically, using specialist words where relevant.

Not all exam boards assess all the AOs as part of the English Literature Shakespeare task. Here is a summary:

Exam Board	Unit	AO1	AO2	AO3	AO4
AQA	Unit 3 CA	✓	✓	✓	✓
Edexcel	Unit 3 CA		✓	✓	
WJEC	Unit 3 CA	✓	✓	✓	

WHAT IS CONTROLLED ASSESSMENT?

Controlled assessment is a way of testing students' knowledge and ability. It differs from an examination in that you will be given the task in advance so you can research and prepare for it, before sitting down to write a full response to it under supervised conditions.

Exam boards differ in the detail of their controlled assessment rules, so do check them out in the board-specific section. However, the general stages of controlled assessment are as follows:

1. The task
  Every year exam boards either set a specific task or offer a choice. Your teacher might adapt one of the tasks to suit you and the resources available. You will be given this task well in advance of having to respond to it, so you have plenty of time to prepare for it.

2. Planning and research

Your teacher will have helped you study your text and taught you how to approach the topics. He or she will now advise you on how to carry out further research and plan for your task.

- During this phase you can work with others, for example discussing ideas and sharing resources on the Internet.

- Your teacher can give you general feedback during this phase, but not detailed advice.

- You must keep a record of all the source materials you use, including websites.

3. Writing up the response

This will take place under timed, supervised conditions.

- It may be split into more than one session, in which case your teacher will collect your work at the end of the session and put it away until the beginning of the next. You will not have access to it between sessions.

- You may be allowed to take an **un-annotated copy** of the text into the session.

- You may be allowed to take in some brief **notes**.

- You may be allowed access to a **dictionary** or a **thesaurus**.

- You may be allowed to produce your assessment on a computer, but you will not be allowed access to the internet, email, disks or memory sticks.

- During this time, you may not communicate with other candidates. The work you produce must be entirely **your own**.

- Your teacher will advise you on how much you should aim to write.

4. Marking

Your Controlled Assessment Task will be marked by your teacher and moderated (supervised and checked) by your exam board.

General examiners' note

Remember:

- you will get marks for responding to the task, but not for writing other material that is not relevant

- you must produce an **individual** response to the task in the final assessment, even if you have discussed ideas with other students previously.

How to succeed in AQA English Literature

If you are studying *A Midsummer Night's Dream* for AQA your knowledge and understanding of the play will be tested in a Controlled Assessment Task. In this task you will have to write about *A Midsummer Night's Dream* and one other text that your teacher will choose. This other text may be a novel, a selection of poetry, another play or even another Shakespeare play. The two texts will be linked in some way and you need to write about both in detail.

> ### Examiner's tip
> You will be assessed on the following objectives when responding to your Shakespeare task: AO1, AO2, AO3, AO4. Refer back to pages 162–3 for more about these assessment objectives.

The task

AQA will give your teacher a number of tasks to choose from. There are two main topics:

1. **Themes and ideas**

   This might mean writing about love or loyalty, reality or fantasy, youth and age, or youth and becoming an adult. For example: *Explore the ways writers present different kinds of love in the texts you have studied* **or** *Explore the ways writers present and use ideas of illusion and reality in the texts you have studied.*

2. **Characterisation and voice**

   This might mean writing about relationships, heroes and heroines, young and old characters, comic characters or even supernatural characters. For example: *Explore the ways the texts show how some characters use their power over others* **or** *Explore the ways the texts show young people growing up.*

Your response

- You have to complete a written response to ONE task. This should be about 2,000 words but remember that it's quality not quantity that counts.

- You have FOUR hours to produce your work. Your teacher will probably ask you to complete the task over separate sessions rather than in a single sitting.

- Your teacher will give you plenty of time to prepare for the task. You can use any resources you like, but do keep a record of them (including websites). You must include a list of these at the end of your task.

- You can work in a small group to research and prepare your material but your final work must be all your own.
- Do watch different versions of the play. You can refer to the different versions when you write your response and you will be given credit for this.
- You can refer to brief notes when you are writing your response, but these must be brief. You must hand in your notes at the end of each session and on completion of the task. You can also use a copy of the play without any annotations.
- You can handwrite your response or use a word processor. You are allowed a dictionary and thesaurus or grammar and spell-check programs. You are NOT allowed to use the internet, email, disks or memory sticks when writing your response.
- You can do the Controlled Assessment Task in January or June. When you have finished, your teachers will mark your work and then send a sample from your school to AQA to be checked.

Examiner's tip

The Controlled Assessment is worth 25 per cent of your final English Literature mark – so it's worth doing it well.

HOW TO GET A GOOD GRADE

1. Select what you write about carefully. It is better to write a lot about a little. Concentrate on one scene in Shakespeare and one chapter in a novel or a single poem, or on two characters, one from a Shakespeare play and one from a novel.
2. Use short, relevant quotations. Every time you include a quotation, consider the language the writer has used and the probable effect on the audience.
3. Never retell the story. You and your teachers already know it. If you find yourself doing this, stop and refocus on the question.
4. Check your spellings, in particular writers' and characters' names.
5. Always remember that Hermia, Helena, Puck, Bottom and all the other characters in the play are not real. Do not write about them as if they are. They have been created by Shakespeare: his play is the important thing to consider.

SAMPLE CONTROLLED ASSESSMENT TASK

Explore the ways writers present and use ideas of love in the texts you have studied.

Here are extracts from responses written by two students. Both are writing about the first appearance of Oberon and Titania in Act 2 Scene 1.

Extract 1 – Grade C response

The first time that the audience sees Oberon and Titania they are having a quarrel over a little Indian boy. Oberon decides that he will send Puck, his servant, to fetch a flower which 'Will make or man or woman madly dote / Upon the next live creature that it sees'. Shakespeare uses alliteration to emphasise the word 'madly'. This shows that one aspect of love in this play is infatuation, the sort of love which just happens and cannot be explained by reason. This is also shown by the word 'dote'. This means to love someone foolishly and for no good reason. Oberon wants to get revenge on Titania and has decided that he will make her look foolish and use love as some sort of a weapon. After Puck has gone, Oberon hopes that Titania will see 'lion, bear, or wolf, or bull' when she wakes up. He gives the audience a list to emphasise that he wants Titania to fall in love with something really horrible.

Annotations:
- Could be developed more
- Good point with relevant quotation
- Could be developed more
- Relevant textual detail
- Explanation of text
- Some awareness of effect on audience

Examiner's comments

- The ideas here are expressed clearly and appropriately.
- The student shows a good understanding of the text.
- There is some indication of awareness of the effects created by the language.
- To raise the grade, this student needs to develop ideas in more detail and to link these details to a more thoughtful consideration of the speech, the ideas of infatuation and jealousy and the more general theme of love.
- As it stands, this is a Grade C response.

Extract 2 – Grade A response

Far from being all that we might reasonably expect of a King, Shakespeare's initial characterisation of Oberon is that of a sulky teenager, thwarted by his partner over an Indian boy. His use of imperatives ('go thy way. Thou shalt not'), the repeatedly plosive consonants of 'Till I torment', and the alliterative 'thee...this' show his mounting anger. 'This grove' is echoed in 'this injury' and it is 'injury' which provides the climax of his parting shot. This anger is left to simmer as Puck is instructed to 'come hither' in direct contrast to the command to Titania to 'go thy way'. Unfaithful partner has been replaced by faithful servant and Oberon is able to reminisce about an incident when Cupid's arrow failed to find its mark and the target passed on 'In maiden meditation, fancy-free'. The double alliteration and the softness of the sounds create an image of innocence and safety: the maiden will not succumb to 'fancy', at least not there and then. However 'fancy' serves as a reminder that love in this play can be both instant and random – the four young lovers blunder in and out of love; Titania is successfully deluded; it is left to Bottom and his mechanicals to show that love can be, in Hippolyta's words, 'strange and admirable'.

Marginal annotations:
- Clear explanation
- Analytic use of detail
- Detailed analysis linked to theme
- Sophisticated insight into theme

Examiner's comments

- In this response the ideas are expressed cogently and persuasively and text references are apt.
- There is evidence of imagination in the development of the interpretation and there is a confident exploration of lines, phrases and even individual words.
- The student has written a lot about a little but has also managed to link this in to a consideration of the ideas which can be found in the whole text, ranging across characters and events.
- This is an example of a Grade A response.

How to succeed in Edexcel English Literature

The response to Shakespeare in Edexcel GCSE English Literature is a Controlled Assessment Task. You must produce your work at school or college under supervision and within two hours, although you may do some preparation for it in advance.

The task

The task will ask you to compare and make links between your own reading of the Shakespeare text and an adaptation. The adaptation can be a film, TV production, musical, graphic novel, audio version or a cartoon, but all must be based on the original play. The task will focus on **one** of the following aspects of the play:

- **Characterisation**
  For example, a study of the importance and development of one of the main characters in the play.

- **Stagecraft**
  For example, looking at ways in which the decisions taken about the staging and set influence the production.

- **Theme**
  For example, following how the action of the play is affected by a central theme such as love, mistaken identity or dreams.

- **Relationships**
  For example, an examination of the difficulties in the relationship between Oberon and Titania, or in those between the pairs of human lovers, Helena and Demetrius, and Hermia and Lysander.

Note that your answer should include some discussion of dramatic devices. These include a range of theatrical techniques and styles used by the playwright to create a particular effect on the audience, such as soliloquies, monologues; juxtaposition and contrast; use of dramatic irony; use of the stage and props; actions and reactions.

Preparing your response

When preparing, you will be able to use a range of resources available at your centre, which may include the internet, TV, DVDs and films, live performances and notes made in class.

You must complete your tasks individually, without intervention or assistance from others. However, you will be able to use: copies of the text without any annotations written in them; notes (bullet or numbered points), but not a prepared draft or continuous phrases/sentences or paragraphs); a dictionary or thesaurus; grammar or spell-check programs.

HOW TO GET A GOOD GRADE

To get a good mark in this response, it is important that you:

- respond to the chosen drama text critically and imaginatively
- make comparisons and explain links with your own reading
- look at different ways that a production or adaptation expresses ideas
- consider what Shakespeare means and how he achieves his effects
- support your ideas by including evidence from the words of the play.

ACTIVITIES

The following approaches will help you to explore *A Midsummer Night's Dream* in preparation for the controlled assessment.

Activity 1: Characterisation

Draw up a page with two columns for two central characters of your choice. List key headings under which to make notes such as how the characters are presented initially, how they are developed; how they relate to other characters and the way they speak. Develop your ideas and support them with brief references. Compare your ideas with a performance or adaptation.

Activity 2: Stagecraft

In a group, plan the production of a performance/adaptation of *A Midsummer Night's Dream*. Give each member of the group a non-acting role in the production, such as being responsible for production, costume and make-up, props, lighting, sound, or set design. Decide on the three most important decisions or tasks that each member has to undertake, and make notes on each of these.

Activity 3: Theme

As you study *A Midsummer Night's Dream* decide on **two** important themes explored through the humans and the fairies and note down moments in the play that deal with these. Give brief references from the text that support them.

Activity 4: Relationships

Draw up two columns, one for Helena and Demetrius, and one for Hermia and Lysander. In these columns note down the changes that take place in their relationships; give yourself key headings to note down your ideas, such as 'positive aspects' of their relationship and 'negative aspects'.

SAMPLE CONTROLLED ASSESSMENT TASK

> - Choose one dramatic device used in the Shakespeare drama text you have studied.
> - Compare your understanding of the dramatic device with the way the same dramatic device is presented in an adaptation.
> - Use examples from the text in your response.

Here and on the following pages are extracts from essays by two candidates who had each watched a modern production of *A Midsummer Night's Dream* modelled on certain features of the famous Peter Brook production, and compared this with their own reading of the play.

Extract 1 – Grade C response

[Annotation: Clear opening, explaining focus]

Shakespeare used many different devices when he wrote A Midsummer Night's Dream to make it come to life. The plot of the play is fantastical, Shakespeare has used real mythical characters like Theseus, as well as fairies and ordinary workmen. In this play, Shakespeare often has one main character describing the action to the audience, as Puck does here: 'Yet but three? Come one more ... Cupid is a knavish lad / Thus to make poor females mad'.

[Annotation: Apt quotation showing depiction of scene]

I watched a production with a simple set, so the audience had to use their imagination as in Shakespeare's time.

[Annotation: Sound point, clumsy expression]

When reading or watching the play you are drawn into a weird world where nothing works quite right and Shakespeare emphasises all bits of performance by even putting a play inside a play. When Bottom and friends act out their play, we see what Theseus and the others think ('The wall, methinks, being sensible, should curse again.') while we think about the play too. This is like being in on a joke with some of the characters in the play.

[Annotation: Good idea, needs development]

Because all of this is half like a fairytale and half like real life, you could make the stage really over the top, but in this production the director didn't do this. Most of the set was completely white and bare with very few props.

[Annotation: Awareness of set and original words]

You have to concentrate on the words more, like when you read the play. You would not know when the scene changes without clues from the actors: 'I know a bank where the wild thyme blows...' This is good. The original set would not have been so flashy as some modern ones.

[Annotation: Fair point, expression could be better]

171

Examiner's comments

- Sound comparisons and links are made in this extract, with appropriate examples.
- There is some clear understanding of the language, structure and setting.
- More detailed analysis of the use of language would have raised the mark.
- Points are made clearly, but there is room for giving them fuller expansion. For example, 'flashy' could have been replaced by references to special effects and elaborate staging.
- Higher grade answers avoid using loose expressions or colloquialisms. For example 'bits' could be replaced by 'aspects'.
- This is a Grade C response.

Extract 2 – Grade A response

A Midsummer Night's Dream, because of its fantastical, mythical setting, lends itself easily to elaborate, creative stagecraft. Shakespeare emphasises aspects of performance crucially in his text with differing dramatic devices (including the 'play within a play'). One interesting aspect of the production I saw, which was inspired by Peter Brook's influential production of 1970, is that its approach to staging is in many ways true to the original staging, without elaborate fairytale forest scenes Shakespeare's language and descriptive speeches were used not only because of the beauty of the language but also to compensate for the very basic staging of Elizabethan theatre: '– Who is here? / Weeds of Athens he doth wear ... And here the maiden, sleeping sound, / On the dank and dirty ground.'

[Margin note: Good link between language and stagecraft]

[Margin note: Confident, perceptive comment]

[Margin note: Close focus on language]

In this production, the director was influenced by Brook as he used minimalist staging, a simple white set, with two levels and two doors. Brook used circus tricks with fairies on trapezes and the director simplified this idea. The human characters on stage were dressed in ordinary, everyday clothes; the fairies were on the higher level, creating distance between them. Thus all their dream-like actions and tricks are beyond the humans, whilst affecting them. Their fairy tricks can dissolve in a minute, once the masks are taken off. 'If we shadows have offended, / Think but this, and all is mended'.

[Margin note: Specific detailed comment]

It is tempting to use elaborate stage effects and many modern performances go that way. This can create a sharp distinction between the mythical landscapes and the primitive setting of the Mechanicals' play. However, Shakespeare's 'wooden O' was always basic, allowing audiences to conjure up their own imaginary world. This simplicity was particularly effective in the production I saw; it made me concentrate on the words and did not distract me. As Theseus says: 'as imagination bodies forth / The forms of things unknown, the poet's pen / Turns them to shapes, and gives to airy nothing / A local habitation and a name'.

[Margin note: Apt quotation, links text to imagination]

Examiner's comments

- The candidate engages very well with the production.
- He/she writes effectively about Shakespeare's text and the dramatic devices used.
- There is perceptive understanding and fully supported ideas.
- This is a Grade A response.

How to succeed in WJEC English Literature

If you are entered for GCSE English Literature you will be assessed on Shakespeare in a Controlled Assessment Task. This task will be a linked assignment, which means you need to write about the Shakespeare play you have studied, in this case, *A Midsummer Night's Dream*, and some poetry you have studied in class. The play and poems will be linked by a theme. The possible themes are:

- love
- family and parent/child relationships
- youth/age
- power and ambition
- male/female relationships/role of women
- hypocrisy/prejudice
- conflict
- grief.

WJEC, the exam board, will specify which themes are set for the year you take the examination, and your teacher will decide which theme to focus on, according to the Shakespeare play and the poems you have studied.

> **Examiner's tip**
>
> Note that you will be assessed on AO1, AO2 and AO3 in this task. Refer to page 162 for detail of these assessment objectives.

The task

The exam board will provide teachers with 'generic tasks'. These are general tasks that your teacher will modify to suit the class and the texts you are studying. For example, the generic task could be:

> Many plays and poems are concerned with the relationship between men and women. Choose one relationship between a man and a woman in the drama you have studied and compare it with a similar relationship in the poetry you have studied.

Your teacher will modify the task and may break it down into three sections, such as:

> - Look at the way Shakespeare presents the relationship between Demetrius and Helena throughout *A Midsummer Night's Dream*.
> - Consider the way romantic relationships are presented in some of the poems in the collection. Choose one poem to write about in particular, but make references to others.
> - What is your personal response to the literature you have studied? In your answer, explore links between the poetry and *A Midsummer Night's Dream*.

Activity

Think about how you would approach the task above, and write a plan for your response to the first part of the task.

You might want to:

- re-read key parts of the text involving Demetrius and Helena
- make notes on how they speak and behave with one another
- make notes on how other characters react to Demetrius and Helena and the effects of this on their relationship.

Preparing your response

- You will have up to fifteen hours to prepare your response, then up to four hours to write it up.
- While you are doing your research and planning, you will have limited supervision; you may use research materials, you can work with others in your class, and your teachers will be able to give you general advice.
- Any worksheets your teacher provides to help you will be sent to the external moderator, and your teacher will have to tell the examination board about the support you have had.
- You are allowed to take an A4 sheet of notes into the final assessment with you. This will be checked to see that it is not a draft or detailed plan of any kind.

Writing your response

- Once you start writing, you will be formally supervised (a bit like in an examination).
- You may complete the assignment over several sessions, in which case, your teacher will collect the work in at the end of each session.
- You are not allowed to discuss your work with others (other students or teachers) during this part of the assessment.
- You will be allowed to use a dictionary or thesaurus if you need to, and you may be allowed to produce the work on a word processor.
- The approximate length for this assignment is 2,000 words but quality is more important than quantity.

How to get a good grade

Be prepared to discuss characters and relationships sensitively in both the Shakespeare play and the poetry. You will be expected to show detailed knowledge of both, through well chosen, brief quotations and direct reference to the texts, in order to back up the points you make.

You should show your understanding of how the texts are written, by exploring, for example, the use of language and its effects. Do not simply try to identify literary features, for instance writing 'There are several metaphors used' or something similar. These features are only of interest if you explain why and how they are used and the effects they create.

Do explain the links and connections between the texts carefully.

Examiner's tip

Remember that you need to show your understanding of the effectiveness of specific words and phrases, so make sure you refer to the texts in close detail.

Sample Controlled Assessment Task

Look at the way Shakespeare presents Hermia's relationship with her father, Egeus, in *A Midsummer Night's Dream*.

Consider the way some of the poets in the collection present relationships between parents and children. Write about the way the relationship between a parent and child is presented in one poem in particular, but make reference to others.

What is your personal response to the literature you have studied here? In your answer, explore the links between the poetry and *A Midsummer Night's Dream*.

On the following pages are extracts from essays by two students, answering the first part of the task.

Extract 1 – Grade C response

Relevant details, but could be better linked to the question

Egeus is the father of Hermia, a Lord in the Athenian court in A Midsummer Night's Dream. He wants his daughter to marry Demetrius, but she is in love with Lysander. The audience meets the father and daughter right at the beginning of the play when he drags them both in front

Clear context

of Theseus, the Duke of Athens, who was busy talking to Hippolyta, the Queen of the Amazons, about their forthcoming wedding. This shows you how worked up Egeus is that he

Valid inference

interrupts his Duke to try to get him to solve the problem of his daughter who is defying him about who she should marry. You can also tell how worked up Egeus is from the way he

Well noted

talks – he hardly lets any of the other people there get a word in and he's blaming Lysander, 'with cunning hast thou filched my daughter's heart'. The way he talks about Hermia it's as if she's dirt under his shoe:

Aware of attitude

'As she is mine, I may dispose of her.'
It turns out that if she will not do as her father wants she

Valid reference, showing understanding of situation

could be either put to death, or will have to become a nun. Even though Hermia knows this, she is still prepared to defy her father rather than marry Demetrius.

Examiner's comments

- This is a lively and engaged start to the Shakespeare part of the task.
- There is awareness of the state of the relationship between Hermia and her father at the beginning of the play.
- There is some use of apt reference to events of the play to support the points made.
- To get a higher grade, points would need to be developed further. There is a tendency to be dependent on telling the story, rather than discussing the way the characters are speaking and behaving.
- This is a Grade C response.

Extract 2 – Grade A response

Strong opening, introducing overview

'The course of true love never did run smooth', as Lysander says to Hermia, and this would also seem to be true of the relationship between Hermia and her father, Egeus, at the beginning of the play. The conflict between them when Egeus feels he has to call on the Duke of Athens, Theseus, for help, has arisen as a result of Egeus's determination that his daughter will do as he says, and marry Demetrius, whilst she is equally determined that she will not do so, as she is in love with another young Athenian man, Lysander. Egeus appears to blame Lysander for bewitching Hermia, to the extent that he has, 'Turned her obedience, which is due to me, / To stubborn harshness'. The language Egeus uses is interesting, as he appears to regard their relationship almost as a sort of business transaction ('due to me'). This impression of the father–daughter relationship is further reinforced when Theseus highlights the consequences of her not acceding to her father's will:

Clear context

Well-integrated reference

Probing language and effect

'You can endure the livery of a nun,

For aye to be in shady cloister mewed,

To live a barren sister all your life,

Chanting faint hymns to the cold fruitless moon.'

The language 'endure', 'shady', 'barren', 'cold', and 'fruitless' used here effectively emphasises the stark choice that faces Hermia should she persist in defying her father.

Analysis and evaluation

Examiner's comments

- This answer really hits the ground running, with supported evaluation right from the start.
- There is evidence of close and analytical interpretation of detail.
- Assured command of material is evident throughout.
- This is a cogent and coherent response.
- This is a Grade A response.

CONTENTS

THE CATHEDRAL BUILDERS OF THE MIDDLE AGES

Alain Erlande-Brandenburg

Thames & Hudson

'As the third year that followed the year one thousand drew near, there was to be seen over almost all the earth, but especially in Italy and in Gaul, great renewal of church buildings; each Christian community was driven by a spirit of rivalry to have a more glorious church than the others. It was as if the world had shaken itself, and, casting off its old garments, had dressed itself again in every part in a white robe of churches.'

Raoul Glaber, *Historia*, c. 1003

CHAPTER 1
A NEW WORLD

Gothic and Romanesque building sites are shown in detail in manuscript illumination. The 15th-century picture opposite illustrates all the stages, from mixing the mortar to laying the tiles on the roof.

The age of pillaging and sacking comes to an end

The raids of the Vikings, or Northmen (Normans), proved far more murderous and dramatic than the barbarian invasions of the 5th century. Repeated onslaughts by well-disciplined troops tirelessly wending their way up streams and rivers brought havoc and devastation. The efforts of Charlemagne's successors to organize the empire were brought to nothing by sieges of towns and monasteries and the very heavy tribute that had to be paid to raise them. The treaty of St-Clair-sur-Epte in 911, which granted to the Northmen a territory that soon became known as Normandy, was to be a decisive factor in Western European history.

The destroyers became builders, founding an advanced national state before going on to conquer other lands in southern Italy and England. The whole of Europe was affected; from this time onwards it was launched on an extraordinary venture, which in the realm of architecture took on a decisively new character.

The architectural explosion of the Middle Ages

Egypt and Rome left a unique architectural heritage, the first over a long period of time, the second over a briefer span, but over a wider area. However, in both places, great works appear as though created in isolation and not as a product of the general will.

Western Europe presents a different picture: architecture does not only spring from political power; it stems from all human beings, monks as well as politicians, peasants as well as lords. It concerns all spheres: urban, administrative, financial and religious, in the town as well as in the country. At first the new

The development of larger sailing ships and long boats with oars that were elegant, steady and did not draw much water (above, left), gave the Vikings great mobility and enabled them to carry out raids – even on horseback.

buildings followed Roman forms, but they soon broke free. The defensive walls constructed in the 4th century to protect the old *urbes* (towns) enclosed an inner area much too small to contain a rapidly expanding population. Throughout the Middle Ages, alterations, improvements and extensions continued to be made.

A new world

This society, which sought to affirm its destiny in stone, experienced a population explosion unprecedented in history. True, it is difficult to give exact figures for this process. It has been suggested the population of Europe almost doubled between the 10th and the 14th centuries, rising from 14,700,000

The population explosion of the early Middle Ages caused cities to burst beyond their defensive stone walls. Outside, suburbs grew up around religious centres, while vast areas remained entirely rural. Moulins, as it appeared in the second half of the 15th century (above), clearly illustrates this development.

around the year 600 to 22,600,000 in 950 and 54,400,000 before the Great Plague of 1348. According to other historians, the figure may have been as high as 73,000,000 at the beginning of the 14th century.

This population explosion was closely linked to two other factors, themselves inseparable: technological advances in agriculture and the growth of the town. The great extension of the area of cultivated land due to intensive clearing reached its peak in the first half of the 12th century; agricultural yield, even if relatively low by modern standards, doubled or even trebled thanks to the three-year rotation of crops and the introduction of the asymmetrical plough, with a mouldboard to turn the soil. Better tools, collars for draught animals and the use of dung as fertilizer all help to explain this great advance, but it was neither regular nor systematic. There were striking differences between one region and another and between one landowner and another. The best yields were to be found on the land of the Cistercians.

The other factor was the town. This was no longer the city of the antique world, the *urbs,* which was essentially political in nature and served to bring peoples together and to blend conquerors and conquered, but the quite different medieval city, which was above all social. It sprang from the great earlier population centres, which had been considerably altered in the 4th century when Rome ordered

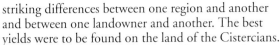

Representations of rural life tend to be as stylized as those of building sites. Four separate actions that happen at different times are represented in one picture: ploughing, sowing, harvesting and threshing. In this illumination from the beginning of the 15th century, the artist nevertheless includes technical details, such as the metal share and coulter on the mouldboard of the otherwise wooden plough.

the enclosure of their administrative sector within powerful defensive walls. From *urbs* the town became *castrum* (a fortress), protecting the surrounding land, which was itself enclosed by a fortified boundary line, the *limes.*

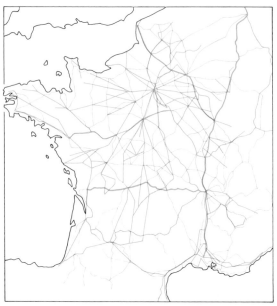

On a map of France, the juxtaposition of the road network created by the conquering Romans for strategic reasons (the fine blue lines) and that of the 16th century (in red) emphasizes the revolution that took place in the country's infrastructure during the Middle Ages. New roads were created, bridges built, canals cut and watercourses made navigable.

The medieval town

The city-wall sheltered the public buildings, which soon came to include the cathedral; most of the population continued to live in the country. In the 10th century the *castrum* was all but abandoned by the civil authorities as well as the population; only the bishop continued to reside there, ensuring permanence and caring for the

maintenance of the few inhabitants. At Beauvais, texts speak of fifty households, about three hundred people. During the 11th century, this picture changed. Towns were born or reborn as a result of the influx of people the country could no longer feed. They were looking for wealth or adventure. A bond was to form between these people of such different backgrounds that would evolve into a kind of urban patriciate.

Once established, this partnership tended to make the towns both economically and commercially active. The town/country relationship was reversed, with the latter now working for the former. Towns became markets and meeting-places, thereby creating a network of commercial links between one another. Then came systems of communication by land or by water: roads were built, supplementing the Roman military routes. This new network was moulded by the needs of commerce and the nature of the topography. In France, it converged on Paris, which became the capital of the kingdom. As for waterways, the development of many

Inside ramparts that had been newly constructed or adapted from earlier structures, as in the amphitheatre at Arles (opposite), urban and rural activities could take place side by side (above). There might, for instance, be a whole area devoted to stock raising, which ensured permanent provisions. From the 15th century, building in stone began to be the norm for the houses of the nobility, as in some of the dwellings belonging to the wealthier members of society at Arles.

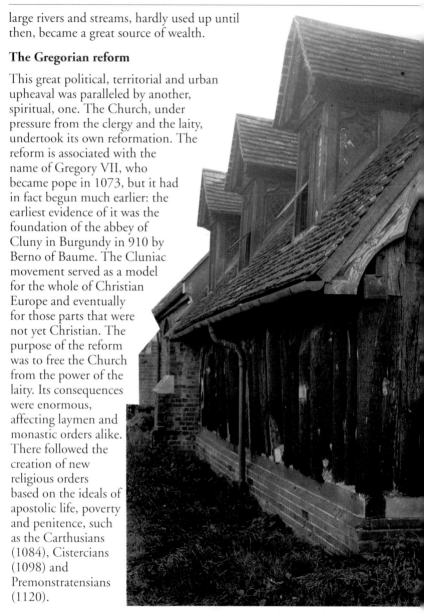

large rivers and streams, hardly used up until then, became a great source of wealth.

The Gregorian reform

This great political, territorial and urban upheaval was paralleled by another, spiritual, one. The Church, under pressure from the clergy and the laity, undertook its own reformation. The reform is associated with the name of Gregory VII, who became pope in 1073, but it had in fact begun much earlier: the earliest evidence of it was the foundation of the abbey of Cluny in Burgundy in 910 by Berno of Baume. The Cluniac movement served as a model for the whole of Christian Europe and eventually for those parts that were not yet Christian. The purpose of the reform was to free the Church from the power of the laity. Its consequences were enormous, affecting laymen and monastic orders alike. There followed the creation of new religious orders based on the ideals of apostolic life, poverty and penitence, such as the Carthusians (1084), Cistercians (1098) and Premonstratensians (1120).

Western Europe was thus transformed to create a more just, more ambitious modern world, in which everyone would find a place in one of three new classes: those who fought, those who prayed and those who worked. This break with the Carolingian era was based upon an unprecedented mastery of technology, which found its supreme expression in the realm of architecture.

Stone versus wood

New requirements confronted society in the 11th century. Architecture had to be rethought in the light of hitherto unknown demands. These came from the administrative sphere with the new road system, which entailed the building of many bridges; from the military sphere with the struggle of

Between the 9th and the 12th centuries a technique of building developed using vertical planks, which were then tied together. The wall was thus made up of jointed elements. The technique evolved into two types differentiated by the presence or absence of corner posts. The south wall of the church at Greenstead in Essex (far left) belongs to the first group. (The rest of the building is of later date.) Inside, posts support the roof. Major buildings were already being constructed in stone. A drawing of the 1060s (above) depicts the consecration of an Anglo-Saxon cathedral, perhaps Wells. The draughtsman has taken care to show the lower part of the walls and the tower as built of ashlar, emphasizing the joints.

great or lesser lords to maintain or extend their might and power; from the religious sphere with the need to receive larger congregations in cathedrals and parish churches and to ensure the life of prayer of monks in new monasteries withdrawn from the world. A taste for comfort and space became evident at the same time. Until now, all building had been of wood, except for the most important monuments, such as those concerned with worship. Little by little wood gave way to stone, unevenly but surely. The mason gradually took the place of the carpenter, whose role was greatly reduced.

Stone replaced wood in military architecture: the earthen motte was topped at first by a keep in wood, and later by one in stone, which remained faithful, however, to the original schema: square ground plan, dominating height and few openings.

The feudal motte

In early times fortresses of earth and wood were raised throughout a large part of Europe. No specialized knowledge was

needed to erect these structures: the earth excavated from a circular moat was piled up in the centre to form a mound, or motte, varying in height and

Above: the motte and keep of Albon in the Drôme.

diameter. Then a tower of wood was erected on the top. The sloping sides of the motte were protected by thorn bushes, the barbed wire of the time. It was not a very effective means of protection, as several scenes in the famous 11th-century Bayeux Tapestry indicate, for it could easily be set alight by the use of burning missiles.

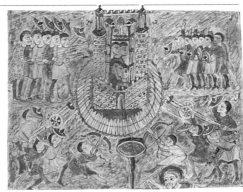

Defences of stone

The development of residential architecture is striking proof of the growth of building in stone.

The feudal motte, which was easy to construct, belonged to the familiar landscape of Western Europe. It could be seen from a long way away. The Bayeux Tapestry, which relates the conquest of England in 1066 by William, Duke of Normandy, gives several examples of mottes, in particular in the episode on the attack on the town of Rennes (opposite), where the motte was scaled by means of a wooden ladder. Mottes were besieged by being surrounded on all sides (above). If the keep was made of wood, attackers tried to set it on fire; if it was of stone, they tried to reduce the defenders by starvation.

This technical advance was closely linked to the desire for increased defences. From the middle of the 11th century, chroniclers draw attention to the use of masonry, as at Brionne, and this became the norm in the next century.

The transition from wood to stone in the construction of bridges was not systematic. It was fairly quick and easy to build a wooden

Nevertheless, the first stone castles kept the rectangular shape of the wooden fortresses. This was not only due to conservatism: they had specific functions – to serve as dwelling places, to contain the great state room or hall as well as the living rooms – so both their shape and their size were determined, at ground level and above.

In the mid-12th century, when the lord gave up the tower for a more comfortable dwelling, it took on a purely defensive character. Its rectangular plan was abandoned in favour of a circular one (as at Provins, Houdan, Etampes and elsewhere).

From 1190, the French king Philip Augustus' architects popularized the idea of the cylindrical tower, an idea occasionally copied in England, as at Conisbrough in Yorkshire. Wood had by then almost entirely disappeared in favour of stone: stone spiral staircases inside the walls, stone-vaulted rooms, and a flat stone roof serving as a platform, sometimes accompanied by a corbelled-out wooden gallery so that the foot of the walls could be overlooked.

bridge, and needed relatively few skilled craftsmen. (This was still the case when the Allied army landed in Europe in 1944.)

Bridges, roads and technical feats

This transition from wood to stone also appeared in the civic sphere. In the Carolingian era, in contrast to the ancient world, bridges were usually of timber. The bridge over the Rhine, built by Eginhard at Charlemagne's request, was made of wood. When it burnt down in 813, a replacement of stone was considered. The project was abandoned after Charlemagne's death and never resumed. Many Carolingian texts mention such wooden constructions, designed to make streams and rivers impassable to Viking boats, while at the same time enabling civilians and soldiers to cross. That dual purpose would last for the greater part of the Middle Ages.

A drawing by Villard de Honnecourt – a rare survival from the 13th century – shows a bridge 17m long, apparently built to cross a mountain river. A roadway structure of timber is held between stone abutments. Stone bridges were intended to be permanent. Technical mastery was needed to ensure their stability, and resistance to air and water. The bridge of Gour-Noir (left), which spans the Hérault River at St-Jean-de-Fos, was constructed to link the abbeys of Gellone and Aniane, around 1030: built of small coursed stones characteristic of that period, it already has side openings to relieve the pressure of floodwater.

In order to promote the new commercial network, many bridges were begun during the 11th century, linking one estate to another. Bishop Arnaud I, who wanted to make his cathedral at Maguelonne near Montpellier more accessible, built a bridge over a

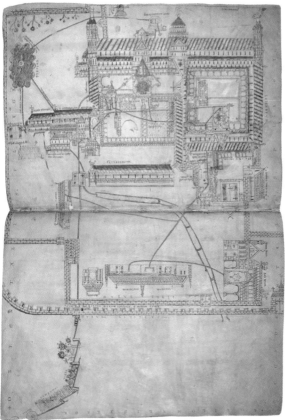

A challenge confronted the architects of the Middle Ages: to gather a large number of people in a limited space and to ensure their well-being. At the beginning of the 9th century, an unexecuted plan for the reconstruction of the abbey of St Gall in Switzerland (below) attempted a dual

PLAN DE SAINT-GALL

(IX⁰ Siècle)

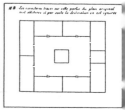

ENTRÉE COMMUNE

BÂTIMENTS DE FERME

kilometre long across the marshes. All these bridges were still of wood. It is difficult to give a precise date for the first stone bridge. It seems likely that at first only the piers were of stone, with a wooden superstructure. The latter was easy to construct, but it had disadvantages: it was relatively fragile and could be swept away in a flood; and it was not well suited to heavy traffic. Master masons clearly turned to Roman models, of which many survived. By the end of the 13th century, bridges were commonly built of stone, with solidly grounded piers and designs that took account of wind- and water-resistance. To make provision for exceptional floods, holes were even built in at a higher level to let the river through. The surviving medieval bridges at Cahors and Avignon both show the engineers' concern over this danger, which was something new, since timber bridges were usually just swept away.

Monastic architecture

In monasteries, churches had always been built of stone, though the nave might be roofed in wood.

function: to organize and reconcile the worldly and the spiritual life. The designer relied on the ancient principle of *insulae* (islands), here centered upon the church. From the 1150s, there survives a plan showing the water circulation system for the monastery of Christchurch, Canterbury (opposite).

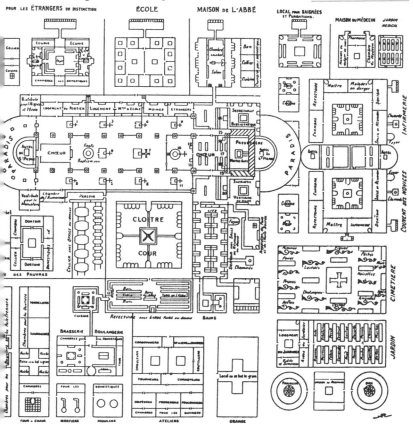

The famous St Gall plan, a drawing of the early 9th century depicting an ideal monastery, shows outbuildings constructed of wood with an abbey church of stone. In the 11th century, outbuildings were already to be found in stone, such as the famous stables at Cluny built by the abbot St Hugh. It was during the 12th century that monastic buildings came to be constructed entirely of stone, a change that gradually worked its way down from the most important buildings to the most humble.

Cistercian barns of the 12th and 13th centuries illustrate this generalization. These huge buildings consist of a stone exterior, divided into nave and aisles either by wooden posts (Froidement), or by stone piers (Maubuisson).

Expanding towns and new fortifications

Finally came urban architecture. In the 15th century, the usual formula for dwellings was a stone ground floor and timber upper storeys, but even before that time façades made entirely of stone were to be found. There are impressive 12th-century examples at Cluny, as well as at the upper town of Provins and at Viviers.

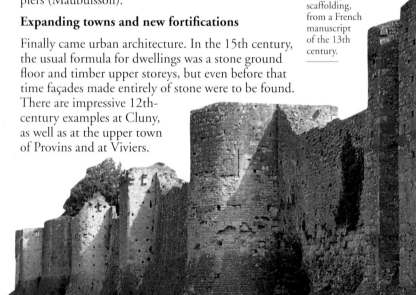

The construction of a tower, using very simple wooden scaffolding, from a French manuscript of the 13th century.

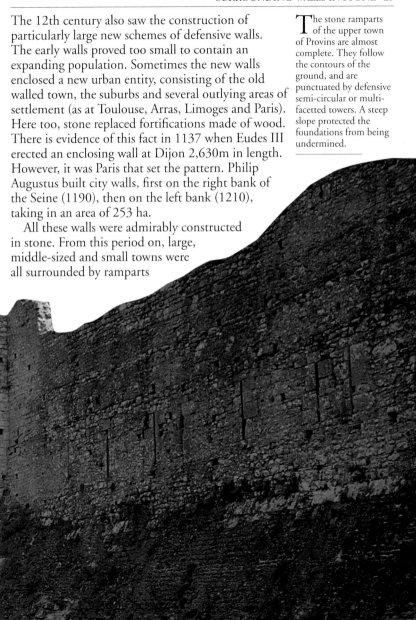

The 12th century also saw the construction of particularly large new schemes of defensive walls. The early walls proved too small to contain an expanding population. Sometimes the new walls enclosed a new urban entity, consisting of the old walled town, the suburbs and several outlying areas of settlement (as at Toulouse, Arras, Limoges and Paris). Here too, stone replaced fortifications made of wood. There is evidence of this fact in 1137 when Eudes III erected an enclosing wall at Dijon 2,630m in length. However, it was Paris that set the pattern. Philip Augustus built city walls, first on the right bank of the Seine (1190), then on the left bank (1210), taking in an area of 253 ha.

All these walls were admirably constructed in stone. From this period on, large, middle-sized and small towns were all surrounded by ramparts

The stone ramparts of the upper town of Provins are almost complete. They follow the contours of the ground, and are punctuated by defensive semi-circular or multi-facetted towers. A steep slope protected the foundations from being undermined.

whose purpose was not just to provide protection. They also united scattered settlements and promoted a sense of identity within the town. In some cities these new walls were quickly outgrown, and new, much larger ones had to be constructed. Charles V enclosed the right bank of Paris – the commercial, rich quarter – within a new wall enclosing 439 ha., making the city the most populous in Europe.

At the end of the Middle Ages towns were composed of several urban units joined together inside an encircling wall whose purpose was as much psychological as defensive. From these disparate units a new community arose.

Building in stone

The adoption of stone was not without difficulties. It cost more; working it required skilled masons; it had to be found, and transported to the site; and to

The wall of Reims (centre) united two towns: the ancient city, at the left, around the cathedral, and the suburb of St-Remi, around the abbey at the right. In Prague (seen in plan far right), three units were grouped together: the castle, isolated on one side of the river, and on the other the Old Town, surrounded by Charles IV's New Town. The Charles Bridge (left) linked them together.

build with it required more
sophisticated technology. To
these inherent difficulties the
fashion for colossal buildings
soon had to be added.

Prague is a good example,
even if it is an extreme case. The
ruler of Bohemia sought to make
his capital the seat of the Holy
Roman Empire, to shift the
political centre of a

somewhat incohesive body towards
the east. In 1348, the Emperor
Charles IV founded a new city on the right bank of
the Vltava which wrapped round the old town.
He built huge streets that were sometimes as much as
25m wide, and 1650 houses, all of stone. Everything
was enclosed within a surrounding wall of 3500m in
length. This desire was not enough in itself to create
a city: he founded 15 parish churches to satisfy the
needs of a population of 85,000 inhabitants, and
established a huge market place and a town hall.
What was remarkable in central Europe was the
determination to build in nothing but stone. This
was exceptional, as was the new cathedral begun
by a French master mason, Matthew of Arras.

The motives of the Emperor Charles IV were
much the same as those of President Kubitschek

There is a link
between the rapid
expansion of cities and
the ever-increasing size
of cathedrals. Cathedrals
emphasized their
importance by taking up
ever more space within
the town. On the
skyline, high civic and
ecclesiastical towers
became a city's emblems.

when in 1957 he launched the construction of a new capital for Brazil, Brasilia, and appealed to one of the great architects of the time, Oscar Niemeyer.

Vast new cathedrals

This love for the colossal, which calls to mind large modern urban projects, was not confined to towns as a whole, but extended to individual buildings. From the beginning of the Gothic era, no one dreamt of building a cathedral less than 100m long. Height also became breathtaking. At Beauvais the distance from floor to vault is 47m; at Strasbourg the spire is 142m high.

This preference for the colossal was also present in parish

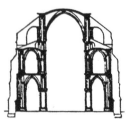

churches, some so large that they became cathedrals, such as Freiburg-im-Breisgau. Churches displayed the same ambition everywhere in Europe, from Ulm in the Holy Roman Empire to S. Maria del Mar in Barcelona, built by shipowners and merchants who sought to compete with the largest buildings of the time and entrusted the project to Berenguer de Montagut in 1328. The same was true of Cistercian abbeys, such as Foigny, 98m long, and Vaucelles, 132m long. Some monasteries were as big as towns; Fontevrault, for example, was divided into four districts around the great church and the churches of St Mary Magdalen, St Lazarus and St John. In England, the Cistercians were equally active – Fountains and Rievaulx in Yorkshire – and in some of the older abbeys the abbot also functioned as a bishop, as at Canterbury. Here again, municipal architecture in no way lagged behind: the 14th-century Charles Bridge across the Vltava in Prague is 513m long.

Diversity and dissemination

It is difficult to estimate today what this architectural activity of the Middle Ages represented. Many buildings have disappeared, some of them a long time ago. Surviving defensive architecture, though eloquent, is only the ghost of an extraordinary reality to which

Stone fostered the human dream of erecting ever higher buildings. The Tower of Babel is the most common illustration of that dream in the Middle Ages, but there are other images. In a drawing by Van Eyck (opposite right), the tower, symbolic of St Barbara, serves as a pretext to represent a masons' lodge. The reality of Gothic buildings bears witness to this enthusiasm for size, whose growing audacity is seen in each generation in the increasing height of cathedral nave vaults: 24m at Laon, conceived around 1160, 37m at Chartres in 1194, and 46.77m at Beauvais in 1225 (opposite and below, left to right).

texts and pictures bear witness. The whole of Europe is covered with important buildings, some of which are decisive in the history of architecture. While the area round Paris was to gain and keep architectural dominance in France, in England there were a number of centres of equal importance – London, Canterbury, York, Lincoln and Bristol. There is no disputing the conclusions to be drawn. 'In a period of three centuries, from 1050 to 1350, several million tons of stone were quarried in France for the building of eighty cathedrals, five hundred large churches and some tens of thousands of parish churches. More stone was excavated in France during these three

Illuminators in the Middle Ages tried to render the finer details of topography not by perspective but by placing different distances one above the other, as in this schematic view of four cities (left).

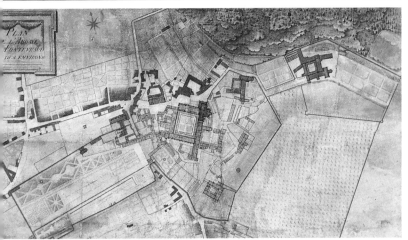

centuries than at any time in ancient Egypt, although the volume of the Great Pyramid alone is 2,500,000 cubic metres.' This extract from Jean Gimpel's *The Cathedral Builders* (1959) has lost none of its relevance. Later histories of medieval architecture have taken account not only of religious but also of civil, military and municipal architecture.

The overall picture has thereby been considerably enriched.

A 15th-century drawing of Montaigut-le-Blanc, in the Puy-de-Dôme (below), successfully suggests the slope of the land, and conveys the dominant impact of the tower. The 18th-century architect who drew the plans of the abbey of Fontevrault (above) was interested in the layout of the various buildings on the ground, not in their effect on the viewer.

'**A** building will never be worthy if the architect is unworthy.'
Thus a king of France, in the second half of the 12th century, defined the importance of the architect when asking an abbot to recommend one. The architect was an intellectual, a man possessed of *scientia* or specialized knowledge, a master builder – never, under any circumstances, a mere executant, trained on the building site.

CHAPTER 2
THE ARCHITECT

Hugues Libergier, architect of St-Nicaise at Reims (d. 1263), is depicted on his tombstone holding the model of the building and dressed in clothes that showed his high social standing. The rod, the set square and the dividers are the only signs of his profession.

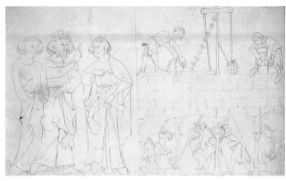

From the 11th century architectural activity took on a special character compared to the preceding period: then it sprang from a royal court. The sovereign, king or emperor was the prime patron. The new era, the Middle Ages, which continued up to the dawn of the Renaissance, is characterized by the diversity of patrons. This explains both its extraordinary richness and its no less extraordinary variety. The sovereign certainly continued to play a leading role, but in his own sphere, in matters concerning palaces or defence works. Some did not hesitate to go beyond that, building or planning whole towns, like the Emperor Charles IV in Prague and King Charles V in Paris in the 14th century. This function was then taken up by the clergy – bishops, abbots or canons; and by the laity – lords, communities, cities and associations. The number of patrons was thus greatly increased.

The patron and the genesis of the project

At the same time, a close relationship grew up between patron and architect, working in concert to bring a complex, ambitious enterprise to completion.

The patron was naturally decisive in the creation of a building: he originated the project, and he had to provide the funds. He chose the architect and ensured the continuity of the works. His death usually caused a crisis: work might stop completely, or slow down, or there might be a change to the initial scheme. The

The relationship between patron and master mason was based on trust. Artists understood this very well and depicted them on an equal footing. In this 13th-century drawing (above left), the king who had built St Albans Abbey is shown talking to his architect.

In a stained-glass window from St-Germer-de-Fly (above), Abbot Pierre de Wessencourt is talking to his architect in the presence of some stonecutters and labourers.

Left: the miniaturist who illustrated a celebrated Latin work on rural life by Petrus Crescentius shows how to build a house in the country under the joint instructions of master mason and patron.

death of Abbot Suger in 1151 stopped the rebuilding of the abbey church of St-Denis at once; work was not resumed until almost a century later, in 1231, when it took a totally different course. The initiation of large construction projects was linked, as it is nowadays, to the presence of extraordinary men of vision, whose ambition sometimes provoked violent negative reactions from those involved in costing the enterprises. Over all these buildings hovers the shadow of exceptional men: some were bishops, such as Fulbert of Chartres at the beginning of the 11th century or Maurice de Sully at Paris in 1160; some were abbots, such as William of Volpiano at St-Bénigne at Dijon, and Notre-Dame at Bernay at the beginning of the 11th century; some were kings, such as Philip Augustus in the 12th century, or Frederick II in the 13th century; some were great lords, such as Fulk Nerra, count of Anjou; some were urban communities, such as Florence, Milan and Siena... Without their strength of purpose, cathedrals, castles, town halls and bridges would never have come into existence. Their construction was an architectural manifestation of piety, indispensable to the life of society, to its flowering and its happiness. Building was also a display of temporal power. Eudes, count of Blois, ordered a bridge to be built over the Loire at Blois in 1033. In that same year, the chapter of Albi Cathedral was compelled to build a bridge, but in return obtained the lordship of it. The consuls of Cahors began the Pont-Neuf in 1251 and the Pont Valentré in 1306. In Florence, Orvieto and Siena, it was the commune that took charge of the cathedral. A lord hoping to atone for his sins might found a hospital. The different origin of the patrons serves to explain numerous problems.

The relationship between patron and master mason was founded on a clear and precise document. Contracts were common by the 13th century. When Hans Hammer was engaged at Strasbourg Cathedral in 1486, a text was drawn up on parchment (below), and five seals were appended: those of the Oeuvre Notre-Dame (the fabric committee), the knight Hans Rudolf von Endingen, the *Altammeister* Peter Schott, the administrator Andreas Haxmacher and the receiver of the Oeuvre, Conrad Hammelburger,

Huge stakes

The realization of the façade of Strasbourg Cathedral went through many changes of plan, due to continuing tension between the bishop and the city, which the contract of 1263 in no way diminished. The first design was abandoned, as often in the 13th and 14th centuries. The city would not allow itself to be excluded from the construction site, which was a symbol of civic pride. In Siena the population of the

the last four signatories to the contract. Hans Hammer designed the cathedral pulpit, among other things.

city undertook the construction of the new cathedral, a circumstance which expressed itself in changes of plan and interruptions. In Milan, the *Fabbrica* or fabric committee grew from 105 members in 1387 to nearly 300 in 1401, making decisions difficult. This process of democratization, which began in cathedral-building in the first third of the 13th century, was generally linked to financial difficulties, which could be lessened if there was common consent.

The patron, whether an individual, a community or an association, was responsible for commissioning the architect after

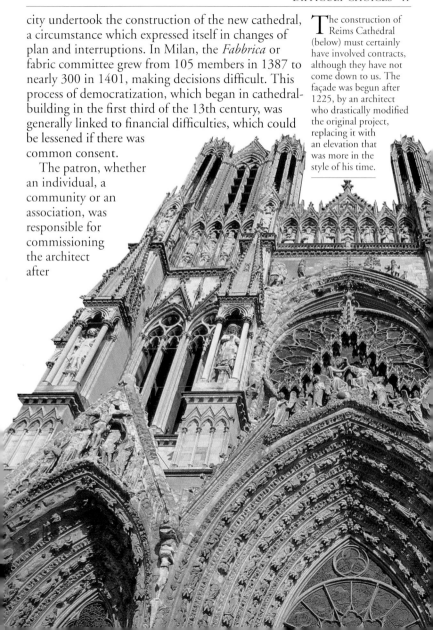

The construction of Reims Cathedral (below) must certainly have involved contracts, although they have not come down to us. The façade was begun after 1225, by an architect who drastically modified the original project, replacing it with an elevation that was more in the style of his time.

The patron was not always a man. Here Bertha, wife of Girart de Roussillon, gives the orders, during the construction of the church of the Madeleine at Vézelay (left). This illumination, painted between 1448 and 1465, shows the stonecutters' lodge next to the building site and the half-finished walls, which are protected from the frost by straw.

describing the project to him. At the end of the 10th century and the beginning of the 11th, the patron often had to face the hard fact that there were few professionals available to respond to the challenge. Great architecture could not be created by men with no more than local experience. Whereas in Carolingian times there were trained architects, they no longer existed because ambitious building projects had disappeared: everything had to be learnt again.

This explains the special position of many patrons: they were forced to become architects themselves to realize their vast plans. They challenged fate, and demanded the utmost of everyone. They were clergy, bishops or abbots, intellectuals familiar with antiquity and its monuments with which they sought to compete. They looked to those ancient structures as models for themselves and for the architects they wanted to convince. The architectural scene, one must remember, was very different from that which exists today: many large ancient monuments still survived, dating from the early years of the Holy Roman Empire or even from late Antiquity. By their very presence and their resistance to the ravages of time, they gave assurance that audacity could succeed.

When King Solomon built the Temple (below), he is said to have employed nearly 200,000 workmen. The builder of Bourges Cathedral (opposite) had a more limited workforce and achieved something just as astonishing.

Men of the Church

William of Volpiano, Gauzlin, Morard and many others were powerful movers and active, stimulating presences in the actual building process. There are revealing documents about Gauzlin at St-Benoît-sur-Loire, which show him after the devastating fire of 1026: he ordered a tower to be built in stone which was to be transported by water from the Nivernais. His demands made difficulties but he succeeded in resolving them. Such patrons demanded sharply jointed ashlar, not rubble-stone roughly broken by hammers, which was commonly accepted. At Auxerre in 1023 the chronicler was enraptured with these *quadris lapidibus* (squared stones). The same patrons were also responsible for developing new types of plan, including that of the ambulatory with radiating chapels, seen in the cathedrals of Rouen, Chartres and Auxerre, which was soon to extend throughout ecclesiastical architecture, though England remained faithful to the square east end.

After the conquest of England by William, Duke of Normandy, intellectuals like Gundulf, who became bishop of Rochester in 1077, took things in hand. He was said to be 'very learned and effective in the matter of building', and was entrusted with the reconstruction of Rochester Cathedral together with

This picture glorifies a great patron at the end of the 14th century. The artist wishes to show the key role of an ambitious patron, who knows how to find architects of great talent. William of Wykeham (1324–1404), bishop of Winchester, founder of New College, Oxford, and of Winchester College, imposed his own style on buildings for which he was responsible.

a monastery for sixty monks, and many other works.

In the 12th century, Hildebert, archbishop of Tours (1125–33), himself measured foundations and decided the dimensions of the palace. In the meantime, however, professional architects had emerged. It became the norm to call on experts, and the clergy, such as Raymond Gayrard at St-Sernin at Toulouse, confined itself to the administration of the project.

A manuscript by the monk André de Mici depicts the new cathedral of Chartres, begun by Bishop Fulbert (1007–28) and completed by his successor, Thierry, in 1037. It was later replaced by the present Gothic building, but the old crypt still exists. In the upper part of the picture, the building is shown from the side, with the façade on the left and the chevet on the right. Below, we are looking down the nave flanked by aisles.

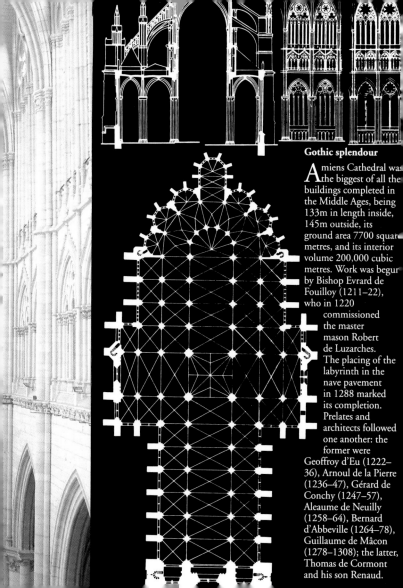

Gothic splendour

Amiens Cathedral was the biggest of all the buildings completed in the Middle Ages, being 133m in length inside, 145m outside, its ground area 7700 square metres, and its interior volume 200,000 cubic metres. Work was begun by Bishop Evrard de Fouilloy (1211–22), who in 1220 commissioned the master mason Robert de Luzarches. The placing of the labyrinth in the nave pavement in 1288 marked its completion. Prelates and architects followed one another: the former were Geoffroy d'Eu (1222–36), Arnoul de la Pierre (1236–47), Gérard de Conchy (1247–57), Aleaume de Neuilly (1258–64), Bernard d'Abbeville (1264–78), Guillaume de Mâcon (1278–1308); the latter, Thomas de Cormont and his son Renaud.

Administration was itself no easy task and it called for particular skills. The Cistercians acquired a reputation in this field: there were men like Raoul at St-Jouin de Marnes, who eventually became abbot of the monastery; St Bernard's own brother, Achard, master of the novices, who supervised the construction of many monasteries, among them Himmerod in the Rhineland in 1134; Geoffrey d'Aignay, who was sent to Fountains Abbey in Yorkshire in 1133; and Robert, to Mellifont in Ireland in 1142. John, a monk from La Trinité at Vendôme, was loaned by his abbot to the bishop of Le Mans, Hildebert de Lavardin, and when his task was over refused to return to his monastery.

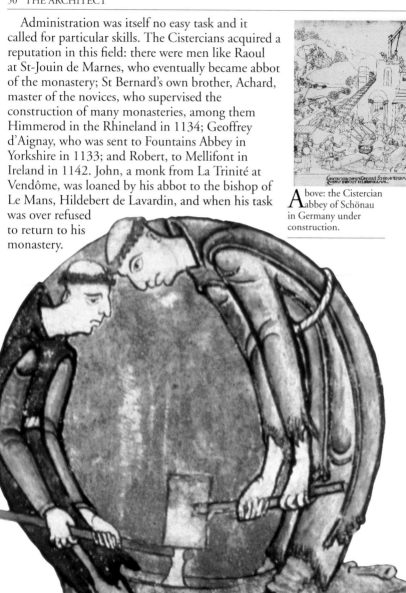

Above: the Cistercian abbey of Schönau in Germany under construction.

PONTIFICI SVMMO CLAVSTRVM OFFERT CONCIO PATRVM, VT FOVEAT IVGI PAPA BEATVS OPE.

A dominant characteristic of the 12th century was professionalism. The Cistercians played a prominent role through concern for economy and profitability. Unlike the monks of Cluny, who were more preoccupied with intellectual life, they regarded manual work as a form of prayer. The manuscript of *Moralia in Job* by Gregory the Great, written and illustrated at Cîteaux in 1111 at the instigation of Abbot Stephen Harding, was like a manifesto with its depiction of the various kinds of work carried out by the monks, (opposite below: woodcutters). From the beginning of the 14th century, the Cistercians promulgated a distinct image of their monasteries, given extra circulation at the end of the 15th century by means of woodcuts. Above: St Robert of Molesmes, St Aubin and St Stephen Harding present a model of Cîteaux to the pope. The monastery is depicted at the bottom, protected by a high wooden fence.

The modern architect

As projects became more and more complex, so it became imperative for the different tasks to be divided between specialists. It was during the second half of the 11th century that the architect established himself in the modern sense as one who, when so ordered by a patron, drew up the project, designed it and was responsible for seeing it carried out. There was no hesitation in citing him by name; we know, for instance, that Gautier de Coorland was chosen by Emma, Queen of England and wife of William the Conqueror, to reconstruct St-Hilaire at Poitiers. The architects of the next generation,

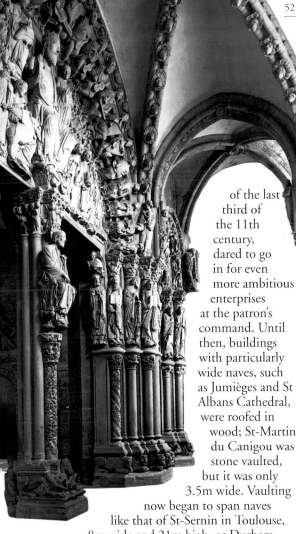

of the last third of the 11th century, dared to go in for even more ambitious enterprises at the patron's command. Until then, buildings with particularly wide naves, such as Jumièges and St Albans Cathedral, were roofed in wood; St-Martin du Canigou was stone vaulted, but it was only 3.5m wide. Vaulting now began to span naves like that of St-Sernin in Toulouse, 8m wide and 21m high, or Durham Cathedral. At the same time, in contrast to ancient Roman architecture, these heavy vaults rested on slim supports. This was doubly experimental, and there were some accidents: a vault collapsed at Cluny in 1120, but the original plan had been to roof the

Santiago de Compostela owes its existence to the pilgrimage which drew crowds of worshippers anxious to honour the body of St James, the holy apostle of Christ, which had miraculously been discovered in this corner of Asturias at the time of Charlemagne. King Alfonso II at once built a church, and the town grew up around it (above). In 1183 the cathedral was rebuilt by Master Mateo, who created the celebrated Portico de la Gloria (left): St James on the trumeau is flanked by apostles and prophets; above in the tympanum is Christ the Judge.

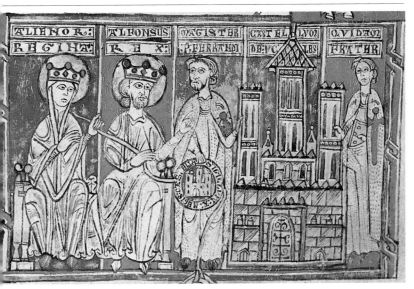

ALIENOR: REGINA : | ALFONSVS REX : | MAGISTER P. FERRANDI | CASTELLVM DE VCLES | OVIDAQ FRATER

abbey church with wood. It is easy to understand how fascinated people must have been with these men who seemed to defy all the accepted rules of building. Many written sources provide evidence for this.

The evidence of history

Aimery Picaud, the author of the most famous medieval text relating to pilgrimage, a guide for pilgrims going to Santiago de Compostela called the *Liber Sancti Jacobi*, written between 1139 and 1173, takes care to mention the designer of the church: 'The stone masons who undertook the construction of the church were Master Bernard the Elder – an inspired craftsman – and Robert, with the assistance of about another fifty lapicides [stonecutters] who all worked actively under the direction of Don Wicart, Master of the Chapter of Segeredo, and the abbot Don Gundesindo, in the reign of Alfonso, King of Spain, and of Diego I, a valiant cavalier and generous man.' The decision to rebuild had been taken in 1077 and the works started

A 13th-century manuscript shows us a meeting between patron and architect. To King Alfonso VIII and his wife Alienor, both of them seated, Master Ferrandi (Pedro Fernández) is presenting the façade of the castle of Uclés, which the king gave around 1170–5 to the Knights of Santiago.

on 11 July 1078. The time taken to set up the workshop shows the difficulties encountered in a country where no enterprise on such a large scale had ever been attempted before. We know nothing about Bernard the Elder, except that recently it has been claimed that he had previously built bridges; it has generally been suggested that he was trained in France because of the French character of the church plan. He did not come on his own, but had with him fifty 'lapicides' – craftsmen who could cut stones, not merely break them with a hammer as was usual in the region. Robert presumably acted as the site architect, while the master of the chapter and Gundesindo administered the project, copying organizational methods that had worked elsewhere.

In the 12th century we find architects were mentioned more frequently and with more flattering comparisons. The architect Garin, in Verdun after 1131, is said to be more learned than his colleagues and compared to Hiram of Tyre, the builder of the Temple of Solomon. Their reputation was such that jealousy was aroused. It is said that the countess of Bayonne had the architect who had just built a tower at Pithiviers beheaded, lest he should repeat the exploit for another patron.

The first Gothic architecture

Might jealousy explain the general anonymity that veils all the architects of the early Gothic period? Perhaps their fame competed with that of the patron. The case of Abbot Suger of St-Denis is particularly striking in this respect. He diligently reported in the minutest detail everything about the reconstruction of his abbey church, while taking care not to mention the name of his architect.

Abbot Suger was an active patron during the reconstruction of the Carolingian abbey church of St-Denis. His death in 1151 prevented him from successfully completing this vast enterprise. The nave which was to have joined the west end of Suger's church to his apse remained unfinished. Proud of his work, he had himself represented in a stained-glass window in the apse, in mosaic in one of the chapels (below), in sculpture at the feet of Christ on the central portal – each time in an attitude of profound humility. The basilica was to transform the Romanesque tradition both in sculpture and in architecture; the ambulatory (opposite) is a manifesto of the new style.

Was he trying to take the credit for the revolutionary construction of the choir, which was to usher in a new style? His silence was deliberate. Nothing was to tarnish his own glory, which he enhanced even more by many portraits of himself. By then the professional role of the architect was in fact well established. In 1175 the bishop and canons of Urgell signed a contract with Raymond the Lombard to complete their cathedral. With four other Lombards he undertook within the space of seven years to finish the work, which involved vaulting the church, erecting belltowers and building a dome.

A written contract now became normal, not only in ecclesiastical architecture but in military architecture as well. When Robert III Gateblé, count of Dreux, wanted to build the castle of

Danemarche, he drew up an agreement with master Nicolas from Beaumont-le-Roger. There he indicated very specifically that the architect was to model his design on the tower of Nogent, and to produce a structure 35m high and 25m in diameter. The contract price was to be 1175 *livres parisis* (livres of Paris), the patron providing stone, sand, lime and water. The architect was completely responsible for the project, since he had to pay the workmen.

Bitter rivalry

The patron did not hesitate to make architects compete with one another. The case of Canterbury Cathedral, devastated by a fire in 1174, illustrates this point admirably. Faced with such a terrible disaster, the monks called in several architects, some English, others from the Ile-de-France, and obtained detailed reports before deciding who to appoint. Their choice fell on William of Sens (from Sens in Normandy), who had impressed them with his analysis of the work that needed to be undertaken, clearly distinguishing the parts that had to be destroyed completely and those that could safely be preserved. Once appointed, he immediately began work, but a crippling fall forced him to take to his bed and eventually return to his homeland. His successor, William the Englishman, carried on with the work and respected the initial

Gothic architecture had begun in the Ile-de-France; in England its appearance was due to the choice of a French architect, William of Sens, for the construction of Canterbury Cathedral. Nothing is known of him before his arrival on the island, but he must already have acquired

ample experience to win over the monks. Left: the much later (15th-century) crossing tower, and (above) the Trinity Chapel, completed by his successor, William the Englishman.

design, which had marked the acceptance by the monks of the new style from the Ile-de-France.

This is how the first fully Gothic building on English soil came to be constructed. For some time its influence was sporadic, and England long retained a fondness for certain Norman features.

Specialized architects

Specialized groups of architects came into being. The arrangement only lasted for a generation, however, since it was closely involved with political events – the fight to the death waged by Capetians and Plantagenets for the control of France. In this field, as in many others, the latter held the upper hand. Henry II of England (1154–89), a Plantagenet, decided to build fortresses in order to secure his vulnerable new territories. The *Pipe Rolls* mention *ingeniatores* (engineers): some of them appear to be English, like Alnoth, while the majority were French – Roger Engonet, Richard, Maurice the Mason, Raoul de Gramont. The castles of Dover, Gisors and many new constructions were their work.

The Capetian king Philip Augustus continued this policy and greatly extended it. Between 1189 and 1206, sixteen architects with specific skills laid the defences of the kingdom by building fortresses linked to recaptured cities.

The king even created a council, over which he presided, to advise him on how best to act quickly and at the lowest possible cost. In Paris, the

English military architects conceived huge self-contained complexes composed of a series of concentric walls and buildings designed to afford protection to each other. In France, on the other hand, the architects of Philip Augustus preferred strong, easily defended castles that were closely linked to towns. Round towers, modelled on those of the Louvre (1190), found in scores of towns, stood as symbols of

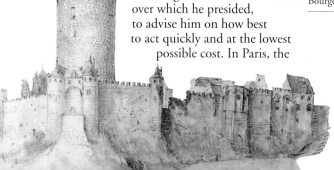

Capetian power. In the same way, all the fiefs of Berry copied the Great Tower of Bourges (below left).

city walls protecting the right bank, strengthened on the west by the tower of the Louvre, were erected in 1190; they included twenty circular towers built to the same design, 31m in height and 15m in diameter. Many towns were surrounded by fortifications on the Parisian model, with well-built walls, regularly spaced towers and a restricted number of entrances. The architects recruited for this huge operation had their own speciality: some constructed moats; eleven of them, referred to in documents as *magistri* (masters),

Dover is a distinctively English fortress. The same type is also to be found in France in Plantagenet King Richard the Lionheart's Château Gaillard in Normandy.

had overall responsibility. When Arnoul II, count of Guines, wanted to fortify Ardres, he called in a geometrician, Master Simon, and asked him to follow the model of the stone defences of St-Omer.

The status of the major 13th-century architects

A radical change occurred at the beginning of the 13th century: the architect could no longer carry all the responsibility. The administrative authorities had to create a financial division to deal instantly with demands that might arise on the building site, to maintain supplies and to pay the workers regularly.

The west rose window of Reims (above) is set in a larger, glazed area, allowing even more light to flood in. The openwork gable below it (opposite) is no less daring, set with statues of the Coronation of the Virgin.

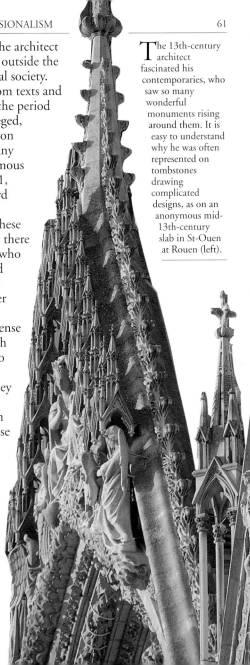

Freed from these tasks, the architect acquired a new status, outside the hierarchy of medieval society.

It is obvious from texts and illustrations of the period that this privileged, powerful position exasperated many people. In a famous sermon of 1261, Nicolas de Biard recorded his irritation: 'In these huge buildings there is an architect who directs by word alone and who seldom or never dirties his hands; however, he receives a much larger recompense than the others. Architects with sticks and gloves in hand say to the others: "Cut me this stone here." They do no work yet they receive much greater reward.' This kind of criticism has been levelled in all ages at men whose genius has conferred on them positions of command and financial ease.

'Rayonnant' architecture

The remarkable new position of the architect is connected with a new period in Gothic architecture, launched in 1231 with the proposed resumption of work on reconstructing St-Denis.

The 13th-century architect fascinated his contemporaries, who saw so many wonderful monuments rising around them. It is easy to understand why he was often represented on tombstones drawing complicated designs, as on an anonymous mid-13th-century slab in St-Ouen at Rouen (left).

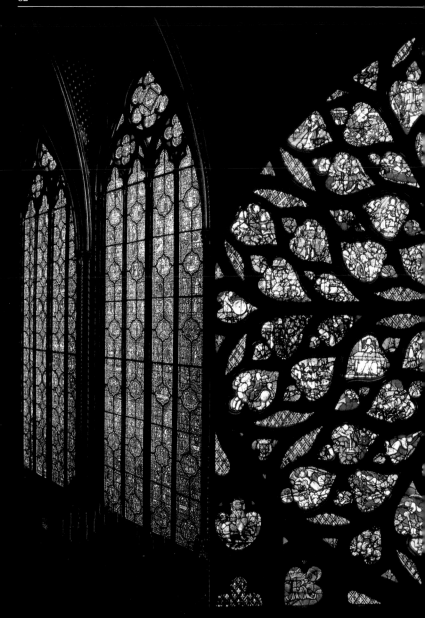

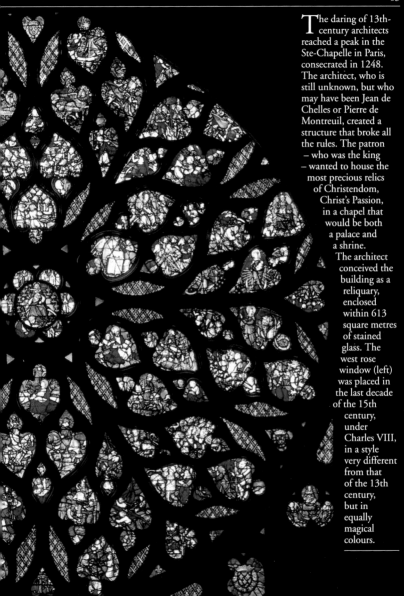

The daring of 13th-century architects reached a peak in the Ste-Chapelle in Paris, consecrated in 1248. The architect, who is still unknown, but who may have been Jean de Chelles or Pierre de Montreuil, created a structure that broke all the rules. The patron – who was the king – wanted to house the most precious relics of Christendom, Christ's Passion, in a chapel that would be both a palace and a shrine.

The architect conceived the building as a reliquary, enclosed within 613 square metres of stained glass. The west rose window (left) was placed in the last decade of the 15th century, under Charles VIII, in a style very different from that of the 13th century, but in equally magical colours.

This style has been given the evocative name of 'Rayonnant', because of the radiating pattern of the rose windows that became almost compulsory in ecclesiastical buildings. To contemporaries it was known as *opus francigenum* (the work of the French), recalling its origin. The manner spread at once through Western Europe: in the Holy Roman Empire there was the nave of Strasbourg, in England Westminster Abbey, in Italy the church of S. Francesco at Assisi, in Sweden Uppsala Cathedral, and, far overseas, in Cyprus, Famagusta Cathedral.

The abbot of St-Ouen in Rouen, Jean Roussel, laid the first stone of a new abbey church (above) in 1318, dreaming, as so many others did, of building the Heavenly Jerusalem on earth. Work went on through two centuries, involving later generations of architects (above left).

It is understandable that contemporaries, struck by this architectural style that made empty space triumph over solid masonry and so flooded the building with light, should have remembered the names of these creative magicians. Some have become as famous as the great heroes of history: Jean de Chelles, Pierre de Montreuil, Robert de Coucy, Peter Parler, Henry Yevele and many others.

Tributes in stone: signatures and tomb slabs

In Notre-Dame in Paris, at the request of the bishop, Pierre de Montreuil inscribed in beautiful Gothic lettering the name of his predecessor, Jean de Chelles, who had laid the first stone of the south transept on 11 February 1258 before his death. In the late 13th century the practice arose of inscribing architects' names in labyrinths laid out on the nave floor. Their installation some time after the facts they record – the labyrinth at Reims dates from the end of the century, that at Amiens from 1288 – explains occasional errors and omissions. Care was taken at Amiens to make clear the order of succession, from Robert de Luzarches to Thomas de Cormont and then the latter's son Renaud, and to include the figure of the patron, Bishop Evrard de Fouilloy. At Reims, archbishop Aubry de Humbert appeared in the centre, surrounded by the master masons, Jean d'Orbais, Jean le Loup, Gaucher de Reims and Bernard de Soissons. Architects were also given titles reflecting not so much their technical mastery as their intellectual worth. Pierre de Montreuil, to whom the monks of St-Germain-des-Prés wished to pay exceptional tribute, is entombed with his wife at his side in the Lady Chapel, which he had built, and honoured with the university title of *doctor lathomorum*, or 'doctor of stones'.

Architects commemorated. Opposite: the tombstone of two master masons, father and son, who worked at St-Ouen in the 15th century. It was put up by Colin, the son, and its inscription mentions only the father: 'Here lies Master Alexandre de Berneval, master of the works and Masonry of our lord the king in the bailiwick of Rouen and of this church, who died in the year of grace MCCCCXL [1490], the V day of January. Pray for his soul.'

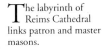

The labyrinth of Reims Cathedral links patron and master masons.

Tombs of esteemed architects were frequently placed inside churches. Tomb slabs recall the most famous of them, though some are illegible through wear by the feet of the faithful: examples are Hugues Libergier at St-Nicaise in Reims, and Alexandre and Colin de Berneval at St-Ouen in Rouen. Their social status is shown in the way they are represented: dressed like great lords, and identified by the tools of their trade, such as compass and rod, or a model of their building.

Images on parchment

Architects are also recorded in a number of manuscripts

which tell us about the building process, concentrating on their role and their close relationship with the patron. It was the patron who gave the orders, which were then transmitted to the workers. Examination of these records provides evidence of the dialectical nature of the relationship between patron and master mason, just as the latter was acquiring greater importance.

The example of Prague is revealing. The future Emperor Charles IV, having decided to endow the capital of Bohemia with a cathedral as large as his political ambition, gave the commission to a French architect, Matthew of Arras. Matthew was active from 1344 to 1352, but then suffered an accident on the building site. In 1354 he was replaced by another architect, the German Peter Parler, who completely transformed his predecessor's project in favour of a German concept. Charles IV had no scruples about including depictions of both in the triforium of the building.

Associates of princes

In France at the same period relationships were

very different, as architects became more like members of the patron's family. Raymond du Temple, who had built the Grande Vis – the great spiral staircase in the Louvre – became an intimate of the king. Charles V stood as godfather to Raymond's son Charlot and in 1376 gave him 220 gold florins 'in recognizance of all the good and pleasant services which our friend, serjeant and mason, Raymond du Temple, has done and is still doing for us daily and which we hope he will continue to do in future, and in order to maintain and keep our godson in studies at Orléans, where he is at present a scholar, and to buy him books and other necessities'.

The cathedral of St Vitus in Prague (opposite right) is a characteristic example of the medieval approach to building. For the Emperor Charles IV (above), it was a matter of creating a work that was significant at three levels: politically, for Prague was the capital of the empire; feudally, for the cathedral was situated in the palace of the dukes of Bohemia; and artistically, a determination that led him to call on a French architect, Matthew of Arras (opposite left). The death of the latter, political developments and the changing ideas of style caused the emperor to turn to a new architect, Peter Parler (left). Unity is preserved, however, in the technique used and is evoked by the placing of busts of the two architects and of the patron in the choir triforium.

This close association between creative artist and patron is found throughout the second half of the 14th century and at the beginning of the 15th in princely courts like those of Dijon and Bourges, London and Milan.

The architect's independence

The accepted, established role of the architect was to have disturbing repercussions for the patron. The most famous architects might be less than punctilious on site, and because they might often be involved with many projects, some far apart, absenteeism became the norm. It became the custom for written contracts to be drawn up, which offered attractive financial rewards but also heavy constraints.

The earliest known contract is the one between the clergy of Meaux and the architect Gautier de Varinfroy: he was to earn 10 *livres* a year for the duration of the work and 10 *sous* a day when present. In return, he undertook not to accept commissions outside the diocese without express permission; not to leave Meaux for more than two months, nor go to the building site at Evreux which he directed, nor to any other construction site in the diocese without the chapter's permission; finally, he was to stay in Meaux.

The 1261 contract between the abbot of St-Gilles-du-Gard and the architect Martin de Lonay, who lived nearby at Pasquières, is no less stringent: he was to earn 2 *sous tournois* (*sous* of Tours) a day on condition that he worked before midday; his keep was the subject of particularly lengthy negotiations; and he would receive in addition 100 *sous tournois* at Whitsun for clothing. In return, he undertook

The Butter Tower of Rouen Cathedral provoked a dispute between the canons and the architect. A council of masters called to settle the conflict produced no resolution. Jacques le Roux finally resigned on 27 January 1508 and was replaced by his nephew, Rolland le Roux. In the end a tower without a spire was built, in accordance with the client's wishes.

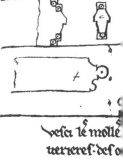

to reside at St-Gilles from Michaelmas to Whitsun. He was not banned from working elsewhere; but he had little opportunity. When Jacques Favran was hired at Gerona in 1312, the contract stated the amount to be paid – 1000 *sous* of Barcelona, on condition he went there every two months – but no longer mentioned any ban on directing work at other building sites.

Artists' rights

Distrust became more and more marked between architects and patrons. At Toul in 1381, the chapter insisted Pierre Perrat renounce ownership of the wooden templates used to determine the moulding profiles

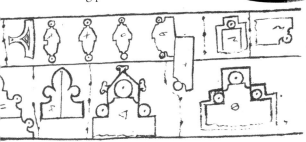

ꝑielef de cele pagne la deuant. def formef ꝛ def def doubliaus. ꝛ def foruolf ꝑ de feure.

of stones. This was the first time that the delicate question of artistic ownership had been raised, and the matter was resolved in the patron's favour. Later, by covenant of 9 May 1460, the architect Hattonchâtel surrendered the drawing for the façade of Toul Cathedral, leaving the chapter totally free over its execution.

At the end of the 15th century, the relationship between the partners was no longer the same, as the balance established in the 13th century was disturbed by some over-strong personalities. The value of technical skill had been proclaimed in stained-glass windows, as at Chartres (above), and in drawings by Villard de Honnecourt (left): stonecutters had achieved decisive status when templates and tools were depicted. However, their role was reduced and eventually disappeared completely, leaving a vast gulf between the patron and the master masons.

'**I**f a master mason has agreed to build a work and has made a drawing of the work as it is to be executed, he must not change this original design. But he must carry out the work according to the plan that he has presented to the lords, towns or villages in such a way that the work will not be diminished or lessened in value.'

Statute of the Strasbourg stonecutters, article 10, 1459

CHAPTER 3
MEANS OF
EXPRESSION

Opposite: detail of a large drawing for the west front of Strasbourg Cathedral, c. 1360–5. Right: an architect's assistant using dividers.

The architect's responsibilities, to provide the design and manage the project, required special skills. In the matter of the design, he had to persuade the patron and avoid any temperamental clashes that might lead to changes of mind and introduce inconsistencies. On site, it was vital for the architect to make himself understood by the different people who had to work together, since if his wishes were interpreted incorrectly the scheme could go wrong. When building in stone, the architect had to produce two kinds of document: one for the patron, to enable him to visualize the final result, and the other for the different craftsmen. Later, we also find another kind of drawing – sketches that show the architect working towards the final design through various changes of mind; and it is probable that such sketches also existed in the Middle Ages, even though we have no written evidence and not one has been preserved. No detailed designs at all are known before the 13th century. From that fact it has been assumed that the medieval architect was happy to communicate in speech, correcting or modifying the initial design as the building went along. Yet this assumption ignores the technical mastery that is evident in the great monuments of the Middle Ages.

Models have often been used as a means of communication between the architect and the patron. The model of St-Maclou at Rouen (below), made after 1521, gives a faithful and complete image of the building. It is made of wood and papier mâché and measures more than lm in height. The model of the pilgrimage

church 'Zur Schönen Maria' at Regensburg (opposite above) was slightly earlier. Made of wood according to a design by Hieber, it is of exceptional quality.

Presentation of the project

The architect had various means at his disposal to let the patron assess his project: drawings representing the complete design and details, and especially models, which were more easily understood. Models were in general use in Antiquity but seemed to have disappeared between the Carolingian era and the beginning of the 16th century in northern Europe. However, there is some evidence of them in Italy in the 14th century and in France in the 15th. In the process of building the abbey of St-Médard at Soissons, a wax model was made.

On tombs, the founders of religious buildings are often shown holding a small model of the edifice. The oldest example, which dates from the middle of the 12th century, is the recumbent

The existence of models before the 16th century is confirmed by the presence of small ones held in the founder's hand on tomb effigies, such as the one from the mid-13th century of a count Palatine, preserved at Nuremberg (below).

figure of King Childebert, founder of the basilica of St-Vincent-Ste-Croix in Paris. From the beginning of the 14th century, the founder may appear on the portal of the church presenting a model of his building, as with the figure of Enguerrand de Marigny on the collegiate church of Ecouis.

Models for patrons were in common use. Easily made of wood, plaster or stone, they might show the complete building or a detail.

Surviving architectural drawings

Drawings were no doubt more expensive because of the high cost of parchment. The oldest to survive come from the Oeuvre Notre-Dame at Strasbourg, the body responsible for building work, composed of the fabric committee of the cathedral and the masons' lodge. One of them dates back to the years 1250–60 and gives us the first design for the west façade planned to complete the nave, itself probably conceived by an architect trained in Paris. The other drawings show changes to this first design, which in the end was never carried out.

Throughout this period, other workshops were equally conscientious in preserving architectural drawings, for instance at Ulm, Vienna, Freiburg-im-Breisgau and Clermont-Ferrand. These show not only façades but

The model of the Rieux chapel, added to the chevet of the Franciscan church in Toulouse between 1333 and 1344, is held by its founder Jean Tissandier. Here the representation is clearly not symbolic, but very specific. Such small-scale models became more and more precise.

also side elevations (Cologne), sections (Prague) and chapels (Strasbourg). There is no doubt about their purpose: the agreement of 1381 for the rebuilding of the belltower of La Daurade at Toulouse involved a 'little roll of parchment'. Better still, the contract for the cloister portal of the Hôpital St-Jacques in Paris, dated 1474, came with an architectural drawing that survives today. It was the work of Guillaume Monnin, stonecutter, and was intended for the hospital governors, to let them judge the final appearance.

How architectural drawings reached the workshop

The drawings submitted to the patron were not detailed enough for the execution of the building. The architect had to produce other detailed drawings to make his ideas clear to the workshop. These generally disappeared during the course of the works, but a few are still in existence, such as a drawing at Strasbourg showing the re-vaulting of Ste-Catherine's chapel, begun by Bernhard Nonnenmacher in 1542. It bears numbers and letters indicating precisely how to cut the stones for the vaulting ribs.

The idea of constructing a belfry between the two tower stumps at Strasbourg Cathedral dates from the years 1360–5. It was given a great deal of thought, reflected in the largest surviving medieval architectural drawing, 4.10m high (left). This also gives a precise indication in colour of the sculptural programme of works (see pages 1–9).

The seal of the Oeuvre Notre-Dame of Strasbourg of 1486 (above), responsible for the fabric of the church and rich in land and income, depicts the façade of the cathedral and emphasizes the belfry.

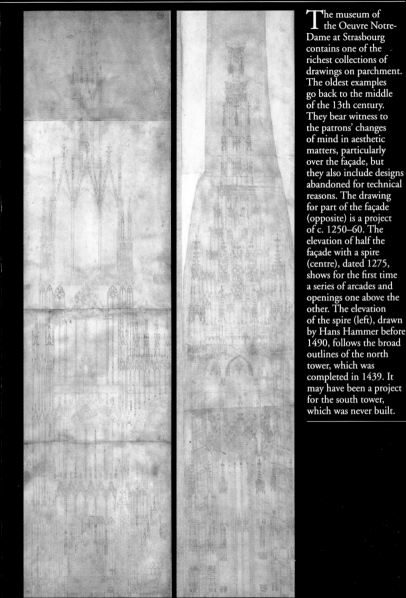

The museum of the Oeuvre Notre-Dame at Strasbourg contains one of the richest collections of drawings on parchment. The oldest examples go back to the middle of the 13th century. They bear witness to the patrons' changes of mind in aesthetic matters, particularly over the façade, but they also include designs abandoned for technical reasons. The drawing for part of the façade (opposite) is a project of c. 1250–60. The elevation of half the façade with a spire (centre), dated 1275, shows for the first time a series of arcades and openings one above the other. The elevation of the spire (left), drawn by Hans Hammer before 1490, follows the broad outlines of the north tower, which was completed in 1439. It may have been a project for the south tower, which was never built.

In another drawing for the west buttress of Strasbourg Cathedral (datable to c.1350–5), the design is shown at three levels – ground, rose window and belfry – superimposed one on the other. Many other drawings exist in which it is very difficult to work out the meaning.

Working drawings

There are some examples, mostly in France, of what have been called tracings, that is architectural drawings painted in stone, to a depth of 2–3 mm, showing an architectural detail to scale. The oldest example recorded, at the Cistercian abbey of Byland (North Yorkshire), dates from the end of the 12th century: the first tracing illustrates a west rose

It was customary to produce full-size working drawings, in order to guide the stonecutters. Some of them, incised in stone, have been miraculously preserved. In the south transept of Reims Cathedral, on the east wall of the triforium is a drawing of the inner side of the central west portal as executed; while on the west wall is a similar drawing of the flanking portal (left above). Though they are diagrammatic they are very precise – to scale, and showing both elevation and ground plan. Drawings of heads – three in the central and two in the side portal – show that the voussoirs were carved. The same system is used in the 20th century in restoration work: in a drawing for the conical roof over the spiral staircase of the Hôtel de Cluny in Paris (left), the mason has shown both elevation and plan, indicating the different courses; markings in colour indicate stones to be replaced.

window, while the second shows the central part of the same window. This procedure – the drawings may be incised or painted on stone – is related to stereotomy, that is to the cutting of stones; this was no longer the concern of the architect but of a specialist, referred to in texts as a dresser of stone.

Working drawings were usually made on perishable material in 'tracing houses' (i.e. drawing offices) – first mentioned in 1324 – and disappeared when the workshop was disbanded. Drawings incised directly into stone – probably never a widespread practice – have been found on the floor (for instance

In the sacristy of the Roslin chapel in Scotland, where construction began in 1450, the north and south walls preserve incised drawings from which the templates for the different ribs and pinnacles would have been made. They appear strangely superimposed, but each would have been clear for its individual purpose.

in the axial chapel of Narbonne Cathedral), on the exterior walls of the choir (at Clermont-Ferrand), and on the walls of the transept (at Reims). In these examples the drawings are full-size. Others are on a reduced scale. In the south transept of Soissons, there are small-scale schematic drawings of two rose windows; one is perhaps that of the west façade of Chartres, the other that of the north transept of Laon. Other examples of small-scale drawings, serving as memoranda for the architect, occur at the hospital of St John the Evangelist in Cambridge, the Benedictine church of Gegenbach and Leighton Buzzard church.

For any architect anxious to maintain control over the project, it was essential to be able to make drawings. A place was put at his disposal, which is sometimes mentioned in documents as a *trasura* – 'tracing house' or drawing office. Such rooms existed at Rouen, Strasbourg and Paris, and some survive in England, in particular at Wells and at York (opposite).

Templates: the workshop's memory

Manuscripts fairly often mention the existence of templates, and they are sometimes illustrated. They are simple units, generally cut out of wood, which give the profile of a base, a rib or any moulding. The earliest depictions, dating from the beginning of the 13th century, occur at Chartres: in the stained-glass window of St Chéron, several templates are shown in the sculptors' lodge, carefully hung up, and we see them again in the medallion recording stonecutters' tools. A little later, Villard de Honnecourt's sketchbook gives particularly valuable information about them. Knowing their importance, Villard drew the different templates used in the construction of the radiating chapels of Reims Cathedral, for mullions,

Tracings were not used only for work in stone. Carpenters today still use the same technique.

vaulting ribs, transverse arches and wall arches. He even indicated by a distinctive sign the direction in which they were to be placed in relation to the grain of the stone. While drawings survive at Strasbourg, Ulm and Vienna, we have nothing at all for other major buildings, and there too Villard de Honnecourt's sketchbook gives important information, particularly concerning work at Reims.

At York a tracing house was specially fitted out by the masons with a fireplace and a closet where the templates are still kept. The tracing floor, 7m x 4m, entirely free of posts or columns, was intended to receive full-size drawings, carried out, as they had to be, by very simple instruments: set square and dividers. On this floor there are still incised drawings (below) that have been identified with the tracery in the side aisles of the minster chancel (c. 1360).

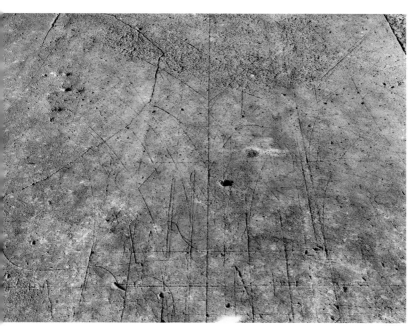

The quality of a building and its construction relied on the workshop's memory. The predictable slowness of the works could easily lead to accidental variations which had to be avoided at all costs. Thus it was necessary to keep a record of such things as moulding profiles in the form of templates. A stained-glass window at Chartres (left) of the early 13th century shows two wooden templates – coloured yellow – hanging below dividers in the stonecutters' lodge.

Villard de Honnecourt

This remarkable collection of drawings, begun by Villard around the 1220s, has been known since the middle of the 19th century. In it he states his aims: 'In this book you will find advice on building in stone, on machines used in carpentry, on the art of portraiture, on drawing, and on the art of geometry.' He never calls himself an architect, and interpretations which assume that he was one only obscure the real personality of the man. He was, above all, an inquisitive person, curious about everything, especially about the technological advances made in his time. In order to satisfy his continual curiosity, he found material where he could, not always at first hand. This accounts for the many errors that have recently been pointed out.

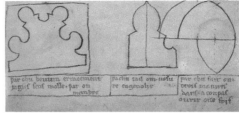

When he says that he had drawn a lion 'from nature', he may have been able to fool his contemporaries, but now it is obvious that he must have been closely copying another illustration; similarly his so-called tomb of a Saracen turns out to be one wing of an antique diptych. He reproduces machines, such as a hydraulic saw, whose mechanism was not always clear to him.

These few reservations do not in any way detract from Villard's genius, which was exceptional for his time, nor do they lessen the light he sheds on it. All but one of his architectural drawings relate to existing buildings, but the differences are too great for them to be straightforward depictions of the actual structure. The drawings of the rose windows at Lausanne and Chartres are so unlike the present windows that it cannot be a case of bad

Villard de Honnecourt drew templates, in particular those used in the construction of the eastern chapel of Reims Cathedral (above). He was equally interested in the latest mechanical developments, such as a saw operated by hydraulic power (below).

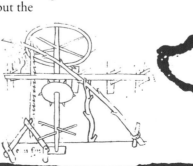

draughtsmanship. The same is true, as all the critics have pointed out, of the exterior and interior elevations and sections of Reims. To explain these differences, which are not mistakes, we have to assume that Villard reproduced an image that he was given.

Inscriptions on certain of Villard's drawings point in the same direction: some features had already been built, he notes, (the radiating chapels) – while some

Villard de Honnecourt stayed for a long time in Reims. There he studied drawings of French and Swiss buildings assembled by the architect in charge as a sort of design archive. Villard copied some of them without worrying whether they corresponded to reality. What interested him most in the depiction of the tower of Laon Cathedral (left and page 106) was the oxen, not the architectural forms.

had still to be built, (for instance one of the crossing piers). It seems likely that the architect of Reims had given him a collection of drawings, including abandoned schemes which, for some reason or another, particularly intrigued Villard. He also provided him with templates used for the construction of the radiating chapels. One even wonders whether the architect of Reims

might have shown Villard drawings of other buildings used to stimulate his imagination before embarking on such a major project. The fact that Villard shows only details, and not complete buildings, lends weight to this theory. In that case, what we have would be eloquent testimony about the conception of a big project, starting with images of existing structures elsewhere to serve as exampla.

Left: Villard de Honnecourt's drawing of the rose window at Lausanne. Above: the window as actually built. His drawing must have been copied from a rejected design.

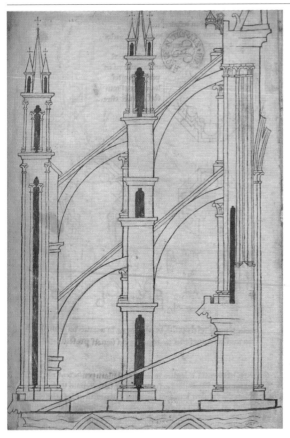

For Reims Cathedral, Villard did not try to record the section and elevation of the finished building, but copied a project that he no doubt knew had been abandoned for reasons now unknown. He seems to have simplified his various drawings so as to retain only certain points: flying buttresses in double flights and double tiers (left), window tracery which he made more legible by leaving out the flying buttresses (opposite right). Comparison with an accurate modern drawing (opposite left) brings out the similarities and differences.

Drawings constituted the living memory of the workshop, and they were indispensable for the patron concerned to avoid changes to the original design: Reims Cathedral, a model of consistency, was started in 1211 but its façade was only begun fifty years later. And as today, the patron could not be expected to make his choice without seeing the design in visual form, whether drawing or model.

'We hereby make known that Estienne de Bonnueill, stone-cutter, came before us undertaking as master mason to build the church of Uppsala in Sweden, who proposed going into that land, according to his words. And it is recognized in law that he shall lead and take, at the cost of the said church, together with him, ten journeymen and ten apprentices as he sees that it shall be to the efficiency and profit of the said church.'

Act passed before the Provost of Paris, 30 August 1287

CHAPTER 4
ON SITE

By the end of the 15th century the era of great cathedral-building was finished, but artists were fascinated by the grandeur of Gothic building sites. Opposite: a miniature by Jean Colombe depicting the reconstruction of Troy. Right: a mason on one of the bosses of Norwich Cathedral cloister.

It is difficult to generalize about the organization of the building site. It varied depending on the date (progress was enormous, but there were also moments of regression), the region, the financial resources available, and finally the men involved, whose talent and technical knowledge were not the same.

Europe of the builders

In stone building the extraordinary progress of northern regions of France – Normandy in the 11th century, the Ile-de-France in the 12th and 13th centuries – cannot be denied. In other regions the appearance of a new style, generally linked to a different technique, follows the arrival of teams of foreigners in the area. To achieve a revolution in art, it is not enough to find a great architect: there also have to be men of high calibre capable of supporting him.

Gothic building techniques spread through highly skilled French architects and technicians called to distant building sites. The organization of craftsmen in guilds was carefully regulated. In Rhodes, the Grand Master of the Hospitallers solemnly received them when the town was besieged by the Turks in 1480 (below). The carpenters come first, before the masons; on the ground are a mortar-trough, dividers, set square, mallet and rasp.

There are telling examples from different countries and different eras. The case of Santiago de Compostela, where Bernard the Elder arrived with fifty stonecutters, has already been cited. When Etienne de Bonneuil was asked to build Uppsala Cathedral in Sweden in 1287, he set off with ten journeymen and ten apprentices – acting as expert technicians – who were recruited in Paris after a contract had been signed. This was also the case in Prague in 1344 with the construction of the cathedral of St Vitus. The future Charles IV called on a French architect he had met

The Tower of Babel, symbol of the vanity of human pride, took on a mythical meaning in relation to architecture in the 15th century. For illuminators and painters it was an excuse to show a stone building of breathtaking height, and also to depict the people and equipment that had built it. Hoists in all their diversity found a favoured place in such pictures.

at Avignon, Matthew of Arras, and persuaded him to build a French-style cathedral in the empire. Matthew set out with a team of technicians he knew he could not find in Bohemia, notably stone-dressers and stonecutters.

The choice of those architects brought a heavy additional cost, which tested the patron's ambition. But it was not always so: William of Sens found men who were capable of fulfilling his demands on the spot when he went to Canterbury, for the English had been trained in building in stone since the time of William the Conqueror.

Organized guilds

Then as now, building in stone brought together on site two major craft guilds: the carpenters and the masons. There are many others whose function is more limited and therefore more difficult to situate. Metalwork was to play an increasingly important role, but its organization into guilds has not yet been analysed. As time went

From the 11th century onwards, carpenters had to yield to masons, and confine themselves to the building of timber roofs, which were of a highly technical nature, but were destined to be concealed by stone vaults. Many have been destroyed by fire, but some remarkable ones survive in England.

The greatest feat of skill was the construction of a spire, which required lengthy calculations and assembly on the ground before setting in place; that of Salisbury Cathedral (left) is one of the most spectacular. Above: a corbel in Gloucester Cathedral showing master and apprentice.

on, progress took the form of great technical advances, though there were some major setbacks. In northern Europe the results were spectacular, and while there were greater developments in masonry construction, we find outstanding timber structures such as the octagon set over the crossing of Ely Cathedral after 1322 by William Hurley. The most stunning examples of work in stone are also to be found in northern Europe during the 14th century.

It was in vaulting that German, English and French architects showed their greatest audacity. The English invention of the fan vault led to the achievement of King's College Chapel at Cambridge, begun in 1446

For the octagon of Ely Cathedral in 1322, the carpenter William Hurley tried to create the illusion of stone in wood by pretending that his two-tier design was a rib-vault. The lightness of the material allowed him to cover a vast space and to light it with a continuous row of high windows.

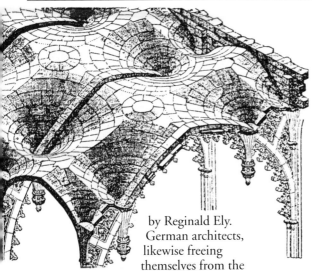

At the end of the 15th century, command of stereotomy (the precise, geometrical cutting of stone) produced some remarkable achievements in most European countries. English architects created the fan vault. Its technical nature disappeared under decoration which looked like a structural rib-system but was in fact incised into the blocks of stone, as in King's College·Chapel at Cambridge (opposite). The sketch of the upper side of the vault of Henry VII's Chapel at Westminster Abbey (left), built a little later in 1502, shows the highest achievement of fan vaulting. As before, it begins with half-cones along the walls, but the vault is almost flat, resting on arches which also support two rows of full cones that terminate in pendants.

by Reginald Ely. German architects, likewise freeing themselves from the over-rigid formula of the quadripartite vault, succeeded in vaulting the Vladislav Hall of Prague Castle by a single span 16m wide and 13m high covered with freely curving ribs. French architects, though less audacious, completely overcame all the problems of the weight of the vaulting in such buildings as St-Nicolas-de-Port, near Nancy, begun in 1481.

Building manuals

This technical mastery was the result of increased professionalism and specialization. It is not easy to reconstruct the process by which this came about, but one can make some headway by studying documents and especially accounts. In the lands of the Holy Roman Empire, the late 15th century saw the appearance of works on building techniques, which became the construction manuals of the Renaissance. In France, the 16th-century architect Philibert Delorme retained something of medieval thought and techniques in what he wrote. The earliest technical treatise is that by Matthäus Roritzer, master

mason of Regensburg Cathedral (1486). Many of these works were limited in their aim, illustrating 'recipes' for details which could only be understood by other professionals. In any case, it is impossible to know whether they circulated beyond a very restricted circle.

Different men, specialized crafts

On site the gap grew between the intellectuals and the minor craftsmen, who were by far the largest in number. Carriers of water, stone and lime are often represented in illuminated manuscripts; they were paid piecerates, or better still by the day, and recruited locally. A significant step higher up the scale came the men who mixed the mortar. Their task was an essential one and demanded great

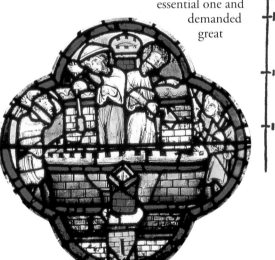

Technical advance from the 13th century, illustrated by a stained-glass window at Bourges (left), to the 15th century was affected by the compilation of manuals. Matthäus Roritzer's shows the importance of geometry. He establishes the elevation from a plan made with the help of dividers and a ruler, achieving 'just proportions'.

conscientiousness. Analysis of the finished stonework shows subtle variations, generally due to differences in training. It is clear from the accounts that pay varied according to training and to the skills involved in the work. Financial comparisons, however, are not easy since gross pay did not exist and wages were topped up by what we would today call payment in kind.

In this 15th-century illustration of the building of the Tower of Babel, the master mason looks like a wizard.

Skilled trades

The masons, who laid the stones from which the walls were built, seem, according to some accounts, to have belonged to a higher rank. The variations, which are not always easy to understand, can be explained by different practices from one site to another.

The stonecutter had an especially important role: he was the essential link between the architect or the warden transmitting the architect's instructions and the actual construction process. He had a decisive effect upon technical development. It was thanks to him that the transition had been made from rustic architecture, in which stone was shaped with hammers, to building with dressed stone, with small vertical and horizontal joints. It was a real revolution, which took place at the beginning of the 11th century in certain exceptional workshops. Chroniclers, who until then had been used to crude buildings, were impressed enough by the

new ones to
express their
wonder. Later,
during the course
of the century,
they became
accustomed to
the sight and had
less to say. Three
elements are essential
to achieve such a result,
then as now: the
stonecutter's initial
training, the way he
made his own tools,
and the choice of the
building material.
Documents, which
are generally not
very explicit,
provide little
information on
these points; the
monuments
themselves are
more instructive.
They show
remarkable
differences,
which can partly
be explained by
a disparity in the skills
of the craftsmen.

Signatures in stone

Masons' marks are a
valuable source of
information. Elegantly incised on
the visible face of the stone, these
signs are evidence of the pride the

man who cut them took in his work, which he did not hesitate to autograph. The same marks appear in a number of different buildings, giving us chronological pointers.

The church of St-Germain-des-Prés in Paris provides revealing evidence. Abbot Morard had begun its reconstruction with a bell-tower porch, which was finished at the time of his death (1014). Work continued with the construction of the chapel of St Symphorien to the south, then with the bell-towers, to the east of the transept, and finally with the nave. The stones are covered with masons' marks, some of which occur throughout the different sections, leading to the conclusion that all these parts were built by a single generation of workmen.

At Tewkesbury in England masons' marks occur that are identical to ones seen in France; the stonecutters had clearly crossed the Channel from one building site to the other. These marks, it must be remembered, were personal signatures just as initials are today. Once the wall was built, they allowed the stonecutter to be remunerated on piecework, while also allowing the quality of the cutting to be judged. Their disappearance was linked to the institution of another form of payment, either by the volume of work done at the bench or by the day, when the chosen technique no longer needed

From the beginning of the 11th century, Parisian stonecutters were determined to put their personal mark on cornerstones. This example (above), shaped like a key, is in the porch of the church of St-Germain-des-Prés. Opposite: architects and masons of the Middle Ages were masters of the technique of replacing the supports in a building, while leaving the upper parts undisturbed. In 1231, for instance, the architect of the new choir of St-Denis retained the early ambulatory vaults, and when he replaced the main arcade piers, he kept the original 12th-century abaci on which the vaults rested. An early 16th-century illumination shows one way of carrying out this delicate operation (left).

such detailed attention. The custom also varied depending on the region and the institution. It is also possible that building enterprises on capitalist lines may have existed just as we know them today. There is no documentary evidence for this theory, but it is worth considering, especially in the case of cities, where there was intense building activity, as in Paris from the 11th century onwards. From the middle of the 12th century, the pace of development grew quicker and never slowed down.

The Cistercian 'mercenaries'

Cistercian architecture sheds interesting light on this point. The difficulties encountered by the Order in

From cutting stone to setting it in its place, medieval representations of building sites depict all the crafts working together at the same time. Images of the Tower of Babel (above) exemplify all this human activity, added to which are mechanical contraptions like the double block crane, here worked by a windlass.

the management of the lay brothers are well known; at the end of the 12th century, the latter finished by revolting against the tasks imposed on them. In the middle of the 13th century, far fewer men entered the monasteries, leading to the employment of outsiders who had to be paid. As early as 1133 St Bernard had begun to hire workers to help the monks erect new buildings at Clairvaux. The Rule of the Order even alluded to people then called 'mercenaries'. They were paid by piecerates and left traces of their passage by signing ashlar blocks at Flaran, Sénanque and many other abbeys. The beauty of the incised marks strikingly matches the quality of the work; the Cistercians had made it a point of honour to recruit the best stonecutters.

Building firms

It seems that these individual marks became those of the master. Five workshops were set up in Paris in 1500 to carry out the construction of the Notre-Dame bridge. At the head of each one there was a master

A 15th-century sculptor represented Cistercians as builders. Left: St Bernard holding a model in his hand to emphasize his role in establishing and building abbeys. An illustration of the second half of the 16th century (below) depicts the construction of the Cistercian abbey of Schönau, near Heidelberg in Germany, and is remarkable in showing monks working alongside other craftsmen.

mason-stonecutter, with fourteen masons under him who inscribed the dressed stones with the master's mark.

One building project amongst many, but one that is more straightforward to analyse than the others, helps in understanding the organization of manpower. It is admittedly a royal building site, that of Beaumaris Castle in Wales. The accounts for 1268–70 indicate the presence of 1630 workmen, 400 masons, 30 blacksmiths or carpenters and 1000 unskilled labourers and carters. Numbers of this order are generally a sign of a well-supplied building site with no financial constraints. The fabric accounts of St Lazare at Autun in France for the period 1294–5 give a few details of pay: unskilled labourers received 7 deniers, the plasterers and men who made the mortar 10–1

deniers, and masons and stonecutters 20–2 deniers. Between the top and bottom of the ladder, the ratio is three to one, underlining once again the strong hierarchical divisions of the time.

The prime material: stone

Building quality depends on the careful choice of materials. In the Middle Ages, just as in Antiquity, people found themselves confronted by this difficult problem, which our age sadly knows only too well when undertaking the restoration of old buildings: the original quarries are exhausted or can no longer supply such good stone. From the 11th century, when a widespread upsurge of building took place on a

Among the concerns of the architect were the transport and handling of stone on the building site. A photograph of the crossing of Reims Cathedral after shelling in 1917 shows the different types of material used in the work: dressed stone, stone carved with mouldings, and rubble. Carrying dressed stone required much attention (opposite) in order to avoid chipping the edges. The transport of rubble did not demand such care (below).

huge scale, patrons and master masons were faced
with the need to find fine stone, to track down timber
for carpentry, and to obtain well-tempered metal.
The supply of good stone was the first
concern of builders in the Middle Ages.
The major preoccupation of
patrons, which they resolved
pragmatically – whether they were
bishops, abbots, kings or lords – was to
have a quarry close at hand and if possible to
own it, in order to exploit it at will without
incurring greater costs.
In some favoured places,
stone could be quarried
on the spot. Defensive
architecture offers numerous
examples of this: at Chinon, Coucy and
Château Gaillard, where the rock still shows
traces of quarrying. Many other castles
less well-known than these were built
with local stone, such as those on
mountain sites. The famous castles of
the Aude region were built of the very
hard limestone that was found on
the spot and easy to cut: only
thus was it possible to create
the eagles' nests of Quéribus,
Peyrepertuse
and
Puylaurens,
situated at
altitudes of
700–800m. It
was also possible
sometimes to
salvage stones
from existing
Late Imperial
structures, such as the fortifications of
Beauvais, or even from more recent buildings.

Quarries

Makeshift sources were no longer satisfactory when ambitions grew larger, and we find many mentions in manuscripts of patrons going to seek out hitherto unknown quarries or those where the workings had been abandoned. At the beginning of the 11th century, in order to reconstruct Cambrai Cathedral, Bishop Gérard I set off in search of a quarry which he finally found at Lesdain, some 10km away from Cambrai. Many other examples could be cited;

Stone was extracted either from an underground mine (opposite left), or in an open quarry (opposite right). The cost was not the same, as the mines had to be shored up with costly timber frames to avoid collapse. The quarryman's trade was a particularly dangerous one and required precise knowledge in the choice of seams and in the calculation of the size of the blocks to be cut. Picks, miners' bars and wooden wedges were the tools used to extract the undressed stone. It is understandable that for reasons of economy, the facing stones were plundered from accessible sections of fine earlier buildings. This exposed the rubble, as can be seen here at the Tomb of Cecilia Metella in Rome (left).

another patron, Abbot Suger, discovered quarries near Pontoise that could furnish stone for the monolithic columns in the ambulatory of St-Denis. To reduce the cost, either the quarry had to be bought (as Chermizy was for Laon Cathedral) or a deal had to be concluded for the period of construction (as was done at Tours, Troyes, Meaux, Amiens and elsewhere). In many cases, by good fortune, the quarries already belonged to the clergy (for instance Lyons and Chartres). However, quarries could also be in private hands and worked commercially, and this must have been the case in Paris, where there were stone outcrops on the slopes above the River Bièvre.

Because of their remoteness, these quarries presented huge problems involving heavy costs. England imported millions of tonnes of stone from Caen across the Channel very shortly after the conquest to construct the cathedral and the abbey church of St Augustine at Canterbury, the royal palace of Westminster, the Tower of London, Battle Abbey and much else before other quarries were discovered near Stamford in Lincolnshire. There remained the crucial question of transport: William of Sens devised new ways of unloading stone from the boats that had carried it.

Transport of heavy material

Once barges had been invented, transport by water was the most practical and cheapest method. For Paris, they came down the Bièvre and took the minor branch of the Seine before discharging at the eastern end of the Ile de la Cité, near the cathedral building site. Streams and rivers were continuously used, such as

Stone was transported by water or by land. By water, there were specially constructed flat-bottomed barges which would approach as near as possible to the building site (above). Overloading could lead to accidents. Although cheaper than transport by road, it was nevertheless inconvenient because of the need to load and unload twice. By land, horses, but even more so oxen, played a key role. Admiration grew for the ox, that strong and placid animal that plodded along the roads in the Middle Ages, and it was justly celebrated in stone by the architect of Laon Cathedral (left).

the Loire, which served to bring stone from the Nivernais to St-Benoît-sur-Loire in Abbot Gauzlin's time. Elsewhere, as at Rievaulx and Bury St Edmunds, special canals were built to avoid re-loading .

Transport by road was sometimes unavoidable, but the shortest way was always sought. When the priory church at Poissy near Paris was built at the beginning of the 14th century, stone extracted from the quarries at Conflans was first transported down the Seine before being brought on site along tracks driven in a straight line through the vineyards. Gradients posed a considerable problem. In order to carry stone from the quarry at Chermizy, 17km from Laon, to the summit of the *arx* or fortress standing some 100m above the plain, it was necessary to use heavy carts drawn by oxen – creatures held in such high esteem that they were depicted on the cathedral towers.

The Middle Ages were particularly inventive in the matter of heavy haulage. The invention of the shoulder collar and the coupling of animals one behind the other in teams allowed horses to pull loads of 2.5 tonnes, when in Antiquity they could only haul one fifth as much. Horses could now draw almost as much as oxen, but they were half again as fast.

The cost of transport was a heavy burden on top of the cost of the building works. Some calculations have been made

• The image of the ox stands for strength and power, the ability to plough intellectual furrows that will receive the fruitful rains from heaven, whilst the horns symbolize invincible and protecting strength.•
Pseudo-Dionysius, c. AD 500

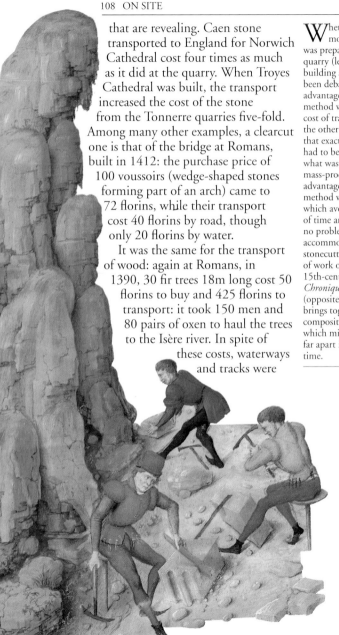

that are revealing. Caen stone transported to England for Norwich Cathedral cost four times as much as it did at the quarry. When Troyes Cathedral was built, the transport increased the cost of the stone from the Tonnerre quarries five-fold. Among many other examples, a clearcut one is that of the bridge at Romans, built in 1412: the purchase price of 100 voussoirs (wedge-shaped stones forming part of an arch) came to 72 florins, while their transport cost 40 florins by road, though only 20 florins by water.

It was the same for the transport of wood: again at Romans, in 1390, 30 fir trees 18m long cost 50 florins to buy and 425 florins to transport: it took 150 men and 80 pairs of oxen to haul the trees to the Isère river. In spite of these costs, waterways and tracks were

Whether dressed and moulded stone was prepared at the quarry (left) or at the building site has often been debated. The advantage of the first method was the lower cost of transport, but, on the other hand, it meant that exact templates had to be sent for what was effectively mass-production. The advantage of the second method was proximity, which avoided loss of time and posed no problems of accommodation for the stonecutters. The vision of work on site in the 15th-century *Grandes Chroniques de France* (opposite above) in fact brings together in one composition actions which might have been far apart in space and time.

Mortar was certainly mixed near the site (below) and at once transported on a man's back before it had a chance to set. The quality of construction was judged by the mortar as much as by the stone.

traversed continually by barges and carts supplying the building sites bustling with activity. The picture becomes even more vivid when one realizes that there were often several building sites close to each other in Normandy in the mid-11th century, in England at the end of the 11th century, and in the Ile-de-France in the second half of the 12th century.

Dressing stone in the quarries versus dressing on site

It is easy to understand that patrons sought to reduce costs by lightening the loads. Blocks came to be both roughed out and cut in the quarry, reviving an ancient custom and making the work easier. Since William of Sens prepared templates and sent them to Caen, there is much information on the practice.

Das die rossen eingehaben in das elsas
kamen vnd gar grossen schaden tarent

A 15th-century picture-story

If transport of materials was a problem, lifting them was an even greater one. Knowledge of machines invented by Roman architects had been lost, but at some unknown time it was rediscovered on very innovative building sites. Differences between regions were probably very great. The *Bern Chronicle* of 1484–5 by Diebold Schilling, shows not only completed structures, like the town walls of Strasbourg, but the crane that stood on the roof of the still unfinished cathedral (opposite). The artist also recorded various types of lifting device, like the claw (left above) or the treadwheel crane that unloaded the barges (left below). Other pictures in the manuscript illustrate different activities on the building site (pages 112–3): stonecutting, transport of rubble in horse-drawn carts, and laying of dressed stones with the aid of a claw.

During the construction of Vale Royal Abbey (between 1277 and 1298), masons were sent to the quarries with their assistants to hew and cut a thousand stones. It was the same for Westminster Abbey in 1253. The stones dressed in this way were the visible elements in masonry: not only facing, but also jambs, tracery and mouldings, whence the care with which they were chosen.

Wood and carpentry

Carpentry posed equal problems, increased by drastic deforestation that had taken place in the 10th and 11th centuries. Tall forest trees became rare. In the 12th century, Abbot Suger recounted with self-satisfaction how he had miraculously discovered wood essential for the roof structure of St-Denis in the forest of Yveline, although experts had told him it was not to be found: the anecdote is quite probably true.

Sovereigns, lords, bishops and abbots adopted a concerted policy of maintaining their forests and looking after timber which was indispensable for building. The Cistercians, seeking to enlarge

their holdings, acted with particular care in this respect, and anarchy was followed by careful management. This did not mean that even in the 13th century architects were not in difficulties. Villard de Honnecourt was sufficiently aware of the problem to demonstrate how to build a bridge with short timbers.

In spite of the triumph of stone, wood remained indispensable. It was used structurally and also for scaffolding. In the middle of the 14th century, 3944 trees were needed to build Windsor Castle.

Patrons did not generally own quarries, but they did own vast forests, at least in the north. They thus concerned themselves with better yields, and a better product, as the cost of transport remained high.

The building of the Ark, directed by Noah as architect, is depicted in the early 15th-century *Bedford Hours* (left) as the construction of a wooden house, with very precise representations of all the carpenters' tools, including plane, awls and saw. Another illumination (above) shows trees being cut down and timbers shaped for a wooden bridge and a roof.

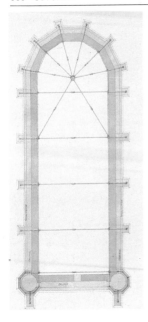

The Ste-Chapelle in Paris, finished in 1248, is tied together at the upper level by two metal chains which encircle it and by metal tie-rods stretched between the buttresses, concealed within the roof. Transverse rods are linked by a tensioning connector; in the apse, a multiple connector receives eight tie-rods. Finally, there are longitudinal chains. In the lower chapel, metal tie-rods link the colonnettes and the exterior walls; the ribs in the apse are themselves reinforced by metal bars which follow their shape. The architect who restored the Ste-Chapelle in the 19th century took care to record the arrangement in plan (left, the upper chapel) and to draw the multiple connector (above).

Metal, an essential building material

The third building material, which is less well known, is not a natural but a man-made material: metal. Mastery of its processes, from extraction in the mine to its use in the final cutting of the stone, has much to do with the progress of architecture. The quality of the stonecutting necessarily depended on that of the tools – on their sharpness and on the temper of the metal, making them more resistant to wear. Here again there were considerable differences between one region and another, and between one building site and another: acquired habits were not easily challenged. The appearance of the specialized stonecutter's hammer in the north during the 12th century was a kind of revolution that some exploited more than others.

The quality of Cistercian architecture from the 1120s onwards is related to the Order's technological inventiveness. They placed importance on metal, both the extraction of the ore and its subsequent processing. At the abbey of Fontenay the forge is not outside, as one might expect, but inside the monastic enclosure: metalworking was thus part of the activity of the monks and not of the lay brothers. This spirit accounted for progress that appeared in spheres other than building, and particularly in agriculture.

It is probable that this experiment spread rapidly; Gothic architecture cannot be understood otherwise. Moreover, metal became an essential element in Rayonnant architecture, when buildings like the Ste-Chapelle in Paris were conceived with a system of iron reinforcements. This type of construction in reinforced stone, which calls to mind the reinforced

Well before the advent of the Rayonnant style, metal had already been used intensively by Gothic architects. The oldest evidence is in Soissons Cathedral, in the south transept (c. 1170). The collegiate church at St-Quentin (left) had tie-rods situated well above the springing of the vault, whose function was to contain the thrust of the vaults. A tensioning connector in the centre allowed them to be tightened or slackened, and they played just as significant a role as the flying buttresses. The tie-rods in the apse were removed at the end of the last century, but those in the nave were retained; after shelling in the First World War, the apse vaults collapsed, while in the nave the ribs survived and only the webs were damaged. When the church was restored after that disaster, the tie-rods in the nave were removed…

concrete of the beginning of the 20th century, demanded a substantial supply of metal and thus of iron ore. Where did it come from in the 13th century? In the 15th century, there is much evidence to show that the metal was imported from Spain at extremely high prices. Whether the same was true earlier is a question that cannot at present be answered.

Machines

After materials, the last element involved in construction is machines, and the physical help they provide. Inventions were made here as elsewhere in the Middle Ages; and where machines are found to go back to older types, as they often did, engineers had the ability to analyse, perfect and simplify them. Machines already existed in Antiquity, when much attention had been given to them, but in the Middle Ages they became indispensable as huge buildings were undertaken without the help of slaves. The study of medieval techniques is difficult because of the

Mariano Taccola, born in Siena in 1381, produced *De machinis libri decem* (Ten Books on Machines) in 1449. He was no more a practical inventor than Leonardo da Vinci, but an inspired compiler who had a sense for the visual. His captions explaining the machines (left) are somewhat naïve:

'Let us suppose that it is a question of raising a bell to a belfry or tower by means of a winch or a hoist. So that the bell may be raised with greater ease, a crate filled with stone is put on the other side. And as the bell goes up, the crate comes down.'

absence of texts and the fact that images while abundant are repetitive. One can never be sure that the painters, illuminators or draughtsmen who depicted a construction site were copying from reality. A number of them, moreover, show the Tower of Babel, which is in the realm of mythology. Nor do the images represent up-to-date methods; they are nearly always out of phase. There are indeed some pictures that are a straight transcription of a specific event: they are exceptional and allow us to follow the rapidity of the development.

Less than 150 years separate the Battle of Hastings – and the Bayeux Tapestry – from the long wars waged by the Plantagenets (Henry II, Richard II, John) against the Capetians (Philip Augustus). The difference is as great as that between trench warfare at the beginning of the 20th century and the amazing technology used in the Gulf War of 1992.

This gap, which has always to be borne in mind in studies of the Middle Ages, is essential to the understanding of this period.

Taccola's explanation of the double cart, also called the great truck (below), is a figment of his own imagination, and it is clear that devices in common use were not always comprehensible. His manuscript demonstrates the

fascination exercised over men of this period by the technical means that had made great architectural achievements possible. A Greek manuscript of the 10th century (above left) shows the sort of model Taccola might have had for his idea of raising a column by means of a winch.

The architectural advantages of warfare

War – it has often been said – encourages the
use of hitherto unknown resources. It promotes
rationalization, as much in the political as in the
architectural sphere. From the second half of the
12th century, machines were invented to besiege
cities or fortresses. The greatest innovation was the
trebuchet (also known as perrier or mangonel), which
hurled stones by means of a counterweight system.
Experiments have shown that a trebuchet manned
by 50 people and with a counterweight of 10 tonnes
was capable of hurling a 100–150kg stone over
a distance of 150m, compared with a Roman catapult
which threw a 20-25k stone 225m.

The siege laid for several months by Philip
Augustus to Château Gaillard, which finally fell,
was maintained by a series of actions where machines
played a great part, some of it psychological. It is
at this period that we begin to find the names of
engineers responsible for devising war-machines
whose construction called for experts in carpentry.
There were immediate consequences for the civilian
world.

Cranes and scaffolding

Lifting devices were in current use in Antiquity. The
Roman writer Vitruvius, whose book on building was
well known in the Middle Ages, gave a reasonably
clear explanation of them. In the Middle Ages they
were greatly improved, owing particularly to the use
of the counterweight and double pulleys. The crane

The distinction
between machines
for military and civilian
use is not always easy to
establish, since the
engineer might serve a
prince both in war and
in the production of
works of monumental
art. The construction of
wooden mantlets or
armoured cars (above)
utilized classic carpentry
techniques.

stood directly on the ground if the buildings were not too tall; otherwise it was placed on a platform. It was made in such a way that assembly and dismantling only required a small crew of men. In addition, some cranes pivoted; in some the overhang of the boom could be as much as 3m; and pulleys arranged in sequence could function as a gear mechanism. Various means were used to power the cranes, the simplest being the windlass whose power was necessarily limited. Then came the treadwheel, also used in Antiquity, which was worked by two men walking inside the wheel, or rotating it by pulling on ladder-like bars on the outer surface. It has been calculated that with a wheel 2.5m in diameter, a man could raise a weight of 550–600kg. Here again the technicians of the Middle Ages proved themselves to be very inventive, enlarging the wheels up to a diameter of 8m, doubling their size, and increasing the number of workers.

Making treadwheels was simple, a fact that explains why they were set up on top of vaults where they survive to this

Conrad Keyser, engineer of King Sigismund of Hungary at the end of the 14th century, compiled a work illustrated with particularly sophisticated machines, such as this one (left), which made use both of a crane and a horizontal beam. Inspired by a military machine, it was meant to bore through the length of tree-trunks to make pipes. The elaborate combination of treadwheel and crane (above) was no doubt also linked to the progress of military technology in the second half of the 12th century.

day, for instance at Beauvais, Châlons-sur-Marne and some churches in Alsace. There was no hesitation in moving them about and adapting them to different roles: the one at Châlons-sur-Marne Cathedral, originally on the first western bay of the nave, above the oculus in the centre of the vault, was reduced in size and moved to the space above the north transept.

The use of these lifting devices had an important effect on the character of scaffolding. In the Romanesque period, scaffolding was heavy, resting on the ground and fixed into the masonry by horizontal poles. It was used in the making of stone vaults. Planks laid on these vertical and horizontal elements constituted both the masons' working platform and a storage space for materials. The scaffolding had therefore to be very solid, and access to it was gained by movable wooden ladders used by the masons and the carriers of stones and mortar.

As in Antiquity, machines for raising weights were extremely simple: the crane and the treadwheel. With the former, as a miniature shows (left), a hook was sufficient for modest weights, while for heavier weights, a claw was needed. The 15th-century illuminator is in error over the mechanics: the ropes should have been pulled from the ground, not from the top of the tower. The treadwheel (opposite) was easy to construct. It could be dismantled and set up again as building progressed, ending up in the roof, where a number are still in existence. The one shown, at the base of the spire of Salisbury Cathedral, dates from the 14th century and is still in working order.

From solid to void

The birth of Gothic architecture is connected
with the arrival of lifting devices that allowed
materials to be raised directly on to the wall.
This was a revolutionary step. Scaffolding no
longer served as a surface on which to put material,
but as the working platform of the individual mason.

Philippe FIX

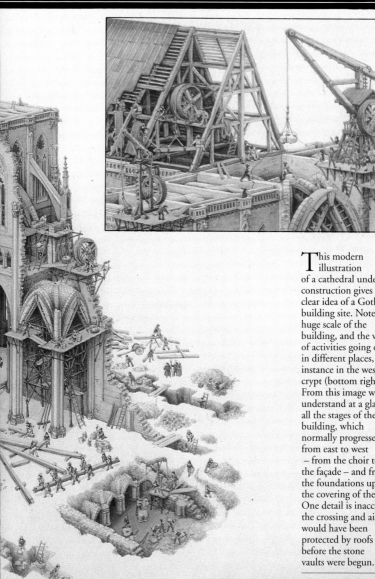

This modern illustration of a cathedral under construction gives a clear idea of a Gothic building site. Note the huge scale of the building, and the variety of activities going on in different places, for instance in the western crypt (bottom right). From this image we can understand at a glance all the stages of the building, which normally progressed from east to west – from the choir to the façade – and from the foundations up to the covering of the roof. One detail is inaccurate: the crossing and aisle would have been protected by roofs before the stone vaults were begun.

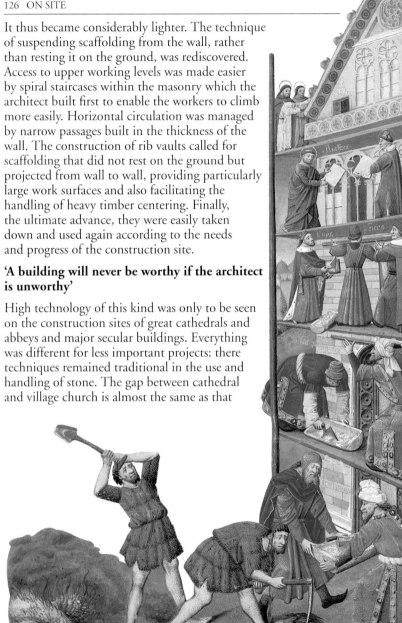

It thus became considerably lighter. The technique of suspending scaffolding from the wall, rather than resting it on the ground, was rediscovered. Access to upper working levels was made easier by spiral staircases within the masonry which the architect built first to enable the workers to climb more easily. Horizontal circulation was managed by narrow passages built in the thickness of the wall. The construction of rib vaults called for scaffolding that did not rest on the ground but projected from wall to wall, providing particularly large work surfaces and also facilitating the handling of heavy timber centering. Finally, the ultimate advance, they were easily taken down and used again according to the needs and progress of the construction site.

'A building will never be worthy if the architect is unworthy'

High technology of this kind was only to be seen on the construction sites of great cathedrals and abbeys and major secular buildings. Everything was different for less important projects: there techniques remained traditional in the use and handling of stone. The gap between cathedral and village church is almost the same as that

to be seen today between the most sophisticated prestige building and a shed from a mail-order catalogue. Not to realize this is to run the risk of grave errors in assessment.

Scaffolding was a major concern for Gothic architects, and they sought to simplify it and make it lighter (below, the construction of an abbey in the 15th century).

The architect of the Middle Ages is curiously like an architect of the Renaissance, the 18th century, and even of the modern world. Strictly tied to the patron who chose him, he tried to satisfy the patron's ambition. On his own, he remained a mere dreamer. His genius could only be liberated when he met a patron who challenged him to put concepts into practice, to realize them. Architecture is born of this duality: patron plus architect.

Opposite: a 15th-century artist depicted the structure of the Church as a building site, complete with accurately drawn tools. The arrangement is hierarchical. The two labourers are Cain and Abel; starting from the bottom, we move from patriarchs up to prophets, on to kings, princes and judges, then to apostles (setting the glazing in place) and martyrs, and finally to the confessors, who are finishing the roof.

DOCUMENTS

Careful examination of medieval buildings reveals little or nothing about the techniques used or the organization of the building site. For this we have to turn to pictures – which are generally late in date and sometimes based on stereotypes – and above all to the documents. The latter are plentiful but sometimes difficult to understand, and to date they have been relatively little used and rarely translated.

The architect

At the beginning of the 11th century, patrons – whether clerics or laymen – could not find architects capable of realizing their grand vision: it was necessary to train them. When, after a generation's training, these master masons had become professionals, they became the object of suspicion and jealousy.

Medieval illuminations depict the privileged position of the architect in society: he is represented holding a measuring rod, dividers or a set square.

Works of Abbot Thierry, successor to Airard, at St-Remi at Reims (Anselm, *Historia*, 1039)

Abbot Airard began a colossal building, so exceptional for its time that he could not see it through to completion. His successor, Thierry, decided to alter it and replace it with something more realistic.

In the year 1005, Airard, inspired by the example of a great number of famous prelates of his time, decided to renew the church which he had in his care. He summoned renowned architects and began, from the foundations, an edifice in dressed stone much more elegant and magnificent than any then being built in France, but which for this reason neither he nor his contemporaries would see completed. Having fulfilled his functions as abbot for about twenty-eight years, he died ripe in years, without having been able to finish his work.

After his death, Thierry, his successor, wished to finish his undertaking; but the task was so enormous it seemed impossible for him to bring it to a successful conclusion. He therefore took counsel of the wisest of the monks subordinate to him, and of the most worthy people in the province of Reims. On their advice he decided on the partial destruction of his predecessor's building, while keeping some foundations whose retention appeared necessary to the architects. Then he began the construction of a simpler but equally suitable church.

It was the fifth year since his promotion to the position of abbot, about 1039, when he undertook this work. Laymen and clergy tried to outdo each other in helping him; several members of the clergy of their own accord used their carts and their oxen for the transport of materials. Foundations were dug where there had been none before, columns from the first, destroyed building were placed upon them, carefully centered arches were built above them, and the basilica began to take shape in the hands of the builders. Then when the gallery walls had been built everywhere and the ridge of the nave had risen to its greatest height, the old church dedicated by Hincmar in ancient times was razed to the ground. A temporary roof was erected over the monks' choir, so that they could attend divine services without being exposed to the weather.

In the midst of all this, in 1045 Abbot Thierry died prematurely after governing his monastery for eleven years and eight months. Herimar, his successor, had been provost of the abbey; in that capacity he had already been one of Thierry's most enthusiastic collaborators in the building of the church and had given him many subsidies from the revenue of the domains which he administered. Hence he did not leave the work of his predecessor in abeyance for long: he completed the south transept, which was already in an advanced state, and also the north, of which only the foundations and the staircases leading to the upper parts yet existed. Finally, with great beams brought from the neighbouring forest of Orbais Abbey, he raised a timber roof over the building, which was then completed in every part.

Victor Mortet, *Recueil de textes relatifs à l'histoire de l'architecture...*, 1911

Construction of Salisbury Cathedral by Bishop Roger (William of Malmesbury, *De gestis regum anglorum*, 1107)

Roger, the Norman bishop of Salisbury, introduced his country's techniques and style into England.

The bishop was a generous man and never considered the expense when he decided what he ought to do, especially when he was carrying out building projects: this can be seen in many places, but especially at Salisbury and Malmesbury. At Malmesbury he had huge structures built, lavish in the sums expended and of very beautiful appearance. The coursing was so precisely realized that the fit of the stones struck the eye and gave the illusion that all the masonry was made up of a single stone. As for Salisbury Cathedral, the bishop had it restored and decorated so richly that it was second to none in England and indeed surpassed many. He could honestly say to God: 'Lord, I have loved the beauty of thy dwelling.'

Victor Mortet, *Recueil de textes relatifs à l'histoire de l'architecture...*, 1911

The building of Lincoln Cathedral by Bishop Hugh

The Metrical Life of St Hugh is a long poem in Latin hexameters probably written in the 1220s, around the time of Hugh's canonization (he died in 1200). The poet's way of looking at architecture is much less literal than that of Gervase, a monk from Canterbury, but is probably a great deal more typical of medieval attitudes. For him, a cathedral is a spiritual entity. Its significance resides in the level of symbolism and allegory that it can be made to yield. He is quite uninterested in the practical side of building, and if Lincoln Cathedral did not exist, it would be hard to reconstruct it from his description. On the other hand, he does convey something of the power and meaning which it must have had for his contemporaries, and which is largely a closed book to us today.

With wonderful art he built the work that is the cathedral church. For in its erection he not only granted means and the labour of his own servants, but the aid of his own sweat. Many a time he carried the hewn stones in a kind of hod, and the lime-mortar also. A handicapped man who was lame and propped on two crutches had the task of carrying that hod assigned to him, believing there must be good presage in it – and thereafter he disdained the help of his two crutches. The day's work, which tends to make the straight crooked, made his crookedness straight....

The old mass of masonry was completely demolished and a new one rose. Its state as it rose fitly expressed the form of a cross. By arduous labour its three parts are integrated into one. The very solid mass of the foundation goes up from the middle, the wall carries the roof high into the air. The foundation is thus buried in the bowels of the earth, but wall and roof lie open, as with proud boldness the wall soars up towards the clouds, and the roof towards the stars. The costliness of the material is well matched by zeal of the craftsmanship. The vault seems to

S t Hugh's choir, Lincoln.

converse with the winged birds; it spreads broad wings of its own, and like a flying creature jostles the clouds, while yet resting upon its solid pillars. The gripping mortar glues the white stones together, all of which the mason's hand has hewn true to the mark. But although the wall is put together from the mass of separate stones, it seems to disdain this fact and gives the semblance of joining in a continuum the contiguous parts. It seems to be the result not of art but of nature, not a thing unified but a single entity. The work is supported by another costly material consisting of black stonework [Purbeck marble], as though it is not content with thus having just one colour.... On being closely inspected this stone can hold people's minds in suspense as they wonder whether it is jasper or marble; but if jasper, then dull jasper, while if marble, an aristocrat of marbles. Of this substance are the shafts, which encircle the pillars in such a way that they seem to be keeping up a kind of ring-dance there. Their outer surface, more polished than a fresh-growing fingernail, presents a starry brilliance to the dazzled sight, for nature has painted there so many varied forms that, if art should toil with sustained endeavour to produce a similar painting, it could hardly copy what nature has done. Thus handsome jointing arranges there in seemly rank a thousand shafts which, strong, precious, and gleaming, render the whole structure of the cathedral durable with their strength while enriching it with their costliness and brightening it with their gleam. For the shafts themselves stand soaring and lofty,

their finish is clear and resplendent, their order graceful and geometrical, their beauty fit and serviceable, their function gratifying and excellent, their rigid strength undecayingly sharp to the touch.

The resplendent procession of windows on the two sides confronts the eyes with puzzles to be worked out. The sequence has depicted on it citizens of the Celestial City and the weapons with which they overcame the Stygian tyrant.

And there are two larger windows, like two luminaries; their circular radiance, looking to north and south, outshines all the other windows with these twin lustres. The others are comparable to common stars, but these two are, the one like the sun, and the other like the moon. Thus two candelabra make the upper reaches of the cathedral bright, with their vivid and various colours imitating the rainbow: indeed, not imitating but surpassing; for the sun, when it is reflected on the clouds, produces the rainbow, whereas those two windows gleam without the sun and flash without clouds….

The foundation is the body, the wall is the man, the roof is the spirit; the division of the church is thus threefold. The body has as its portion earth, the man has the clouds, the spirit has the stars….

Illuminating the world with heavenly light is the distinguished band of the clergy, and this is expressed by the bright windows. There is a ranking order on either side, which can be remarked: in the clerestory range the rank of canon, and in the aisle range that of vicar. And since, while a canon is handling the world's affairs, his vicar is perpetually and diligently carrying out the divine offices, the top range of windows shines illustrious with flower-petals, signifying the varied beauty of the world, while the lower range presents the names of the holy fathers. The twin windows that offer a circular light are the two Eyes of the cathedral; and rightly the greater of these is seen to be the bishop and the lesser the dean. For north represents the devil, and south the Holy Spirit and it is in these directions that the two Eyes look. The bishop faces the south in order to invite in, and the dean the north in order to

avoid; the one takes care to be saved, the other takes care not to perish. With these Eyes the cathedral's face is on the watch for the candelabra of heaven and the darkness of Lethe.

The Metrical Life of St Hugh
Translated by Charles Gaston, 1986

Contract of the master mason Gautier de Varinfroy for Meaux Cathedral (1253)

Very soon patrons and master masons were bound by contracts, which came into common use in the 13th century.

The bishop, dean and chapter of Meaux send greetings in God to all those who read this letter. We hereby announce that we have entrusted to Master Gautier de Varinfroy of the diocese of Meaux direction of the building works of our church under the following conditions: he is to receive ten *livres* each year, as long as we ourselves, our successors and the said chapter allow him to work on the said site. In the event of him falling long and continuously ill so that he could no longer work, he is not to receive the said ten *livres*. He is also to receive three *sous* a day while working on the building site, or when he is sent on errands in connection with the works. In addition, he cannot accept any work outside the diocese without our permission. Over and above this, he will receive wood from the building site which cannot be used there. He will not have the right to go to the site at Evreux or to any other site outside Meaux, or to remain there longer than two months, without the permission of the chapter of Meaux. He will be obliged to live in the town of Meaux and he has sworn that he will work faithfully on the above-named building site and will remain loyal to it. Drawn up in the year of Our Lord 1253 in the month of October.

Roland Recht, Les Bâtisseurs des cathédrales gothiques, 1989

Fortification of Ardres by Arnoul II, count of Guines; the role of Master Simon and the workmen on the building site (1200–1)

The problem of professional status arises as soon as there is a demand for specialized architects.

Arnoul II, count of Guines, resolved to fortify Ardres in imitation of the walls (*fossatum*) protecting St-Omer. He surrounded the town with a protective wall, the like of which had never been made by arms nor seen by eyes in the whole land of Guines. A large number of workers were gathered to make and dig out the moat. The geometrician Master Simon, directing the work, and walking as a master with his measuring rod, as was the custom, here and there measured the work that had already been planned in his mind, less with his measuring rod than by eye. He had houses and barns demolished; he cut down orchards, flowering trees and fruit trees; he pulled down many buildings that had formerly been made available to travellers at great expense; he broke up gardens of vegetables and flax; he destroyed and beat down the fields to make roads. He did not bother about those who became angry and cried out aloud, nor about those who grumbled silently about him. The peasants, given block and tackle, with waggons used for transporting marl and with dung carts, brought stones to spread on the roads.

The choir of Meaux Cathedral.

The trench diggers were seen working with their hoes, the diggers with their spades, the pioneers with their picks, the demolition men with their mallets, the navvies and the levellers with their trenching tools, the workmen working on the facing, the beaters (who rammed down the soil), each with the equipment and instruments that were most suitable and necessary for them. Carriers and porters were to be seen, and the turfers with long pieces of sod which had been cut and lifted from the meadows on the master's orders. The serjeants and the lord's agents, armed with knotty sticks, called out at times to the workmen, and at times urged them on to do the work in the manner that the foremen, who went on before, had carefully laid down.

Gabriel Fournier
Le Château dans la France médiévale, 1978

The building site

Building sites are often depicted in late medieval illuminations, but we have little sense of what they were really like. There are very few documents — whether accounts or literary texts — that can resurrect this rich, living and vivid world for us. For building work to be carried out successfully, many classes of people, chiefly professionals, have to be brought together.

Seal of the Strasbourg masons' lodge in the 16th century.

Construction of Noyers Castle (*Gesta pontificum Autissiodorensium*, 1106–1206)

The author of The Acts of the Bishops of Auxerre *describes in minute detail the construction of a castle.*

We have thought it useful to describe the works which Hugues de Noyers carried out at the castle (*castrum*) of Noyers, which is part of his heritage and which has been made famous through the deeds of his ancestors … and to describe the efforts he has made for the improvement of the fortifications of that place and the considerable expenditure he has made there. At the top of the walls of the lower town, situated at the bottom of the mountain and bathed on every side by the Serein River, he built solid firing devices in masonry or very strong wood. On the mountain slope above the town, although the castle (*castrum*) was inaccessible from this quarter owing to the nature of the site, he set about creating trenches dug deep into the mountain rock, as well as fortified gateways. Higher up, at the top of the mountain where the central part of the fortress (*presidium*) stands, a large area was prepared to make a site suitable for the installation of war machines. In addition to the ancient walls of the castle (*munitio*) – of which the outer one was solid (it had been built by Bishop Clérembaud's brother shortly before his death) – he erected another, higher wall behind the interior one, which was thicker and stronger, and in the middle he built a strong tower (*turris*). Along the outer wall he made deep trenches, digging out the rock, and forward of that he had further

On the construction site, it was crucial to coordinate the work of the different trades.

excavations made in the mountain to keep the enemy away from the principal part of the fortress (*presidium*) by numerous obstacles and barriers. He made projections in the outer wall; their upper part was covered with beams of extreme thickness. Those inside, therefore, need not fear missiles, no matter how heavy, nor catapults nor any other devices of the enemy, but in safety they would deny access to the trenches to any assailants coming from the front, as well as access to the wall to which these defences were attached. Outside the ramparts of the principal part of the fortress (*presidium principale*), he constructed a palace (*palatium*) of great beauty, which completed the defences of the principal part of the fortress (*presidium munitionis*). It was a pleasant lordly residence, which he decorated with taste with numerous ornaments. He had subterranean passages made leading from the wine cellar – which lay beneath the tower (*turris principalis*)

– to the palace situated lower down, so that to get wine and other provisions it would not be necessary to go in or out of the principal part of the fortress. While provisions were let down in baskets to the foot of the wall of the central part of the fortress, wine and water [were conveyed], with great care, through lead pipes that were very cleverly fashioned. Thus supplies assembled for the castle garrison were kept there under heavy guard and in complete safety, and after protecting them with bars to make them safe from all threat, they were able to serve and satisfy all needs on demand. Furthermore, he equipped the principal part of the fortress (*presidium*) with weapons, war machines and other devices necessary for defence. At great expense, he bought the houses of the knights and others which lay within the ramparts of the upper fortress (*munitio*) and he reassigned the property to his nephew. Thus, both in this part of the fortress and in the main building of the palace, as a measure of safety, the arrival of those who wanted to see the lord in his palace (*palatium*), situated outside the surrounding wall of the principal part of the fortress (*principale presidium*), would not arouse suspicion. And since any non-resident could be excluded in time of danger, the lord of the castle was no longer compelled to let any man enter the upper ramparts (*infra septa superiora*) without being sure of his allegiance. Also for this reason he removed the parish church of the locality (*municipium*) outside the walls (*extra septa*), allowing only a chapel for the lord within the upper part [of the fortress]....

Victor Mortet, *Recueil de textes relatifs à l'histoire de l'architecture...*, 1911

Accounts for the work done at the Collège de Beauvais in Paris by the executors of Jean de Dormans (1387)

This document perfectly evokes everyday life on the building site: publicizing the work to be done and calling for tenders, site meetings, payment of the workers in kind...

Item, to apply and execute the said decision and order of our said lords, shortly afterwards the said Master Raymon [of the Temple] made and set out a report detailing the form, the materials, the style and the thickness of the said building, and had it copied by his clerk, so that the work and the specification should be known by all the warranted and competent workers who would care to make and execute this work at a lower price.... Several working masons, having seen the report and taken note of it, tendered for the said work and several times lowered their asking price. Nevertheless, after much barter and many discussions, the said contract, for its better profit and

Where there was no good building stone, brick was used for structural purposes.

greater utility, according to the opinion and decision of the said Master Raymon, was awarded to and remained with the first masons whose prices had already been reduced, and who were at work every day, while waiting for any who might close the said deal for a lower price, as has been said. ...

On Thursday, feast day of the beheading of St John, Master Raymon came to the workshop and saw the masons, the hewers and the others ... he examined minutely and measured all the excavations from the base up to ground level....

Because stones from Gentilly were arriving in great numbers in several carts, there was no time to examine them properly; a poor stonecutter who was in the workshop all the time was assigned to check whether they were satisfactory, and, for this work, he was given, *ex gratia* ... four *sous*....

At the time of this work, in summer, since the days were long and it was hot and they were bringing stones, lime, sand and other materials, it was advisable to give those who were working water to drink several times to stop them grumbling....

On Friday eighteenth day of October, it was the feast-day of St Luke, and although on this day all work should cease according to the commandments of the Church ... the workshop was nevertheless kept at work...

Let it be known that one day amongst others, whilst the foundations of the said walls were being laid, being the time when the frosts were coming and the season when masonry could be done was coming to an end, some of the masons, while they were going to lunch, asked and prayed that while they were taking their hour lunch break, the

hewers should continue to work. The said hewers ... wanted to have their hour's break in the same way. So they gave the said hewers food and drink in the trench itself so that they went on working without any interruption; for this ... four *sous*.

On the day of Lent, when the masons and labourers were in the workshop, they demanded all together that, according to the custom in workshops where work is continuous, all the workmen and labourers should be given a favour, that is the meat of one sheep which they would all eat together....

Around Whitsuntide, the masons and labourers in the workshop who worked there permanently asked all with one voice as a mark of favour and kindness, which is the custom on every established and continuously working site like this one ... whether they could eat together on the day of the Ascension of Our Lord and receive an advance on the expenses of the said workshop. The said Master Raymon, being the employer and master of the corps of masons and of all the labourers and their judge in this matter, wished to decide this ... and so he decided ... that if it pleased the said College to do thus and not otherwise, the said masons and labourers would dine together.... There came to this meal the said Master Raymon, as their employer, as well as his wife and several well-known and honourable persons...

Around the twentieth day of July, M. de Beauvais passed through this workshop, visited the workers and inspected the work; he commanded his steward to give the workers a tip of one *franc* each.

Gustave Fagniez, *Etudes sur l'industrie et la classe industrielle à Paris au XIIIe et au XIVe siècles*, 1877

Materials

In order to construct buildings comparable to the monuments of ancient times, it was essential to find seams of fine stone which could be easily extracted and cut. In the 11th century, the location of quarries had been forgotten, in England as in France: the land had to be surveyed for this purpose. There was a similar problem in finding timber for the carpentry work: it was necessary to plant large species of trees and wait until they matured.

Bricks were manufactured on the site for convenience and economy.

Construction of Battle Abbey, near Hastings (*Chronicum monasterii de Bello*, 1066)

The transport of materials was one of the concerns of the patron and the master mason. In England, stone was scarce. It had to be imported from Normandy.

Since at the time the king was worried about the transport of building materials, the same monks suggested to him that the place where he had decided to build the church, being on a hill, was on soil that was arid, dried out and without water; and that for these reasons it was advisable, if he thought fit, to choose a more suitable location for a work of such importance. When the king heard this, he was indignant and left immediately, commanding that the foundations of the sanctuary should be laid more rapidly still on the precise spot where his victory had been acknowledged after he had killed his enemy. And as the monks, who did not dare to oppose him, made the lack of water a pretext, the magnanimous king replied, it is said, to their objections with these memorable words: 'If by the grace of God my life is spared, I shall see the abbey established on this very spot, supplied with wine in greater quantity than any other major abbey is supplied with water.' The monks again began to complain of the poor location, saying that no suitable building stone was to be found anywhere in the area for some distance, all the ground being covered by forests. So the king offered to meet all the costs by drawing on his own resources, and he even sent his ships to transport stone from the town of Caen by sea in sufficient quantity for the projected work. And when the monks, following the king's decisions, had transported part of the stone from Normandy by boat, it is said that at the same moment a nun had a revelation: if they dug in a place revealed to her in her vision, they would find a great quantity of stone for the projected work. So they went and looked, as they had been commanded to do, and not far from the area designated for the church they discovered stone in such rich quantity and quality that evidently a treasure had been buried there in former times by the will of God in order to provide the material for the intended building. At last the foundations were laid of this work which was of great importance in the eyes of the times and then, following the king's decision, the high altar was carefully sited on the very spot where King Harold's ensign, known as the 'standard', had been seen to fall....

Victor Mortet, *Recueil de textes relatifs à l'histoire de l'architecture...*, 1911

The architect's first priority was to find stone and timber, here for the construction of Bern in the 12th century.

The search for wood for St-Denis (Abbot Suger, *De Consecratione*, 1140)

The best-known text on the subject of the difficulty of finding wood is by Abbot Suger, patron of St-Denis.

In order to find the beams, we consulted all those who work with wood in our area as well as in Paris, and they all replied that, in their opinion, because of the lack of forests, beams could not be found in these regions, but we should have to get them from the region of Auxerre. They were unanimous in that view; as for us, we were overwhelmed at the prospect of all the effort and the great delay that this would involve. One night, having returned from matins, I thought as I lay on my bed that I should myself go round the neighbouring woods, and look everywhere to see whether I could find the beams and avoid the delay and the extra work. And so, putting aside all my other cares, I set off early in the morning with the carpenters and the dimensions of the beams and made my way quickly to the forest of Yveline. Passing through our lands in the valley of the Chevreuse, I called together our officials and those who had charge of the land and all those who knew the forests well, and I asked them to say under oath whether we had any chance of finding beams of these dimensions in that area. They began to smile, and certainly would have burst out laughing if they could have, astonished that we should not know that nothing of that size was to be found in all those lands, especially since Milo, the Lord of Chevreuse, who was our vassal and who held half the forest in addition to another fief, and who for a long time had waged war with the king and Amaury de Montfort, had left nothing untouched or in a good state, having himself built three-storeyed defensive towers. We ourselves rejected everything that these men said, and with bold confidence we set out through the forest; in about an hour we found one beam of the right dimensions. What more was needed? At about nones or a little earlier, pushing our way through the woodland, through the thick forest, through the thorn bushes, to the astonishment of all those present, who were gathered together, we discovered twelve beams. It was the number that we needed. We had them carried to the holy basilica and placed them with joy on the roof of the new work, to the praise and glory of the Lord Jesus who had procured them thus for himself and his martyrs, having chosen to protect them from the hands of robbers.

Abbot Suger
De Consecratione, 1140

Contract made with Master Jean de Lohes, mason, for the building of the castle at Bapaume in Flanders (1311)

Some contracts are extremely precise concerning the materials to be used in construction.

To all those who will see and hear the present letters, greetings from Thomas Brandon, bailiff of Arras. May all know that the mason Jehan [Jean] de Lohes has appeared in person before us and before the men of Madame d'Artois, that is Master Girart de Saleu, Jehan Testart and Jehan d'Estainbourg, and that he has acknowledged that he is to make for the castle of Madame d'Artois at Bapaume the masonry for a hall which will be 80 feet [24 metres] long and 70 feet [21 metres] wide on the inside. All round, there will be walls 5 feet [1.5 metres] thick and 40 feet [12 metres] high. On one side, there will be an arch adjoining the chapel as is suitable with an opening equal to the width of the chapel. The arch will be decorated with roll mouldings; there will be four large windows at the ends of this hall, and four on the two sides, if as many are desired, as wide as is necessary. And there will be six double windows and six ordinary ones with frames on the inside. There will be two fireplaces in this hall, wherever it is wished they should be put. In the middle of the hall, lengthwise, there will be two freestanding columns and two attached to the wall, which will support three [transverse] arches in due manner, as high as they can be below the roof timbers, the spandrels of these arches being entirely masonry right up to the roofing. This central [transverse] wall will be 40 feet [12 metres] high like the others. The walls all round and the central wall will have entablatures both inside and outside, as is suitable. The aforesaid columns will be given bases and capitals. At the ends of the hall, there will be two gable ends as high and as wide as is necessary for them to fit the roof structure well. These gables will be crowned with French copings, as is suitable, and decorated on these copings with bosses, balls and fleurons in sufficient quantity. At the four corners of the hall there will be turrets, as wide as is necessary, and a fifth turret in the centre, on the courtyard side. The four corner turrets will spring from the entablature, while the other will spring from the ground; inside there will be a spiral staircase leading up to the wall-passages. All around the said hall, there will be crenellated wall-passages, with walkways which will allow people to come and go. The two gables will be set back inwards so that the wall-passages will be outside the gable ends as they should be. In this hall there will be as many door-frames as is desired. The four turrets will be as high as the wall-passages, and will be crenellated like the rest of the building. If it were desired to raise the turrets 10 feet [3 metres] above the passages, it should be done, and entablatures made all round so that the roof timbers could rest on them, if that is what is wished. The four columns in the hall will be of sandstone; the said Jehan is to furnish them at his own expense, except for the transport, the copings and the capitals being worked with bosses and leaves. The two free-standing columns will be all of one piece, 15 feet [4.5 metres] long if that length is suitable and eighteen spans in thickness; the two half-columns will be made of stone blocks and bonded to the walls. There will be as many gargoyles as are necessary for drainage purposes and, on the gables, as many openings as there should be. For the foundations, the said Jehan must go at his own expense 3 feet [almost 1 metre] down below the ground; if it should prove necessary to go deeper,

that would be at Madame's expense.

All that is said and estimated above is to be done by the said Jehan de Lohes at his own expense, for the workers as well as for the work, for the consideration of three hundred *livres parisis* [livres of Paris], which he will receive for the said work. All the materials are to be provided on the site: to wit stone, lime, sand, fencing, pulleys, rope and whatever is necessary to this work. He is to provide labour to put up the fencing, and furnish the four columns at his own expense, as has been said, except for the transport, which will be charged to us. If the cost of the said work exceeds [the agreed cost] by ten *livres parisis*, nothing of that will be paid to the said Jehan, but he must work for the agreed salary; if the excess were more than ten *livres parisis*, he will be paid this on top of his salary, with an exemption of ten *livres*. The said Jehan must take the cut stone that is already available to use for the said work, and that at the price obtaining before work commences; he is to deduct this price from his salary. He is to finish the said work in a correct and satisfactory manner in the present season, if he can.

J.-M. Richard, *Mahaut, comtesse d'Artois et de Bourgogne (1302–29)*, 1887

Contract for roofing Troyes Cathedral (11 October 1390)

Payment for work relating to the supply and use of building materials – in this case slates and nails and roofing timber, was the subject of very stringent contractual agreements.

Jehan Nepveu, called the slater [Escaillon], living in Reims, and

his brother Colart, living in Troyes…
recognized that they have entered into
contract with venerable and discreet
persons the dean and chapter of the
church of Troyes to cover the roof of
their church from the great pillars of the
great crossing as far as the pillar which is
beside the well…and they should
supply the slate and nails and put them
to use, by contract for piecework [made
with my lords] £350 t. [*livres tournois*].

And the said worshipful persons
[i.e., the dean and chapter] are, and
will be held, responsible for delivering
to them planks of wood in sufficient
quantity for the said roofing; and in
addition to pay them, for the above
contract, three hundred and fifty *livres
tournois* [livres of Tours] in money that
is legal tender on the day; of this sum,
the said brothers had and received from
the said worshipful persons, through
the masters of the ecclesiastical works,
in the presence of the said jurors,
one hundred *livres tournois*; the two
hundred and fifty *livres* remaining will
be paid to them by the said worshipful
persons in the following way: that is,
on the next feast day of St Andrew
the Apostle one hundred *livres tournois*,
twenty days after the following
Christmas another hundred *livres
tournois* and the fifty remaining *livres
tournois* when they have finished the
said roofing. Giving their word to the
said jurors, under pain of arrest, of
being put and kept in prison, and
against a guarantee of all their goods
and the goods of their heirs, movables
and real estate, now and to come,
submitting and giving as guarantee the
said goods to the judgment and decree
of our Lord the King, of his men and
of all other men of justice, the said
brothers have undertaken, each for all,

Making glass for stained-glass windows
required large quantities of sand and
powerful furnaces.

to make, accomplish perfectly, finish
and successfully conclude all the above-
mentioned things and each of these
things in the manner stated above,
without any shortcoming, without
deviation or causing deviation, on
pain of having to reimburse and pay
in return all costs and damages which
might arise or depend on this: the said
brothers renouncing, in everything
which touches this, all regional custom
and practice, all resort to castellany and
provostship, all appeals, all other
opposition that could be made against
these letters or against their terms,
and renouncing any action declaring
the general renunciation invalid….

Bibliothèque de l'Ecole des Chartes,
1862; first paragraph translated by
Stephen Murray in *Building Troyes
Cathedral,* 1987

Report on the abbey church of St-Ouen at Rouen (1440)

The four piers supporting the crossing tower of the abbey church were giving cause for concern. An expertise, or professional assessment, was held. The architect, Colin de Berneval, successor to his father Alexandre, was relieved of all responsibility for the problem.

Below is the report of Simon Le Noir and Jehan Wyllemer, masters of the works in masonry and carpentry of our Lord the King in the bailiwick of Rouen, of Jehanson Salvart, master of works of the cathedral church of Our Lady at Rouen and of the said town, of Jehan Rouxel, juror of our Lord the King, and of Pierre Bense, master masons, all of whom have said and signified to the reverend father in God my lord the abbot of St-Ouen and to the prior, the bailiff, the overseer of the granary, to the master of ecclesiastical works of the said place of St-Ouen, how dangerous their church is, in view of the great load which weighs on the four piers of the tower and on the four great transverse arches. These piers are not buttressed by their shifts and supports [?] on the side towards the crossing, and as a result they bulge out in those places and are very dangerous; for if the said piers or the great transverse arches should shift ever so slightly, the church would be in a position where the tower would collapse and the whole of the choir would follow. To avert this danger, the said masters and workmen unanimously advise that as quickly as possible and without any interruption the shifts and supports [?] of the crossing, on which work has already begun, should be completed, so that the piers of the tower, the transverse arches and the abutting piers should all be made secure, being linked more strongly together. In order to be able to carry out this reinforcement rapidly, the masters and workmen named above declare that it would be wise to sell or to pawn chalices or objects of value to get money so that work could begin at once, and the church might be made safe; the which church is at the present moment in very great danger. The master of the works, hearing the said report, instantly asked the said masters and workmen to put this report in writing on a sheet of parchment and sign it with their signatures or the seals which they used in their royal offices; and in the presence of my lord the abbot, of the prior, of the bailiff, of the overseer of the granary and of the said masters, he resigned the office of the works, so that if the church was not made safe and some disaster occurred, no-one could turn against him or say that it was in some way his fault. Present at this report was Colin de Berneval, appointed by my lord the abbot and by the monks named above to be the worker in masonry for their church in the future, as his father, the late Alexandre de Berneval, had been in his time. The said Colin de Berneval asked if he could hold in his possession a copy of the said report, for his indemnity in the future. This was done on Monday the twenty-third day of January, in the year of Grace 1440.

Bibliothèque de l'Ecole des Chartes, 1862

Building techniques

Architects, who realized the extent of their abilities in the first third of the 11th century, proved to be not only great creative artists but also remarkable technicians. They had to devise new solutions to overcome difficulties. Very soon some of them began to produce 'expertises', or professional assessments.

Prague Cathedral retains the metal tie-rods that have ensured its stability since the 14th century.

Reconstruction of Cambrai Cathedral (*Gestum pontificum Cameracensium,* 1023–30)

Like all the patrons of his generation, Gérard I, Bishop of Cambrai, tried to force the hand of fate.

The Lord Bishop Gérard first entered the town. When he saw that the buildings of the monastery of St Mary were as small as they were decrepit and he suspected their ancient walls were cracking, he swiftly conceived the project of putting them into a more satisfactory state, if only he were given the necessary time, with the help of God. But he could not undertake the project before the year of the Incarnation 1023 … because he was prevented … by internal as well as external conflict. But then, trusting in divine mercy and reassured by the prayers of many of the faithful whom he had taken into his confidence, he gave orders to demolish the old walls. Once the necessary funds were pledged, he devoted all his energy to reconstructing a building that presented such great difficulties, for he had a fear of leaving the work unfinished, either because death might overtake him, or because some other reason might hinder him from completing it. In this respect, he realized that among the obstacles that might delay the project he had at heart, none was more difficult to overcome than the slowness of the transport of columns, cut a long way from the town, almost at the thirtieth milestone. And so he prayed Divine Mercy grant him assistance nearer at hand. One day while riding his horse, he explored the hidden depths of the earth in many surrounding places. At last, with the help of God who never fails those who put their trust in Him, he had a trench dug in the village that has always been known as Lesdain, four miles [over six kilometres] from the town, and found stone suitable for the columns. And this was not the only place: on digging nearer, to be precise on the estate [*villa*] of Nigella [Noyelles], he had the joy of finding good quality stones of another kind. Giving thanks to God for this find, he devoted all his zeal to this pious work. And to cut short the story, in the space of seven years, with the help of Divine Mercy, he brought this huge work to its conclusion, that is in the year of the Incarnation of Our Lord 1030.

Victor Mortet, *Recueil de textes relatifs à l'histoire de l'architecture...*, 1911

Construction of the castle of Ardres, near St-Omer (*Chronicle of Lambert of Ardres*, 1060)

All construction involves destruction. In this case a group of buildings was moved from one place to another, wooden buildings being dismantled and re-erected.

How Arnould, seneschal of Eustace, count of Boulogne, had all his buildings at Selnesse transported to the tall keep at Ardres. Arnould, seneschal of Eustace, count of Boulogne, seeing that everything smiled upon him and turned to his advantage, almost as he wished, had a sluice-gate made in a marsh in the neighbourhood of Ardres almost a stone's throw from a mill, and then a second sluice. Between the two, in the middle of the marsh, which was deep, muddy and copiously filled with water, extending almost to the foot of a hill, he fortified a very high motte or 'keep' that rose above a line of defence [*in munitionis signum*] and above a dyke. And from what the inhabitants say, a tame bear ... transported the materials intended for the keep of this fortress between the hill [*altitudo*] and the motte. It is said that in a hiding-place perfectly concealed within this dyke a good-luck amulet was hidden, to remain there for ever; it was a lump of very pure gold. Arnould had the periphery of the outer fortification surrounded by a very solid ditch, the mill being included within the fortification. Soon, in accordance with his father's old plan, he had all the buildings at Selnesse pulled down and destroyed, then he had the keep at Ardres equipped with a bridge, gateways and all the necessary buildings. From this day, once the vast residence of Selnesse had been demolished and razed to the ground and all its buildings dismantled and moved to Ardres, the very memory of Selnesse disappeared with its castle; so that first at Ardres and then everywhere, Arnould became known as the protector and lord of Ardres.

Victor Mortet, *Recueil de textes relatifs à l'histoire de l'architecture...*, 1911

The rebuilding of Canterbury Cathedral (*Chronicle of Gervase of Canterbury*)

In 1174 the whole east end of Canterbury Cathedral was destroyed by fire. It was witnessed by one of the monks, Gervase. His account of the rebuilding over the next ten years, included in his history of the archbishopric, is the most complete, most vivid and most informative of all the documents on medieval architecture that have come down to us.

Meantime the brotherhood sought counsel as to how and in what manner the burnt church might be repaired, but without success; for the columns of the church, commonly termed the *pillars*, were exceedingly weakened by the heat of the fire, and were scaling in pieces and hardly able to stand, so that they frightened even the wisest out of their wits.

French and English artificers were therefore summoned, but even these differed in opinion. On the one hand, some undertook to repair the aforesaid columns without mischief to the walls above. On the other hand, there were some who asserted that the whole church must be pulled down if the monks wished to exist in safety. This opinion, true as it was, excruciated the monks with grief, and no wonder, for how could they hope that so great a work should be completed in their days by any human ingenuity.

However, amongst the other workmen there had come a certain William of Sens, a man active and ready, and as a workman most skilful both in wood and stone. Him, therefore, they retained, on account of his lively genius and good reputation, and dismissed the others. And to him, and to the providence of God was the execution of the work committed.

And he, residing many days with the monks and carefully surveying the burnt walls in their upper and lower parts, within and without, did yet for some time conceal what he found necessary to be done, lest the truth should kill them in their present state of pusillanimity.

But he went on preparing all things that were needful for the work, either of himself or by the agency of others. And

The choir of Canterbury Cathedral.

---

when he found that the monks began to be somewhat comforted, he ventured to confess that the pillars rent with the fire and all that they supported must be destroyed if the monks wished to have a safe and excellent building. At length they agreed, being convinced by reason and wishing to have the work as good as he promised, and above all things to live in security; thus they consented patiently, if not willingly, to the destruction of the choir.

And now he addressed himself to the procuring of stone from beyond the sea. He constructed ingenious machines for loading and unloading ships, and for drawing cement and stone. He delivered moulds for shaping the stones to the sculptors who were assembled, and diligently prepared other things of the same kind. The choir thus condemned to destruction was pulled down, and nothing else was done in this year.

As the new work is of a different fashion from the old, it may be well to describe the old work first and then the new. Edmer, the venerable singer, in his Opuscula, describes the ancient church built in the Roman manner, which Archbishop Lanfranc, when he came to the See, utterly destroyed, finding it in ashes. For Christ Church is recorded to have suffered thrice from fire; first, when the blessed martyr Elfege was captured by the Danes and received the crown of martyrdom; secondly, when Lanfranc, abbot of Caen, took the rule of the church of Canterbury; thirdly, in the days of Archbishop Richard and Prior Odo.... Leaving out, therefore, all that is not absolutely necessary, let us boldly prepare for the destruction of

this old work and the marvellous building of the new, and let us see what our master William has been doing in the meanwhile.

The master began, as I stated long ago, to prepare all things necessary for the new work, and to destroy the old. In this way the first year was taken up. In the following year, that is after the feast of St Bertin (Sept. 5 1175) before the winter, he erected four pillars, that is, two on each side, and after the winter (1176) two more were placed, so that on each side were three in order, upon which and upon the exterior wall of the aisles he framed seemly arches and a vault, that is three [bays] on each side.... In the third year (1176/7) he placed two pillars on each side, the two extreme ones of which he decorated with marble columns placed around them, and because at that place the choir and [transepts] were to meet, he constituted these principal pillars. To which, having added the keystones and the vault, he intermingled the lower triforium from the great tower to the aforesaid pillars, that is, as far as the [transept], with many marble columns. Over which he adjusted another triforium of the other materials, and also the upper windows. And in the next place, three [bays] of the great vault, from the tower, namely, as far as the [transept]. All which things appeared to us and to all who saw them, incomparable and most worthy of praise. And at so glorious a beginning we rejoiced and conceived good hopes to the end, and provided for the acceleration of the work with diligence and spirit. Thus was the third year occupied and the beginning of the fourth.

In the summer (1178), commencing from the cross[ing], he erected ten pillars, that is, on each side five. Of which the first two were ornamented with marble columns to correspond with the other two principal ones. Upon these ten he placed the arches and vaults. And having, in the next place, completed on both sides the triforia and upper windows, he was, at the beginning of the fifth year, in the act of preparing with machines for the turning of the great vault, when suddenly the beams broke under his feet, and he fell to the ground, stones and timbers

accompanying his fall, from the height of the capitals of the upper vault, that is to say, of fifty feet [fifteen metres]. Thus sorely bruised by the blows from the beams and stones, he was rendered helpless alike to himself and for the work, but no other than himself was in the least injured. Against the master only was this vengeance of God or spite of the devil directed.

The master, thus hurt, remained in his bed for some time under medical care in expectation of recovering, but was deceived in this hope, for his health amended not. Nevertheless, as the winter approached, and it was necessary to finish the upper vault, he gave the charge of the work to a certain ingenious and industrious monk, who was the overseer of the masons; an appointment whence much envy and malice arose, because it made this young man appear more skilful than richer and more powerful ones. But the master reclining in bed commanded all things that should be done in order. And thus was completed the [bay] between the four principal pillars. In the keystone of this [bay] the choir and [transepts] seem as it were to meet. Two [bays] on each side were formed before the winter; when the heavy rains beginning stopped the work. In these operations the fourth year was occupied and the beginning of the fifth. But on the eighth day from the said fourth year, on the ides of September, there happened an eclipse of the sun at about the sixth hour, and before the master's accident.

And the master, perceiving that he derived no benefit from the physicians, gave up the work, and crossing the sea returned to his home in France. And another succeeded him in charge of the works; William by name, English by

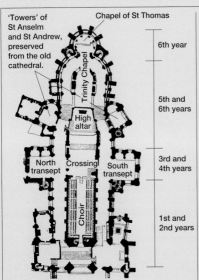

'Towers' of St Anselm and St Andrew, preserved from the old cathedral.

Chapel of St Thomas

6th year

Trinity Chapel

5th and 6th years

High altar

North transept   Crossing   South transept

3rd and 4th years

Choir

1st and 2nd years

P lan of the eastern part of Canterbury Cathedral to show the work carried out in successive years according to Gervase.

nation, small in body, but in workmanship of many kinds acute and honest. In the summer of the fifth year (1179) he finished the [transepts] on each side, that is, the south and the north, and [built the vault] which is above the great Altar, which the rains of the previous year had hindered, although all was prepared. Moreover he laid the foundation for the enlargement of the church at the eastern part, because a chapel of St Thomas was to be built there....

Moreover, in the same summer, that is of the sixth year (1180), the outer wall round the chapel of St Thomas, begun before the winter, was elevated as far as the turning of the vault. But the master had begun a tower at the eastern part outside the circuit of the wall as it

were, the lower vault of which was completed before the winter.

The chapel of the Holy Trinity above mentioned was then levelled to the ground; this had hitherto remained untouched out of reverence to St Thomas, who was buried in the crypt. But the saints who reposed in the upper part of the chapel were translated elsewhere, and lest the memory of what was then done should be lost, I will record somewhat thereof. On the eighth idus of July the altar of the Holy Trinity was broken up, and from its materials the altar of St John the Apostle was made; I mention this lest the history of the holy stone should be lost....

It has been above stated, that after the fire nearly all the old portions of the choir were destroyed and changed into somewhat new and of a more noble fashion. The differences between the two works may now be enumerated. The pillars of the old and new work are alike in form and thickness but different in length. For the new pillars were elongated by almost twelve feet [about three metres]. In the old capitals the work was plain, in the new ones exquisite in sculpture. There the circuit of the choir had twenty-two pillars, here are twenty-eight. There the arches and everything else was plain, or sculptured with an axe and not with a chisel. But here almost throughout is appropriate sculpture. No marble columns were there, but here are innumerable ones. There, in the circuit around the choir, the vaults were plain, but here they are arch-ribbed and have keystones. There a wall set upon the pillars divided the crosses from the choir, but here the crosses are separated from the choir by no such partition, and converge together in one keystone, which is placed in the middle of the great vault which rests on the four principal pillars. There, there was a ceiling of wood decorated with excellent painting, but here is a vault beautifully constructed of stone and light tufa. There, was a single triforium, but here are two in the choir and a third in the aisle of the church. All which will be better understood from inspection than by any description.

This must be known, however, that the new work is higher than the old by so much as the upper windows of the body of the choir, as well as of its aisles, are raised above the marble tabling.

And as in future ages it may be doubtful why the breadth which was given to the choir next the tower should be so much contracted at the head of the church, it may not be useless to explain the causes thereof. One reason is, that the two towers of St Anselm and St Andrew, placed in the circuit on each side of the old church, would not allow the breadth of the choir to proceed in the direct line. Another reason is, that it was agreed upon and necessary that the chapel of St Thomas should be erected at the head of the church, where the chapel of the Holy Trinity stood, and this was much narrower than the choir.

The master, therefore, not choosing to pull down the said towers, and being unable to move them entire, set out the breadth of the choir in a straight line, as far as the beginning of the towers. Then, receding slightly on either side from the towers, and preserving as much as he could the breadth of the passage outside the choir on account of the processions which were there frequently passing, he gradually and obliquely drew in his work, so that from the opposite the altar, it might begin to

contract, and from thence, at the third pillar, might be so narrowed as to coincide with the breadth of the chapel, which was named of the Holy Trinity. Beyond these, four pillars were set on the sides at the same distance as the last, but of a different form; and beyond these other four were arranged in a circle, and upon these the superposed work (of each side) was brought together and terminated. This is the arrangement of the pillars.

The outer wall, which extends from the aforesaid towers, first proceeds in a straight line, is then bent into a curve, and thus in the round tower the wall on each side comes together in one, and is there ended. All which may be more clearly and pleasantly seen by the eyes than taught in writing. But this much was said that the differences between the old and new work might be made manifest.

Now let us carefully examine what were the works of our mason in this seventh year (1181) from the fire, which, in short, included the completion of the new and handsome crypt, and above the crypt the exterior walls of the aisles up to their marble capitals. The windows, however, the master was neither willing nor able to turn, on account of the approaching rains. Neither did he erect the interior pillars. Thus was the seventh year finished, and the eighth begun.

In this eighth year (1182) the master erected eight interior pillars and turned the arches and the vault with the windows in the circuit. He also raised the tower up to the bases of the highest windows under the vault. In the ninth year (1183) no work was done for want of funds. In the tenth year (1184) the upper windows of the tower, together with the vault, were finished. Upon the pillars was placed a lower and an upper triforium....

Translated by Robert Willis in
<i>The Architectural History of Canterbury
Cathedral,</i> 1845</div>

The 'Expertise' of 1316 (on Chartres Cathedral)

The 'Expertise' of 1316 is a report prepared by a group of architects – Pierre (i.e. Jean) de Chelles, master of the works of Paris, Nicolas des Chaumes, master of the king's works and Jacques de Longjumeau, master carpenter of Paris – who were asked by the worried canons of Chartres to inspect the cathedral.

....My lords, we say to you that the four arches which help carry the vault are good and strong, and that the piers which carry the arches [are] good, and that the keystone which carries the summit [French *la clef qui porte la clef,* literally 'the keystone that carries the keystone'] [of the vault] is good and strong; and it would not be necessary to remove more than half of your vault, at the place[s] where one will see what is needed. And we have noted that the scaffolding would move from above the tracery of the glass [French *enmerllement;* probably the assemblage of stones in the window tracery]; and this scaffolding can be used to help cover your rood screen and the people who will pass beneath it, and to hold the other scaffolds to be constructed in the vault, which one can see will be required and needed.

Here are the defects which are in the church of Notre-Dame at Chartres, seen by Master Pierre de Chelles, Master of the Works of Paris; Master Nicolas des Chaumes, Master of the Works of our lord, the King; and Master Jacques de Longjumeau, Master Carpenter and officer of Paris, in the presence of Master Jean de Reate, canon of Chartres, originally from Italy; Master Simon, Carpenter; and Master Berthaud, officer of the aforementioned work, upon the order of the dean.

First: we have seen the vault of the crossing; repairs are necessary there; and if they are not undertaken very shortly, there could be great danger.

Item: we have seen the flying buttresses which abut the vaults; they need pointing up, and if this is not done at once, much damage may ensue.

Item: there are two piers which support the towers which need repairs.

Item: repairs are needed on the porch piers and a plank should be provided in each side opening to carry what lies above; and, on the outside, one of the jambs will be moved above the dado on the corner pier and the other jamb will be moved above a reworking of the fabric of the church; and the plank will have a support so as to reduce the strain; and this will be done with all the ties that are needed.

Item: we have seen and devised for Master Berthaud how he will [re]make the statue of the Magdalene where it now is, without moving it.

Item: we have looked at the great tower [the south tower] and see that it has real need of important repairs; for one of its sides is cracked and creviced and one of the turrets is broken and coming apart.

Item: the needs of the front portals follow – the coverings are broken and in pieces; wherefore it would be good to put an iron tenon in each to help hold them up, and it should be

well-seated so as to remove the danger.

Item: for the advantage of the church, we have noticed that the first scaffolding will be moveable from above the tracery of the windows so that the vault of the crossing may be redone.

Item: for the advantage of the church, we have noticed that the post that carries the little angel [the statue at the point of the roof covering the hemicycle] is all rotten and cannot join the other pier of the nave of the minster, for the pier of the minster is broken on the upper side of the assemblage of the beam; and if they want to work well, [the masters] will put two trusses with

The flying buttresses of Chartres Cathedral play a role that is primarily structural.

those which are on the chevet and will put the little angel on the second of these trusses; and the larger part of the beam, which is on the afore-mentioned ridge, could be put inside.

Item: the belfry, where the little saints are [the bells, which were usually given saints' names], is insufficient, for it is very old, as is the one where the large saints are; repairs to them are necessary at once.

Item: the roof of the minster needs four new tenons, [to replace those] which now are rotted at one end; they can be repaired, if you do not want to replace them, in the manner which we explained to your masters.

Translated by Robert Branner in *Chartres Cathedral*, 1969

Record of the visitation to Troyes Cathedral (*Deliberations of the Chapter*, 1362)

The report on Troyes Cathedral reveals the structural problems for the architect.

This is the record of the visitation made by Master Pierre Faisant, mason, to the church of Troyes, in the year 1362, on the Saturday after the feast day of St Martin in the winter [12 Nov.].

1. First, it is to be known that all the gutters of the low vaults are to be repointed, that is, those [the gutters] around the choir of the said church.

2. Item, in several places the entablatures [balustrades] which are by the gargoyles are to be redone and re-erected.

3. Item, it is necessary to make 1 flying buttress by the chapel of my

lord the bishop toward the court [south side of the choir] which will spring above the gutter and it is necessary that it [the flyer] should go as high above the rear tail as up to the base of the first pinnacle, and this only involves 1 single flying buttress.

4. Item, further, it seems to the said master who has looked at the new work of Master Jehan de Torvoie…that there is no fault except that the flying buttresses are placed too high, that is to say the upper flying buttress, and it seems to him that it is necessary to demolish the said work to the height of the pinnacles which rise from the angles, and [he] is for saving the [old] masonry completely throughout, and to do this and to put things right according to his profession will easily cost 250 florins.

5. Item, further, another thing, that there is a problem with the new flying buttress toward the house of the great archdeacon [north side of the choir], and he will show it, if need be, for, if the work is augmented with plaster and cement, it is not at all adequate. [He] says on this oath that although it might be uglier, it would not be any less strong or less worthy on that account.

6. Item, it seems that the pillars of the balustrade of the high gutters [of the clerestory wall] are fragmented and without cement and the [rain] water is running down the walls.

7. Item, in several places, that is to say in the joints in the passageways, the [rain] water is running down through the walls, and this must be remedied.

8. Item, the four gutters of the bell tower need to be fixed, that is at the joints above the flying buttresses, there is a major defect and it should be remedied.

9. And the said masters are at your disposal to be your own workers, if necessary.

Translated by Stephen Murray in *Building Troyes Cathedral*, 1987

Report on the building of Milan Cathedral

Milan Cathedral was begun soon after 1386. It was on a vast scale, and the Lombard architects (called 'the Masters' in the following document) found themselves out of their depth. In 1399 a Frenchman, Jean Mignot, was put in charge and made serious criticisms, which they attempted in vain to answer (see below). In February 1400 a conference was called, at which several notable architects from France, Italy and Germany gave their opinions. Extracts from their report are given in the second half of the piece.

1400 Sunday, 25 January. Master Jean Mignot has stated to the council here present that he has given in writing to the said council a note computing to date all the reasons and every motive which lead him to say that the aforesaid work lacks strength, and he does not wish to give other reasons.

Final statements were given by aforesaid Master Jean on the 25th day of January.

Master Jean Mignot points out to you excellent lords of the workshop council of the Milanese church with respect and pure truth that as he had demonstrated in writing elsewhere and among other matters, the defects of said church, he reiterates and affirms that all the buttresses around the church are neither strong nor able to sustain the weight which rests upon them, since they ought in every case to be three times

The nave of Milan Cathedral.

the thickness of one pier in the interior of the church. The Masters reply:

Concerning the first statement, they say that all the buttresses of said church, are strong and capable of sustaining their weight and many times more, for many reasons, since one braccio of our marble and *saritium*, whatever its width, is as strong as two braccia of French stone or of the French church which he gives to the aforesaid masters as an example. Therefore they say that if aforesaid buttresses are one-and-a-half times [the size] – and they are – of the piers in the interior of the church, that they are strong and correctly conceived, and if they were larger they would darken said church because of their projection, as at the church in Paris, which has buttresses of Master Jean's type, and since they can be an obstruction [there are] other reasons.

Moreover, he [Mignot] says that four towers were begun to support the crossing-tower of said church, and there are no piers nor any foundation capable of sustaining said towers, and if the church were to be made with said towers in this position it would infallibly fall. Concerning the claims, however, which were made by certain ignorant people, surely through passion, that pointed vaults are stronger and exert less thrust than round, and moreover concerning other matters, proposals were made in a fashion more willful than sound; and what is worse, it was objected that the science of geometry should not have a place in these matters, since science is one thing and art another. Said Master Jean says that art without science is nothing [*ars*

sine scientia nihil est], and that whether
the vaults are pointed or round, they
are worthless unless they have a good
foundation, and nevertheless, no matter
how pointed they are, they have a very
great thrust and weight.

Whereupon they [the Masters] say
that the towers which they wanted to
make are for many reasons and causes
[desirable]. Namely, in the first place, to
integrate aforesaid church and transept
so that they correspond to a rectangle
according to the demands of geometry,
but beyond this, for the strength and
beauty of the crossing-tower. To be sure,
as if as a model for this, the Lord God is

seated in Paradise in the center of the throne, and around the throne are the four Evangelists according to the Apocalypse, and these are the reasons why they were begun. And although two piers of each sacristy are not founded, but begin at ground level, the church is truly strong nevertheless for these reasons, that there are projections upon which the said piers stand, and the said projections are of large stones and joined with iron dowels as was said above other statements, and that the weight on these three [sic] towers falls evenly on their square, and they will be built properly and strong, and what is vertical cannot fall; therefore they say that they are strong in themselves, and for that reason will give strength to the crossing-tower, which is enclosed in the center of those towers. Therefore said church is truly strong.

Moreover he [Mignot] recognizes that their premises are willfully conceived, nor do those who disagree wish to give in to the right and the betterment of said church and workshop, but want to win their case either for their own profit or from fear, or else from obstinacy, since they would like to continue in spite of defects. For this reason said Master Jean requests that four or six or twelve of the better engineers who are expert in these matters might be brought together, either from Germany, England, or France, otherwise said work will certainly fall, which would be a great loss in every way....

Whereupon they [the Masters] say and reply in the same statement, that where it says that the science of geometry should not have a place in these [matters], the above-mentioned say: if he [Mignot] invokes, as it were, the rules of geometry, Aristotle says that

the movement of man in space which we call locomotion is either straight or circular or a mixture of the two. Likewise the same [writer] says elsewhere that every body is perfected in three [ways], and the movement of this very church rises *ad triangulum* as has been determined by other engineers. So they say that all [the measurements] are in a straight line, or an arch, therefore it is concluded that what has been done, has been done according to geometry and to practice, and even he [Mignot] has said that science without art is nothing; concerning art, however, replies have been made already in other statements.

1400–21 February. On 21 February 1400, in his palace there came before the most reverend Archbishop of Milan numerous deputies and members of the council of the Cathedral, and Simonetus Negrus, Johannes Sanomerius, and Mermetus de Sabandia [Savoy], all three French engineers and [they] were queried on the questions set forth in writing below as to what they would say and decide under oath since they are in transit to Rome.

First it was asked on this question by the above-mentioned lords if it seemed to them that this church was adequately founded to sustain and carry the weight belonging to said church.

We the aforesaid engineers and masons say that we have seen and reviewed all of said church, and especially we have seen the foundations of two piers exposed, which two piers should sustain and abut the apse of said church, and are inadequately and poorly founded. And one of these is more than a foot at fault inside the work, and of poor material. All the piers of said church both inside and outside are to be reviewed down to the lowest base and all those

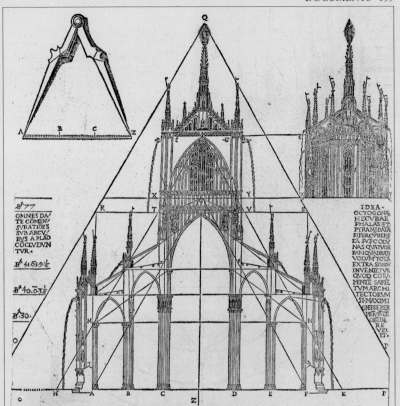

S ection through Milan Cathedral analysed according to the medieval proportional system
called *ad triangulum* advocated by Paul Mignot.

which were badly founded as are the
aforementioned, are to be refounded of
large blocks of well-laid stone, and their
bedding should be well leveled and
planed and joined, and buttressed by
dovetailing into the other foundations
well inside, and built in with a mortar
bath. These foundations should be made
two braccia or more beyond the plumb
line of the bases of the piers, coming to
one braccio at the surface by a setback.

Furthermore, it was asked and the
question was put if the aforementioned
two piers outside the apse of said church
are strong enough to sustain and
buttress against all its weight.

We state that if one founded two
piers for carrying two flying buttresses,
that the church would be made
stronger....

Furthermore, it was asked and the
question was put if all the other piers of

said church seemed to us to be good.

We state that if they were to be made now they could be made better.

Furthermore it was asked if all the aforesaid piers could carry and transmit their loads as they are (now).

We reply that it seems so to us providing a good mason were available to change the mouldings and load-bearing members above the capitals, and to make this moulding proper and lighter, as it should be, since some of these piers are not well aligned....

Furthermore we note that there are cracks and holes cut through from the circular openings [probably stairwells] of the corner pier of the sacristies of this cathedral to carry off the rain water that is shed from the roofs of the sacristies and chapels, and this is unsound. It is necessary that they be closed and cemented up and that additional, new gargoyles be made....

(Signed) Symonetus Nigrus, Johannes Sanomerius, and Mermetus de Sabaudia.

1400–8 May. In the name of God and the Virgin Our Lady Saint Mary, in the year 1400 on the 8th of May. I, Bertolino of Novara, who have been sent by the illustrious and most high prince, my lord, the Duke, for certain views and disagreements brought up by some of the masters in the construction and commission of the church of our lady, St Mary, which disagreements and opinions the overseers of the said construction have given me in writing, and I have seen and examined, and besides, I have been with the masters and engineers who are at present on this said construction, to see the disagreements with my own eyes from every angle. And besides this looking, I had the foundations of the said church dug into at certain points to see the said foundations, so as to be clearer about the doubts brought up about the construction. Briefly answering, I said that the church should have had a truer proportion around the foundations, and in certain other places above ground. But it is not to be scorned on that account, in fact it is to be praised for a most beautiful big building, but in my opinion it would have to have an addition made for permanent strengthening as follows:

First, because the buttresses of the body of the church are not as large as is needed, considering the breadth and height of the said church, the first nave should be reduced to the form of chapels with partitions between one chapel and another, with some openings through which one could see the Host from either side of the church. By doing this the greatest strength would result in the other three naves, on account of these thrown arches, it would have a sounder base, and the body of the church would be beautiful and more wisely rational because it would match the size of the crossing.

Further, there would be need to make a chapel at the apse of the church toward the cemetery, which chapel would be attached to those two buttresses on the right side, making it as small as possible and not damaging anything already built, and this chapel would result in more strength, and in this area could be placed that tomb which it is said my lord, the Duke, wishes to make, and with the tomb installed in this place it could be located straighter, because the choir would turn out larger.

Master Bernardo of Venice, Master Bertolino of Novara.

From Elizabeth G. Holt (ed.), *A Documentary History of Art*, 1957

Contract for building the nave of Fotheringay Church

In the 15th century, Fotheringay Church, in Northamptonshire, was rebuilt to serve as the church of a college founded by one of the sons of Edward III. As was normal, the choir was built first. In 1435 it was time to start on the nave and a contract was drawn up with a builder called William Horwood, who was told to follow the design of the choir that had already been built (but which no longer exists).

This contract made between William Wolston, squire, Thomas Pecham, clerk, commissioners for the high and mighty prince, and my right dread lord, the Duke of York, on the first part, and William Horwood, free-mason, dwelling in Fotheringhay, on the other part, witnesses that the same William Horwood has granted and undertaken, and by this same has contracted, granted and undertaken to make up a new nave of a church joining to the choir, of the college of Fotheringhay, of the same height and breadth that the said choir is; and in length eighty feet [24 metres] from the said choir downward, within walls a meter-yard [thick] a meter-yard of England, counted always as three feet. And in this covenant, the said William Horwood shall also make well all the ground work of the said nave, and take it and excavate it at his own cost, and as slowly and as adequately as it ought to be, overseen by masters of the same craft. The material that belongs to such a work is sufficiently provided for him at my said lord's cost. And to the said nave he shall make two aisles, and do the ground work and excavation of them in the aforesaid manner, both the aisles to

be in accordance with the height and breadth of the aisles of said choir, and the height of the aforesaid nave; the ground of the same nave and aisles to be made within the end with rough stone under the ground tablestones; and for the ground stones b...ments [*sic*]; and all the remainder of the said nave and aisles to the full height of said choir all made with clean-hewn ashlar in the outer side to the full height of the said choir. And all the inner side to be of rough-stone, except that the bench-table-stones, the sills of the windows, the pillars and capitals that the arches and pendants rest upon, shall all be of freestone wrought truly and duly as it ought to be.

And in each aisle shall be windows of free-stone, agreeing in all points to the windows of the said choir, but they shall have no bowtels at all. And in the west end of either of the said aisles, he shall make a window of four lights, agreeing with the windows of the said aisles. And to either aisle shall be as square embattaillment of free-stone through out, and both the ends embattailled butting upon the steeple. And either of the said aisles shall have six mighty buttresses of free-stone, clean-hewn; and every buttress finished with a pinnacle, agreeing in all points to the pinnacles of the said choir, save only that the buttress of the nave shall be larger, stronger and mightier than the buttress of the said choir.

And the clerestory, both within and without, shall be made of clean ashlar grounded upon ten mighty pillars, with four responds; that is to say two above joining the choir, and two beneath joining to the end of the said nave. And to the two responds of the said choir shall be two perpeyn-walls joining of free-stone, clean wrought: that is to say, one on either side of the middle choir door. And in either wall, three lights, and piscinas on either side of the wall, which shall serve for four altars, that is to say one on either side of the middle door of the said choir and one on either side of the said aisles.

And in each of the said aisles shall be five arches above [*sic*] the steeple, and above every arch a window and every window to be of four lights, agreeing in all points to the windows of the clerestory of the said choir. And either of the said aisles shall have six mighty arches butting on either side to the clerestory, and two mighty arches butting on either side to the said steeple, agreeing with the arches of the said choir, both in table-stones and crestis, with a square embattaillment thereupon....

And to the west end of the said nave shall be a steeple standing [high above] the church upon three strong and mighty arches vaulted with stone. The said steeple shall have in length eighty feet after the meter-yard of three feet to the yard, above the ground from the table-stones, and [measure] twenty feet square within the walls, the walls being six foot thick above the said ground table-stones. And to the height of the said nave [of the church], it shall be square, with a large door, which shall be in the west end of the same steeple.

And when the said steeple comes to the height of the said battlement, then it shall be changed and turned in eight panes and at every angle, a buttress finished with a pinnacle agreeing to the pinnacles of the said choir and nave; the said chapell [to be] embattailled with a large square embattaillment. And above the door of the said steeple, a window rising in height as high as the great arch

of the steeple and in breadth as wide as the nave will come out to be. And in the said steeple will be two floors, and above each floor eight clerestory set in the middle of the wall, each window of three lights, and all the outer side of the steeple of clean wrought free-stone; and the inner side of rough stone. And in said steeple shall be a stair-way, serving up to the said nave, aisles and choir, both beneath and above....

And for all the work that is devised and rehearsed in this same agreement, my said Lord of York shall find the carriage and materials, that is to say, stone, lime, sand, ropes, bolts, ladders, timber, scaffolds, machines, and all kinds of materials that belong to the said work, by which the work will be well, truly, and duly made and finished in the manner as it is above devised and declared. The said William Horwood shall have of my said lord, three hundred pounds Sterling; of which sum he shall be paid in the manner as it shall be declared hereafter; that is to say, when he has excavated the ground of said church, aisles, buttresses, porches, and steeple, hewn and set his ground table-stones, and his string-courses and the wall thereto within and without as it ought to be well and duly made, then he shall have six pounds, thirteen shillings, four pence. And when the said William Horwood has set one foot above the ground table-stone, also the outer side as well as the inner side throughout all the said work, then he shall have payment of a hundred pounds Sterling. And so for every foot of the said work, after it be fully wrought and set as it ought to be and as it is above devised, until it comes to the full height of the highest pinnacles and battlement of the said nave, hewing, setting, raising [the tower] of the steeple after it has passed the highest embattaillment of the said nave, he shall have but thirty shilling Sterling, until it be fully ended and completed in the manner as it is above directed.

And when all the work above rehearsed and devised is fully finished, as it ought to be and as it is above agreed to and devised between the said commissioners and the said William, then the said William Horwood shall have full payment of the three pounds Sterling if any be due or left unpaid thereof to him.... And if it be that the said William Horwood not make full payment to all or any of his workmen, then the clerk of the work shall pay him in his presence and stop as much from the said William Horwood's hand as the payment amounts to that shall be due to the workmen.

And during all the said work, the setters shall be chosen and taken by those that shall have the control and supervision of the said work for my said lord. They are to be paid by the hand of the said William Horwood, in the form and manner above written and devised. And if it should be that the said William Horwood will complain and say at any time that two setters of any of them, be not profitable nor adequate workmen for my lord's profit, then with the oversight of the master-masons of the country they shall be judged. And if they be found faulty or unable, then they shall be changed and others taken and chosen by such as shall have control of the said work by my said lord's order and command.

And if it be that the said William Horwood makes not end of the said work within reasonable time, which shall be set clearly by my said lord, or

The nave of Fotheringay Church.

by his counsel in form and manner as is above written and devised in these same agreements, then he shall yield his body to prison at my lord's will, and all his movable goods and heritances at my said lord's disposition and order.

In witness, & the said commissioners, as [well as] the said William Horwood have set their seals interchangeably to these present contracts, the XXIVth day of September, the XIIIth year of the reign of our sovereign lord King Henry the Sixth, after the conquest of England.

From Douglas Knoop and G. P. Jones, *The Medieval Mason*, 1933

Machines

Texts concerning the making of machines are less numerous than those on architecture.

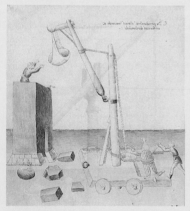

A crane inspired by a war machine, by Mariano Taccola, a 15th-century Sienese 'engineer'.

Construction of a crane at Arles (notary's draft, 1459)

In the year shown above [1459], on the seventh day of the month of June. It is hereby notified to everyone, etc.:

That the Reverend Master Alziarius Bartholomei, master of theology, venerable prior of the convent of the Order of Preachers [i.e. Dominicans] at Arles, has made payment and disbursement to Master Guyot Perissis, building timber merchant, living in Arles, here present, etc., for him to construct from new and to make in good building timber, new and suitable, a good and fitting crane able to carry and to support a weight of one hundred Arles quintals, with the object of erecting the new church which the said convent is having built and constructed in praise and honour of God and the glorious Virgin Mary of Succour, begun on the flank or side of the church of the said convent, and in order to raise the stones and other materials necessary to the construction of this church, with and under the clauses set out below.

And that in the first place, the said Master Guyot is held and obliged to build well and construct in due form the said crane, to have it assembled and placed on the site of the said church, during the length of the present month of June, and to make it of a height of eight rods, in such a way that it can be used both inside and outside; and that the said lord prior must at his own cost and expense maintain and clean the site where the said crane is to be installed. It has been agreed similarly that the said lord prior must at the expense and cost of his convent have all the pieces of ironwork necessary for the said crane, and must execute all repairs necessary to these same pieces of ironwork at the expense of the said convent.

It has been similarly agreed that the said lord prior or his convent shall give in payment to the said Master Guyot for the said crane in such fashion as he has promised to make it, for the timber as well as for his own labour, forty-eight florins, that is to say two florins at once as deposit and payment, and the remaining forty-six florins to be paid within fifteen days, once the said crane has been manufactured and tried out [*probatum*], to see whether it is suitable or not [*si fuerit sufficiens*], from the day when it will have been installed on its site: the which two florins as deposit and payment, to be deducted from the said forty-eight florins, the said Master Guyot has acknowledged to hold and to have received from the said lord prior, with no exceptions etc. ...

Sealed at Arles in the said convent, in the cloister range next to the library, in presence of the witnesses: Pierre Jacquin, boatman, Master Byon Alvernhas, mason, citizens of Arles living there, and myself, Bernard Pangonis, notary, etc. ...

B. Montagnes
Architecture dominicaine en Provence,
1979

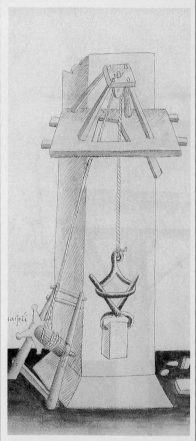

Another crane by Taccola, based on an invention by his friend the architect Filippo Brunelleschi.

THIRTY-ONE GREAT CATHEDRALS

BRITAIN

Bristol, late 13th century. Unique in Britain as a 'hall' church, the aisles as high as the central vessel, with buttresses in the form of bridges across the aisles carrying the thrust of the vault.

Canterbury. East end rebuilt in the late 12th century (see pp. 147–53). Largely French in style, but uses the English material Purbeck marble. Retains nearly all its stained glass. The nave was rebuilt in Perpendicular style in the 14th century.

Durham, 11th–12th century. The most complete survivor from the period when all English cathedrals were rebuilt following the Norman Conquest. Has its original nave, transept and choir, covered with the earliest high rib-vault in Europe.

Ely. Romanesque nave and transepts, 12th century. Octagon over the crossing built in the Decorated period, mid-14th century, with unique use of diagonal light.

Exeter, late 13th–early 14th century, a period when England's Decorated style led the rest of Europe. Intricately patterned rib vault and windows with curvilinear tracery.

Gloucester. Choir and south transept of the Romanesque church remodelled in the 14th century, originating the Perpendicular style, straight tracery covering the walls and expanding into the vault.

Lincoln. Rebuilding begun a few years after Canterbury, using the same elements but no longer in a French way. Of a number of quirkily individual features, the most surprising is the so-called 'crazy vault' of the choir. See pp. 131–4.

Peterborough. Romanesque nave (12th century) and Romanesque painted ceiling. Characterized by extreme length, an English feature.

Salisbury. Stylistically the most consistent of English cathedrals, built within forty years (1220–60), the tower and spire a little later.

Westminster Abbey. Begun by Henry III (mid-13th century) as the coronation and burial church of the English kings. The most French of English great churches; the series of royal tombs from Henry III to Elizabeth I makes it of unique historical interest. The early-16th-century Henry VII Chapel is the last and most ingenious of fan-vaulted structures.

Wells. Begun at the same time as Canterbury and shares many of its features. The Decorated retrochoir (late 13th century) is a fascinating vista of complex spaces.

FRANCE

All the following were begun in the century 1150–1250:

Amiens. Follows the pattern of Reims, its two-towered façade decorated with fine sculpture.

Beauvais. The most ambitious of all Gothic cathedrals, with a vault higher than any other – in fact too ambitious: the vault collapsed and had to be rebuilt, and the cathedral never progressed beyond the crossing.

Bourges. The most original of the group in design. It has double aisles, the nave arcade being so high that the inner aisle has a complete three-storey elevation (arcade, triforium, clerestory) of its own.

Chartres. Best preserved of all medieval cathedrals. Elaborate sculptural ensembles on the west front and both transept porches. A dazzling display of stained glass.

Laon. Notable especially for its twin-towered west front with figures of oxen, drawn by Villard de Honnecourt (see pp. 84 and 106).

Paris, Notre-Dame. Set the pattern for cathedrals in the Ile-de-France: double aisles, four-storey elevation, chevet with radiating chapels, two-tower façade, quadripartite vaults.

Reims. Coronation church of the French kings with notable sculpture and the earliest use of bar-tracery.

GERMANY AND CENTRAL EUROPE

Cologne, 13th century. A French cathedral on German soil. Unfinished in the Middle Ages, finished according to the original design in the 19th century.

Prague, 14th century. Begun by a French architect and taken over by a German. Like Cologne, its nave was built only in the 19th century.

Ulm, 14th century. Specifically German in having a single west tower and spire, also completed in the 19th century.

ITALY

Florence. Arcade arches even broader than Siena (nave of four bays only), 14th century. Brunelleschi's octagonal dome of the 1420s is the last great work of the Italian Middle Ages and first of the Renaissance.

Milan, begun 13th century, finished 19th. The only Italian cathedral comparable to the Gothic of the north, and partly designed by northern masters. On a vast scale, of white marble with a wealth of figure sculpture, curvilinear tracery and pinnacles. See pp. 156–60.

Monreale, late 12th-century Sicilian Romanesque. Union of Byzantine and Western influences, with marble columns, a wooden roof and mosaic decoration.

Pisa, 11th-century Tuscan Romanesque. Exterior covered with dwarf galleries on miniature columns. (This applies also to the famous Campanile and Baptistry, which form a monumental group.)

Siena, 13th–14th centuries. Has the broad arches of Italian Gothic and the local speciality of horizontal banding in white and green. Crossing surmounted by hexagonal dome.

SPAIN

Burgos, built from the 13th to the 15th centuries. The west towers and spires were designed by a master mason whose family came from Cologne.

Gerona. Choir begun as a cathedral with nave and aisles, but in the 15th century the whole nave was thrown into one space (no arcades) covered by the widest Gothic vault in the world.

León, 13th–14th century. Basically French Gothic. Retains much stained glass.

Santiago de Compostela, 12th century. Built as the focus of a pilgrimage. Belongs to a French church type, with barrel vault and no clerestory.

Seville, 15th century. Embodies the Spanish characteristic of extreme width; covers the largest area of all medieval cathedrals.

FURTHER READING

ARCHITECTURE

Aubert, Marcel, *Romanesque Cathedrals and Abbeys of France*, 1965

Bony, Jean, *The English Decorated Style*, 1979

—, *French Gothic Architecture of the 12th and 13th Centuries*, 1983

Frankl, Paul, *Gothic Architecture*, 1962

Grodecki, Louis, *Gothic Architecture*, 1979

Harvey, John, *The Perpendicular Style*, 1978

Street, George Edmund, *Some Account of Gothic Architecture in Spain*, 1865

Von Simpson, Otto, *The Gothic Cathedral*, 1962

Webb, Geoffrey, *Architecture in Britain: The Middle Ages*, 1956

White, John, *Art and Architecture in Italy, 1250–1400*, 1966

Wilson, Christopher, *The Gothic Cathedral: The Architecture of the Great Church 1130–1530*, 1990

BUILDING TECHNIQUE

Andrews, Francis B., *The Medieval Builder*, 1974

Coldstream, Nicola, *Masons and Sculptors*, 1991

Fitchen, John, *The Construction of Gothic Cathedrals*, 1961

Gille, Bertrand, *Engineers of the Renaissance*, 1964

Gimpel, Jean, *The Cathedral Builders*, trans. Teresa Waugh, 1983

—, *La Révolution industrielle du Moyen Age*, 1975

Harvey, John, *English Medieval Architects* (2nd ed.), 1987

—, *The Medieval Architect*, 1972

Knoop, Douglas, and G. P. Jones, *The Medieval Mason*, 1933 and 1949

Recht, Roland, *Les Bâtisseurs des cathédrales gothiques*, 1989

Salzman, Louis Francis, *Building in England down to 1540*, 1952

Schock-Werner, Barbara, 'L'Oeuvre Notre-Dame, histoire et organisation de la fabrique de la cathédrale de Strasbourg', in Roland Recht, *Les Bâtisseurs des cathédrales gothiques*, 1989

CRAFTSMEN

Barral i Altet, Xavier (ed.), *Artistes, artisans et production artistique au Moyen Age*, 1986–9

Binski, Paul, *Painters*, 1991

Brown, Sarah, and David O'Connor, *Glass-painters*, 1991

Grodecki, Louis, and Catherine Brisac, *Gothic Stained Glass: 1200–1300*, 1985

Harvey, John, *Medieval Craftsmen*, 1975

GENERAL

Bagley, John Joseph, *Historical Interpretation: Sources of English Medieval History*, 1965

Branner, Robert, *Chartres Cathedral*, 1969

Clifton-Taylor, Alec, *The Cathedrals of England*, 1986

Coulton, George Gordon, *Medieval Village, Manor and Monastery*, 1960

Cowen, Painton, *Rose Windows*, 1992

Evans, Joan (ed.), *The Flowering of the Middle Ages*, 1985

—, *Life in Medieval France*, 1925

Favier, Jean, John James, Yves Flamand and Jean Bernard, *The World of Chartres*, 1990

Huizinga, Johan, *The Waning of the Middle Ages*, trans. F. Hopman, 1965

Loyn, H. R. (ed.), *The Middle Ages: A Concise Encyclopaedia*, 1989

McEvedy, Colin, *The Penguin Atlas of Medieval History*, 1961

Martindale, Andrew, *Gothic Art*, 1967

Norman, Edward, *The House of God: Church Architecture, Style and History*, 1990

Southern, Richard William, *The Making of the Middle Ages*, 1953

TEXTS

Abbot Suger on the Abbey Church of St Denis and its Art Treasures, trans. and ed. Erwin Panofsky, (2nd ed.), 1979

Holt, Elizabeth G. (ed.), *A Documentary History of Art. I. The Middle Ages*, 1957

The Metrical Life of St Hugh, trans. Charles Gaston, 1986

Mortet, Victor, *Recueil de textes relatifs à l'histoire de l'architecture…XIe–XIIe siècles*, 1911

—, and Paul Deschamps, *Recueil de textes relatifs à l'histoire de l'architecture…XIIe–XIIIe siècles*, 1929

The Sketchbook of Villard de Honnecourt, ed. Theodore Bowie, 1982

Willis, Robert, *The Architectural History of Canterbury Cathedral*, 1845 (contains a translation of Gervase's account of the rebuilding)

LIST OF ILLUSTRATIONS

The following abbreviations have been used:
a above; *b* below; *c* centre; *l* left; *r* right; BN
Bibliothèque Nationale, Paris.

COVER

Front Construction of the Tower of Babel.
Rudolf von Ems, *Weltchronik*, 2 MS. theol. 4.
Gesamthochschulbibliothek Kassel, Landes-
und Murhardische Bibliothek, Kassel
Spine Construction of a tower. Ms. Lat. 99. BN
Back Rebuilding of a town. *Chroniques de
Hainaut*, Ms. 9242. Bibliothèque Royale Albert
I, Brussels

OPENING

1–9 Design for the central part of the façade
of Strasbourg Cathedral (details). Inv. no. 5.
Musée de l'Oeuvre Notre-Dame, Strasbourg
11 Foundation of an abbey. *Life of St Hedwig
of Silesia*, Ms. Ludwig XI 7. J. Paul Getty
Museum, Malibu

CHAPTER 1

12 Girart de Roussillon, Construction of twelve
churches by Girart and his wife. Cod. 2549.
15th century. Österreichische Nationalbibliothek,
Vienna
13 Construction of a temple. *Psalterium Aureum*,
Cod. Sang. 22. Bibliothèque de l'Abbaye de
St-Gall
14 Vikings landing in England. *St Albans Psalter*,
St Godehard, Hildesheim
14–5 Moulins in the 15th century. Guillaume
Revel, *Armorial of Auvergne*, Ms. fr. 22297. BN
16–7 Representation of rural life, showing
ploughing, sowing, harvesting and threshing
18 A map of Roman and 16th-century roads in
France. After Jean Hubert and Charles Estienne
18–9 The amphitheatre at Arles. Engraving,
1686. BN
19 Scene in a town. Marco Polo, *Le Livre de
Marc Paul des merveilles d'Asie et d'Inde*, Ms.
fr. 2810. BN
20–1 Church at Greenstead, Essex. Photograph
21 Consecration of a church. *Lanalet Pontifical*,
Ms. A 27. Drawing. 1060s. Bibliothèque
Municipale, Rouen
22 The motte and keep of Albon, Drôme.
Photograph
22–3 The town of Rennes and soldiers of
William the Conqueror. Bayeux Tapestry.
11th century. Musée de la Tapisserie, Bayeux

23 Siege of the abbey of St-Germain d'Auxerre.
Haimon, *On Ezekiel*, Ms. lat. 12302.
BN
24–5a Construction of a wooden bridge.
Romance of Alexander. Collection Dutuit, Musée
du Petit-Palais, Paris
24–5b The bridge of Gour-Noir (c. 1030) on
the Hérault River. Photograph
25 A bridge. Villard de Honnecourt, *Album*,
Ms. fr. 19093. Drawing. 13th century. BN
26 Plan of the water circulation system for the
monastery of Christchurch at Canterbury, Ms.
R-17-1. 1150s. Trinity College Library,
Cambridge
26–7 Unexecuted plan of the abbey of St-Gall.
9th century. After Encyclopaedia Universalis,
Atlas d'architecture
28 Construction of a tower. *Histoire universelle*
or *Bible en français*, Ms. fr. 9685. Drawing.
13th century. BN
28–9 Stone ramparts of the upper town of
Provins, Seine-et-Marne
30–1 Wall of Reims. Engraving. 17th century.
BN
30b Charles Bridge, Prague. Photograph
31 Plan of Prague in the Middle Ages
32l Section of Laon Cathedral
32r Jan van Eyck, *St Barbara*. Drawing. 15th
century. Musée Royal des Beaux-Arts, Antwerp
33l Section of Chartres Cathedral
33r Section of Beauvais Cathedral
34 Founding by the Trojans of Venice,
Sycambre, Carthage and Rome. Jean de Coucy,
La Bouquechardière or *Chroniques*, Ms. fr. 2685.
BN
34–5 Montaigut-le-Blanc in the Puy-de-Dôme.
Guillaume Revel, Armorial d'Auvergne, Ms. fr.
21297. 15th century. BN
35 Plans of the abbey of Fontevrault.
18th century

CHAPTER 2

36 and 37 Tombstone of Hugues Libergier,
architect of St-Nicaise at Reims. Notre-Dame,
Paris
38 Construction of St Albans Abbey. *Life
of Offa*, Ms. Cotton Nero D I. 13th century.
British Library, London
38–9 Petrus Crescentius, Construction of
a country house. *Ruralium commodorum,*
Ms. add.. 19720. British Library, London
39 A stained-glass window from the abbey
church of St-Germer-de-Fly (after Du
Colombier)

CHAPTER 3

INDEX

PHOTO CREDITS

TEXT CREDITS

Alain Erlande-Brandenburg, who studied at the Ecole Nationale des Chartes,
is the director of the National Archives of France, director of studies at the Ecole
Pratique des Hautes Etudes and professor of history of art at the Ecole des Chartes,
all in Paris. He was chief curator of the Musée National du Moyen Age, chief curator
of the Musée National de la Renaissance, of which he was a founder, and assistant to
the director of the Musées de France (1987–91). He has gained an international
reputation for a number of important publications on the Gothic era. He is responsible
for an enlightening work on the new conception of the history of art: *La Cathédrale*,
1989. He is the president of the Société Française d'Archéologie.

*To my colleagues at the Société Française d'Archéologie with whom I have
– over the past twenty-five years – discovered the greatness and the
beauty of medieval architecture. In community of spirit.*

Translated from the French by Rosemary Stonehewer

First published in the United Kingdom in 1995 by
Thames & Hudson Ltd, 181A High Holborn,
London WC1V 7QX

Reprinted 1997, 1998, 2000, 2002, 2005, 2007, 2009, 2010

English translation © 1995
Thames & Hudson Ltd, London

© 1993 Gallimard

British Library Cataloguing-in-Publication Data

A catalogue record for this book is available
from the British Library

ISBN   978-0-500-30052-7

Printed and bound in Italy by Zanardi Group

To find out about all our publications, please
visit **www.thamesandhudson.com**. There you
can subscribe to our e-newsletter, browse or download
our current catalogue, and buy any titles that are in print.